# WITHOUT
## A
# PADDLE

DAVID MOFFATT

# WITHOUT A PADDLE

## TALES FROM THE TYNE AND RIVERS FAR AWAY

Matador
9 Priory Business Park,
Wistow Road, Kibworth Beauchamp,
Leicestershire. LE8 0RX
Tel: 0116 279 2299
Email: books@troubador.co.uk
Web: www.troubador.co.uk/matador
Twitter: @matadorbooks

ISBN 978 1785891 687

British Library Cataloguing in Publication Data.
A catalogue record for this book is available from the British Library.

Printed and bound in the UK by TJ International, Padstow, Cornwall
Typeset in 11pt Aldine401 BT by Troubador Publishing Ltd, Leicester, UK

Matador is an imprint of Troubador Publishing Ltd

 David was born in County Durham and brought up in the Northumbrian seaside town of Whitley Bay. He attended St. Cuthbert's Grammar School in Newcastle and went on to do a degree in Agriculture at Newcastle University. He obtained a Royal Society Leverhulme Scholarship to work for a year on a Royal Society/ Royal Geographical Society expedition to Central Brazil.

His work on the expedition was recognised by his receipt of the Royal Geographical Society's Mrs Patrick Ness Award for Scientific Exploration and Investigation. Completing his PhD at Newcastle, David then worked for the Ministry of Overseas Development in West Africa and Indonesia. In 1976 he joined ULG Consultants in Warwick, an international consultancy in Rural Development where he stayed for 25 years, half that time as the Managing Director. He eventually returned to hands-on consultancy on a free-lance basis.

David is married with two children and seven grandchildren and splits his time between his homes in Warwick and Corbridge from where he and his wife roam the coast and moors of his native Northumberland.

*Dedicated to the memory of Angie –*
*the girl from Bermondsey*
*1946 – 2007*

# CONTENTS

# PROLOGUE

In a lifetime of travel to far-flung parts of the world I have encountered many great rivers. The tales that I tell here are from just a few of them. But all these rivers and all these tales are just threads woven into the canvas of the river that fashioned me. So my tales must inevitably take us back to the Tyne as the backdrop to my travels.

The Tyne starts its life as two rivers. Rising close to the borders of Scotland is the North Tyne, now dammed to form Kielder Water, the largest manmade lake in the United Kingdom. Built to support the northeast's growing industrial base, its completion coincided neatly with the virtual cessation of big industry on Tyneside. Leaving Kielder Water, the North Tyne continues its journey through the sparsely populated countryside of Northumberland to its confluence with the South Tyne. This rises as a tiny spring on the Alston Moors in Cumbria, an area of wild, dramatic beauty. The two rivers meet close to the market town of Hexham and flow through an increasingly urbanised landscape to what was once the industrial heartland of the northeast. So polluted was the Tyne in the first half of the twentieth century that a definition of someone who enjoyed the greatest of good luck was that if he fell in the Tyne he would come up with a salmon in his mouth. Now, no matter how feebly lady luck may smile on you, a fall into the Tyne would more than likely find you a salmon, recognised as it is as the best salmon fishing river in England.

I was born in 1944 in Rowlands Gill, a former coal-mining village lying four miles south of the Tyne in what was then County Durham. Nearly six years later we edged closer to the Tyne, to Whitley Bay just two miles north of its mouth, which is where I grew up. My secondary education was pursued at a school whose anthem proclaimed it to be our 'Alma Mater by the Tyne' though it was less a 'sweet mother' than a wicked stepmother as far as I was concerned. Quite unable to cut my umbilical link to the Tyne, I continued my education at what was then Kings College of the University of Durham, subsequently to become Newcastle University. My mother, who had some pretensions to snobbery, could never understand why I took a Newcastle University degree rather than the more prestigious 'Dunelm', but I belong to the Tyne not to the Wear.

# PART 1

## THE RIO DAS MORTES

*The Rio das Mortes – the River of the Deaths – rises in the Serra de Jeronymo, near to Cuiabà, the capital of the state of Mato Grosso and the city regarded as lying at the exact centre of South America. It is the major tributary of the mighty Araguaia which, after joining forces with the Tocantins, finally discharges into the Atlantic Ocean alongside the Amazon. In its upper reaches it is known as the Rio Manso – the Tame River – and is believed to owe its very different name further downstream to an incident that occurred in 1660. Gold was known to exist in the region populated by the Xavante Indians and that year a party of São Paulo bandeirantes – the famous explorers of the interior – started to extract vast quantities of gold from the river. A second exploration party followed hot on the heels of the first. The two rival parties met and fought out a battle of such savagery that they were nearly all wiped out. The river ran red with their blood and became known thereafter as the River of the Deaths. Still, the explanation did little to persuade my mother that by going to the Rio das Mortes I wasn't flirting with death.*

# CHAPTER 1

# VULTURES

For a long time three vultures had been circling above me, menacing black silhouettes against the peerless blue sky. Now emboldened by the approaching evening, they swooped down to the small clearing in which I crouched at the bottom of a deep hole. I could hear them shuffling around the clearing, sometimes casting slanting shadows over me and occasionally peering down into the hole, ugly birds with their unkempt plumage and scrawny necks. Just me and the three vultures, and I appeared to pose no threat to them, only the promise of a meal when I eventually expired, as must any animal that had fallen into such a hole. For this was unforgiving territory – the middle of the Brazilian state of Mato Grosso, the land infamously associated with Colonel Percy Harrison Fawcett[1] who, in 1925 with his son Jack and another companion, disappeared without trace while pursuing their quest to locate a long-lost civilisation. Their fate remains one of the world's great enduring mysteries and now I sat close to Fawcett's last known base of Dead Horse Camp. Two years after their disappearance another expedition was dispatched to discover what had happened to Fawcett and his party. Its leader, Commander Dyott, concluded: '*That Colonel Fawcett and his companions perished at the hands of hostile tribes seems to me and all my party beyond dispute*'.

---

1   Exploration Fawcett, 1924, arranged from his manuscripts, letters, logbooks and records by Brian Fawcett

However, Fawcett's disappearance has never been irrefutably explained and to this day remains a source of conjecture, with theories that range from the party being devoured by cannibals to their finding a paradise that they couldn't bear to leave. So despite Commander Dyott's conclusions, since his pronouncement 40 years before, more than a hundred would-be rescuers or researchers had died in thirteen expeditions sent to uncover Fawcett's fate[2]. In 1961, just six years before I ventured into Fawcett territory, Richard Mason, a member of a British expedition working a little further to the north on the Rio Irriri, was clubbed to death by an unknown tribe of Indians, exploding the myth that there were no longer tribes living in the area outside the knowledge or jurisdiction of the Indian Protection Service.

I squinted into the setting sun; night came quickly in Mato Grosso, the passage from light to the absoluteness of the dark happening almost instantaneously. It was time to make my move. Using hand and foot holds fashioned with a geological hammer I scrambled out of the pit, hauling behind me a pack filled with the soil samples that I had spent the last few hours meticulously collecting. The vultures shuffled disconsolately away – a totally wasted vigil.

I was a member of the latest expedition to Mato Grosso, but our goal was not to find the remains of the missing Fawcett. It was to study an environment untouched by modern civilisation, before it was destroyed forever by a road that was to be driven through it linking the new capital, Brasilia, to the Amazon, allowing rich land grabbers and the landless poor to swarm all over this virgin territory.

In response to an invitation from the Brazilian government, the Royal Society and the Royal Geographical Society had

2    Brazilian Adventure by Peter Fleming, 1933

mounted the Xavantina/Cachimbo Expedition, and the Times, continuing a long association with the Fawcett tale, funded this to the tune of £40,000 in exchange for exclusive rights to report on the progress of the expedition. Ostensibly funding the expedition's scientific objectives, it was not difficult for the sceptical to conjecture that their extravagant funding may have been based less on the newsworthiness of scientific exploration and more on the basis of the fate of Colonel Fawcett, Richard Mason and the other hundred or so people that had disappeared in the same area. Taking a cynical view, it looked a reasonable gamble that somebody – maybe the entire expedition – would be killed, disappear or get kidnapped by some hitherto unknown tribe. Assigned as The Times' special correspondent for the expedition was Anthony Smith, an adventurer, tall and prematurely bald, who had motor-cycled across Africa and ballooned over the Alps and was raring to explore what was universally recognised as one of the last great unexplored wildernesses in the world. So it would be naïve to imagine that they didn't privately nurture the hope that the expedition would provide at least some exciting, copy-selling incident. Their special correspondent quite overtly did so, and it was difficult sometimes not to feel that The Times also hovered, waiting for the drama, sometimes with less patience than the vultures.

My job was to determine how the soils influenced the complex pattern of distribution of a hitherto undisturbed habitat – not the stuff of a Boy's Own adventure nor in truth of the middle pages of The Times. And unless I was kidnapped by Indians or attacked by a jaguar on my way back to base camp, I was going to provide little copy that day which would excite the hovering Times, its special correspondent or its readers. In reality there was little danger; I was only a couple of miles from our base camp on a route that I had travelled a number of times, though particularly as the red sun started its final precipitous descent below the horizon I felt that little frisson as the sounds of the night started to take over from the sounds of the day. In this confusion of sound it was not hard to conjure up images of the sort that would provide that elusive copy for The Times.

Odd, really, that I should find myself sitting in a deep hole in the middle of Brazil for I am a Geordie, with roots deep in the banks of the Tyne, and there was little in my childhood that suggested at first glance that I might become an explorer. I was a small child, very small, and grainy photographs from the time show a child with a generally anxious look. My father was in the wartime Royal Navy and stationed in India when I was born. My mother, despite eventually raising five children, was never the most maternal of women, and had horrified the midwife when I was born by declaring that she was too tired to see me and would see me in the morning. After three daughters, her first son, and she couldn't be bothered to see me. I was over a year old before my father saw me, by which time I had my revenge on my mother's early rejection of me by having her wrapped round my little finger.

I was very much a loner. There were few children of my own age in the village and I did not anyway go out of my way to seek their company. I had relatively little interaction with my three older sisters, except for the youngest whom I used to lock in the toy cupboard. Perhaps because of my diminutive stature I was deemed to be somewhat delicate and was pronounced as suffering from bronchitis. Whether I was delicate, whether I did suffer from bronchitis, I cannot say, but I took full advantage and avoided any formal schooling till we moved home when I was nearly six.

Somehow in those austere post-war years my parents had tracked down a second-hand pedal car. It was well past its prime, but with a good clean-up and a coat of green paint it was the best birthday present a three–year–old could have had. I recall my early childhood as being spent pedalling my car up and down the lane in front of the house. And here perhaps is the clue to my later life. Perched alongside me in my little green car was Teddy, and Teddy was a frequent visitor to South Africa. There he braved all manner of hardship and danger as he went in search of gold. Never mind that to the unimaginative eye the gold comprised penny and halfpenny coins, scrounged from my mother, in one of my father's Gold Block tobacco tins; for me it was gold from the darkest corners of South Africa discovered by my intrepid teddy bear and transported in my little green car. Teddy sits now on a chair in my attic office with a recently refurbished body, clutching his gold and musing no doubt on his most recent trip to South Africa when the search for gold was replaced by the search for goals, though England supplied few of those.

It wouldn't take a great child psychologist to realise that this small, anxious and loner child nurtured the desire for adventure but, too timid to seek this himself, travelled through the safe proxy of his teddy bear. How that would change.

# CHAPTER 2

# AN UNLIKELY EXPLORER

It was a bitterly cold but dazzlingly sunny February day when my tutor summoned me. I was in my last of four glorious years in the Agriculture Faculty at Newcastle University – glorious not for any outstanding academic achievement but glorious for the fun I had had – and I was acutely aware that the reality of the outside world was getting perilously close. I had applied to the North East office of the National Agricultural Advisory Service and to the Northumberland section of the Soil Survey of England and Wales, though my great hope lay in conning money out of the National Research Council to fund me through a PhD. This would involve no more travel than short forays from Newcastle to collect samples of soil from the estuary of the Solway Firth and would have kept me in the cloistered confines of academia.

The new Faculty of Agriculture building at Newcastle University was an impressive glass tower and the low February sun streamed through my tutor's office windows. I could see him only in silhouette as he leaned his back against the broad windowsill. He didn't invite me to sit, which would anyway have been difficult as every available surface was covered in aerial photographs showing thousands of square miles of apparently featureless forest. *'Here be dragons,'* I thought, as I gazed down at them.

'How would you like to go to Brazil?'

'Brazil?' I had heard of it of course, who hadn't? Two times winner of the World Cup and prevented from a justifiable attempt at the hat-trick in 1966 by the violence of a Portuguese side which pushed, pulled and hacked them out of the game, particularly targeting the great Pele who was eventually stretchered off the field. But at least it helped to clear the path for England's glorious victory. And who hadn't heard of the Maracana in Rio de Janeiro, at one time the greatest football stadium in the world capable of holding 200,000 people? Brazil; there was a song by Frank Sinatra about there being an awful lot of coffee in it. So yes, of course I had heard of Brazil and I knew it was one hell of a long way from Newcastle.

The scene laid out in my tutor's office at a virtual 10,000 feet below me was in the State of Mato Grosso, the central State of Brazil, and through it there was to be built a road linking the new capital of Brasilia with the Amazon. My tutor's finger drew the imaginary line of the road across the aerial photographs and stabbed at possible sites for a base camp. The University had been invited to provide that part of the Xavantina/Cachimbo expeditionary team that would study the soils, and they were looking for someone barmy enough to go and spend a year working in the middle of the jungle. I tried observing my tutor from a different angle to see if I could give substance to the silhouette. Was he just having a joke? Brazil? The Mato Grosso? Twelve months in the middle of nowhere?

I was having a fraught love life, and Newcastle United was languishing in the lower reaches of the first division, bottom on New Year's Day 1967 after a 4 – 0 thumping at Spurs the day before. We had been bumped out of the League Cup in the first round and out of the FA Cup in the third round, and could well be in the second division next season. Could I face another season back in the second division? How long could I sustain my love life? I squinted into the bright

February sunshine then gazed down at the endless expanse of forest 10,000 feet below me; the idea of a year in the middle of nowhere seemed suddenly appealing.

'Thank you, yes, that would be great.'

There was the promise of a scholarship to come back to the University to do a PhD, so perhaps by then Newcastle would have picked themselves up and my girl troubles would have resolved themselves one way or another. Yes, a year in the wilderness could be the answer to a lot of problems.

There were a few hurdles to jump. First I had to persuade the Royal Society Leverhulme Trust that I was a worthy candidate for a Leverhulme Scholarship. I composed a suitably persuasive application and then faced the rigours of an interview by a panel of eminent Fellows of the Royal Society and of the Royal Geographical Society. Not that the interview itself particularly fazed me, indeed I have always rather enjoyed interviews, they are a bit like being onstage. The real problem lay in having to go to London for it. Of course I had been to London before – twice in fact; but both times it was to attend the Smithfield Show and I travelled in a group that included people with a rudimentary understanding of how to get round London. This time I would be on my own, and failing to find the venue for the interview would hardly have been a good start for someone proposing to find his way round the Mato Grosso. I got there by dint of asking people at every point along the route from Kings Cross to Piccadilly. My last enquiry proved particularly fruitful when the object of my enquiry offered to escort me for the final leg of my journey and deposited me right at the imposing door of the Royal Society's headquarters at Burlington House. I had always been led to believe that southerners were an unfriendly and unhelpful lot and I thanked my guide profusely.

'That's alright,' he said, 'anything for a fellow Welshman'. Funny that the Geordie accent can be confused with the Welsh one.

Whether it was the well-crafted application, my on-stage performance at the interview or it had all been stitched up beforehand in the corridors of Burlington House I will never know, but a couple of weeks later I received a letter with the prestigious Royal Society emblem advising me that I had been awarded a Leverhulme Scholarship. The finances were carefully itemised:

| | |
|---|---|
| *Personal Allowance* | *£208* |
| *Kit Allowance* | *Up to £40* |
| *Subsistence in São Paulo or Rio at £5 per day* | *Up to £280* |
| *Return fares to São Paulo or Rio (two visits)* | *£56* |
| *Expedition expenses (contribution towards return fare to Brazil, travel and maintenance in the field and use of expedition's equipment)* | *£916* |
| *Total* | *£1500* |

and a cheque for £584 was to be dispatched to me. I am not sure who was most overjoyed to see it – me or my bank manager, to whom I was heavily in debt. However, my Bank Manager's joy was rather short-lived when I asked for most of the money to be transferred to Brazil.

The second hurdle was a medical, and I don't mean your ordinary pop-into-your-GP-and-let-him-count-your-arms-and-legs-and-say-aaaahh-type-medical. This was more serious stuff; clearly they weren't going to have people let loose in the Mato Grosso who were not in the rudest of good health. I was summoned to attend the Admiralty and there to be medically examined by Commander Doctor somebody or other; something like that anyway. It meant another trip to

London; much more of this and I would develop a craving for jellied eels. This time a cousin who lived on a houseboat in London agreed to accompany me. Some years later I was to visit her on her houseboat; it was fine when I arrived but as the evening wore on the tide came in and the houseboat started bobbing on the changing tide. She always claimed that I was the only person she knew who had ever been seasick on a houseboat.

The Admiralty was, happily, firmly on the shore and I was ushered into a waiting room and presented with the most daunting form I had ever seen. This could take a very long time and I had been harbouring the hope that if I got through the medical quickly I could be back in Newcastle in time for a match that evening. However, I quickly realised that it wasn't as bad as it looked – mainly a catalogue of all the diseases known to man and tick-boxes to say if you had ever had them. In those happy days I had succumbed to almost nothing. The fourth of five children, I had rolled around with my siblings as they went through the usual panoply of childhood maladies without ever even contracting any of these. I rattled through the list in no time, checking the 'no' boxes. The only other occupant of the room was someone of similar age but who had clearly been less fortunate on the health front, as he worked his way slowly through the form making frequent marginal notes. I easily won the race to pass my completed form to the nurse and was ushered into the Commander's den. He worked his way painstakingly through my form before eventually fixing me with a penetrating stare.

'Mr Moffatt, do your bowels function normally?' Obviously well-functioning bowels were rather important for people intending to go and live in the Mato Grosso.

'Absolutely, never miss, go like clockwork,' I assured him.

'Why then, Mr Moffatt, have you ticked the box that says

no?' Got me there, the trick question lurking in amongst all the 'no' answers was one that required a 'yes'.

Beneath that nearly impassive military demeanour, in eyes that would forever look as if they were peering at you from under a peaked cap, I am sure I detected a little triumphant smile; no doubt not the only person to get caught on that one.

My blood pressure was a bit low.

'Do you ever faint?'

'No.'

'Ah well, better than high blood pressure, but you should still stop smoking.'

When he hit my knee with his hammer it jerked with great ferocity and my ears had wax in them, obviously not a good thing, might prevent me hearing Indians or jaguars creeping up behind me, and I was despatched to the nurse to have them syringed. And that was it; I stepped onto Whitehall and into a terrifying roar of traffic in my newly syringed ears. Odd, nobody has ever since suggested any need to de-wax my ears, and talking later to others who had attended the Commander's surgery, they apparently were all declared as needing their ears syringed. Maybe he really was concerned about those soft-footed Indians or maybe he just had a thing about waxy ears.

Only one hurdle to jump – I had to make sure that I got the right degree, which inevitably meant that fun had to take a back seat to work at least for a while. Largely I got it right and got through my final exams without too much difficulty. Well, all but the soil chemistry practical. That was my last exam, but most of my closest friends in the faculty finished their exams the day before me and understandably set out to celebrate – the celebration of the end of exams forever, after so many years of them playing such a pivotal role in our lives. It would have been churlish for me not to join them on such an important occasion. My recollections of the evening are a little hazy, though I do remember that it involved a trip down to Yorkshire for reasons that presumably seemed good at the time but less good as we returned to Newcastle some five hours before the start of my exam. Recollections of the exam are almost as hazy as those of the celebrations of the previous night. I went through it in a fog. I had been reasonably confident that I could handle a soil chemistry practical in whatever state, since they all seemed to follow much the same pattern and were little more than following a recipe. Unfortunately that year the examiner had thought up a little twist; nothing that someone with eight hours of sober sleep under his belt wouldn't have coped with, but that was not the state that I was in. It brought me down a class on my degree, but still I managed enough to claim my ticket to Brazil.

As soon as my exams were over and a few administrative ends were sorted out at the University, I was off to the Royal Agricultural Show site in Warwickshire. This had been an annual pilgrimage for me, as it afforded the most immediate opportunity of earning the money desperately needed to repay my substantial overdraft at the end of each academic year. Once that source of income came to an end, I was left with little time to prepare for my forthcoming adventure. I was acutely aware of my ignorance of Brazil and decided that the priority was to learn something about the country. I perused the travel section at my local bookshop and, passing over rather weightier tomes, I lighted upon 'How to Tango' by George Mikes.[3] Within the first few pages I knew that I was going to be at home in Brazil. George Mikes writes: *'Oh yes, this is the Land of the Future all right. The Land of Tomorrow. But will it remain the Land of the Future forever?'* Brazil, I concluded, was just like Newcastle United – perpetually one for the future.

---

3    How to Tango by George Mikes, 1966

One of my girlfriends, the proud owner of a car, had offered to take me down to the airport via a stop in London at the Royal Society, to be loaded up like some giant pigeon with mail that I was to carry out to Brazil. I craned my neck to look back at Newcastle as we crossed the Tyne Bridge. I have my own definition of a Geordie; as you approach Newcastle from the south there is a curve in the road where suddenly you can see the city in front of you. If that sight gives you goose bumps, a lump in your throat, or a missed heartbeat, then, no matter where you were born, you are a Geordie at heart, though the younger generation say that these days it is the Angel of the North that induces those reactions. Now I was crossing the Tyne Bridge with the city receding into the distance and wondering what the hell I was doing leaving it behind.

On this, my first ever flight, I departed for Brazil on one of the most beautiful planes ever built. Sadly, for all its elegant lines and having been launched only five years before, the VC10 was already a doomed aircraft, a classical series of political and administrative bungles having effectively handed the long range aircraft market to the United States with their Boeing 707 and Douglas DC8. But as an object of beauty neither held a candle to the VC10. Kindly, fate had given me a very pretty girl in the seat next to mine. She was going to Lisbon, she replied in response to my enquiry. Now, if I have one criticism of George Mikes' otherwise excellent book, it was that it had no map that told me where exactly in the world Brazil was, so I had only a vague notion. Still, I was surprised that she should be travelling to Australia via Brazil. I settled down to what promised to be a most agreeable flight. Beer was served and a splendid cold collation of smoked salmon, chicken, cheese, a dessert and red wine. They looked after economy class passengers in those days, because aside from a tiny elite who flew first class everybody else was economy. There was no business class or club class or super economy, you were all just economy and treated as valued passengers, not as cattle in the way that most economy travellers are today. The captain announced our imminent descent to Lisbon. Dammit, of course, it was Brisbane that I was thinking of that was in Australia and I felt a real sense of regret as my pretty companion for such a short leg of the journey disembarked.

The second stop, in Las Palmas, was prolonged in the hope that the fog apparently enveloping Rio's airport would clear before we got there. It didn't and so we were initially diverted to São Paulo.

Stepping into the tropics for the first time was an unforgettable experience. Now of course with docking jetties it is different, but then it meant stepping through the door of the plane to be assailed by a wall of heat, the glare of the sun, but most of all by the smell of jet fuel, mixed in with which somehow was a tantalising smell of coffee and a curious hint of disinfectant. On the occasions in later travels that I have stepped straight from the plane into the tropics there always comes back to me a vivid memory of that first time in São Paulo; I see it, I feel it, and in true Proustian fashion the smell transports me back as if I was again stepping off that plane at São Paulo.

The modern way is quite different. As you walk from your jetty to the baggage hall, warmth seeps through the windows; gusts of heat and smells waft through the curtains through which the baggage conveyors disgorge their mounds of luggage or through opening doors as passengers scurry out, gratefully clutching their bags. Now the tropics sneak up on you gradually; then it was the full frontal assault and perhaps I knew, as that first wave of heat and glare and smell hit me, that I was addicted already.

George Mikes had prepared me to some extent for the warmth of Brazilians towards even total strangers, while at the same time acknowledging that those same Brazilians would run you over in their Volkswagen Beetles simply because you were within range. In Brazil, Beetles, I was told by the head of the British Council, are like bottoms; everybody has one but nobody talks about it. I wandered somewhat aimlessly around the lounge where it seemed that transit passengers mingled relatively freely with people awaiting the arrival of their friends. A young man, maybe a little older than me, and a man I took to be his father addressed me in English – did I look so obviously English? – and invited me to join them for that most Brazilian of occasions, a 'cafesinho' – did I look so obviously like a man that desperately needed a coffee but had no local currency with which to purchase one? The 'cafesinho' or small coffee is a drug, a social occasion, an expression of welcome and somehow a proud statement of being Brazilian. It is strong and bitter although many Brazilians will load it with sugar so to its attributes may be added a source of instant energy. George Mikes recounts how in a small civil war some years previously all firing always stopped between 2.00 and 3.00 pm – it was time for the 'cafesinho'. People, it seemed, were prepared to sacrifice their lives for the cause but not to sacrifice their 'cafesinho'.

My new companions watched in some fascination as I rolled a cigarette to accompany my 'cafesinho'. I had taken to rolling my own the previous summer when, during the vacation, I had a job driving a lorry on the pea harvest in Lincolnshire. It was a job with a high tedium quotient, shuttling between the farms and the pea viners and working the sort of very long hours that would no doubt be illegal today. I quickly realised that if I was not careful I would spend more on cigarettes than I was earning, so I started to roll my own. This meant that I couldn't smoke at all while I was actually driving, having little chance of ever developing the one handed cigarette roll so expertly demonstrated by B-movie cowboys. I continued the practice after I finished the job, having decided that it did reduce both cost and consumption, though lacking any vestige of manual dexterity, my hand-rolled cigarettes were always badly misshapen and with entrails of tobacco spilling from either end.

The older man went to pay for the 'cafesinhos' and returned with four packets of cigarettes.

'For you,' he said 'I am sure you will get to like Brazilian cigarettes.' I was overwhelmed that a total stranger should be so generous, even having been faced with the grim sight of my laboured efforts at rolling my own, and I thanked him profusely. He shrugged:

'We don't have much to offer,' he said. 'Just a little friendliness, a little kindness.' Of course, quite possibly he owned half of São Paulo; you could never be sure with the Brazilians.

We finally landed in Rio's Galeão airport some six hours behind schedule, where I was met by a charming Brazilian from the staff of the British Council, who were the expedition's guardians in Brazil. The fact that he had been at the airport since early that morning and been given almost no information on what was happening to the flight seemed to bother him not the slightest. Despite the fact that I had long since missed my connection to Brasilia we nevertheless jumped into his car and hurtled at high speed to the domestic airport located in the middle of the city. I had never seen anything like it, with planes taking off over the water what seemed like every few seconds. I was left in the car and he disappeared into the airport, eventually to emerge half an hour later triumphantly waving a ticket at me; he had got me a seat on the evening flight to Brasilia.

In those days Brasilia was a fantastic sight, like some vast skeleton. Being hacked out of the red earth that characterises much of the interior of Brazil, the air was constantly filled with fine red dust which, while leading to serious risk of pulmonary disorders, created the most spectacular sunsets. You could see the bones of a great metropolis in the wide boulevards and huge skyscrapers, but between these were large expanses of the scrub, which were slowly giving way to the new capital and the temporary slums of the labourers. I wondered whether the skeleton would ever become a real body or would it be like the cathedral they had started to build but which now stood a skeletal superstructure, ten years after construction had started. Was Brasilia to be, to paraphrase George Mikes, the city of the future, and always remain so?

# CHAPTER 3

# INTO THE UNKNOWN

The expedition had officially started on 1ˢᵗ April 1967 with the departure to Brazil of the leader Iain Bishop and his bride of only six months. April Fool's day seemed a slightly odd choice of start-date, given the aura of impending doom that The Times managed to convey as surrounding the expedition. Under a headline of *'Braving Wilds Where Others Have Died'*, the photograph in The Times shows a smiling couple waving at the foot of the steps to the plane. Iain, slightly overweight with thinning hair, looks rather more than his 29 years. A zoologist at Leicester University, he was to run the expedition for two-and-a-half years. The previous September he had married Angie. She was twenty and came from Bermondsey. She had started training as a nurse but not completed it, and when Iain met her she was a barmaid in a London pub that he frequented from time to time. She was attractive, gregarious and full of fun. Nobody could have been less well equipped to spend two-and-a-half years marooned in the Mato Grosso than this girl from Bermondsey, and I have often wondered how much this traumatic start to married life was to blame for the sadness of her later life and tragedy of her death.

The Bishops met me at the airport and whisked me first to the British Embassy flat in which they were ensconced during their extended sojourn in Brasilia. After a couple of drinks and a few instructions on what I could and couldn't do, I was escorted to a pleasant enough but rather down-market hotel where I was to stay for the night or two before continuing my journey. The night or two became a week in which I trailed along behind the Bishops and got to know them well. Iain was kind and very anxious that I was okay. He did, however, have one bête noire. To such a family-focussed society as Brazil was then, it was inconceivable that we did not in some way constitute a family group, or that someone as apparently young as me could possibly be in Brazil alone, and most people would ask him if I was his son, sometimes if Angie and I were his children. Nothing riled him more than the suggestion that someone only six years his junior was constantly taken to be his son. He never translated the exchanges for me but even without translation it was easy to guess from the red flush and sharp reply when the question had been asked.

The expedition came under the patronage of the Central Brazil Foundation. The Foundation had been established in the 1940s and was a powerful organisation responsible for all major developments in central Brazil. One of its flagship projects was to construct the road that would ultimately link Brasilia with Amazonas. The Foundation apparently owned a plane which, in theory, was to transport me to Xavantina where the advance party of the expedition was currently based. Every day we were told that the plane would be here tomorrow – 'amanha' – we should just wait. If I had known Brazil then as I got to know it later I would have realised that there quite possibly was no plane, or that it needed a spare part that had to come from America and anyway they hadn't got the money to pay for it. Or maybe they really did have a functional aircraft but it was occupied on more important tasks like transporting politicians or influential businessmen to golf courses or discreet resorts with their paramours. Whatever, the possibility of it ever transporting me to Xavantina was nil.

It is not by freak chance that in Brazil the verb 'esperar' means to wait but also means to hope. In Brazil you are rarely waiting for anything with that rock solid certainty that what you are waiting for will actually happen, and therefore waiting always implies a sense of hoping. At home, when I was waiting for a bus I was doing so knowing for almost certain that it would come. In Brazil if you wait for a bus you are by the very same word also hoping that a bus might arrive. After eight frustrating days, Iain eventually reached the inevitable conclusion that the plane almost certainly would never materialise. Did the man in the Foundation's office, who so confidently assured us every day that the plane would be there tomorrow, know that? Almost certainly yes, but the Government of Brazil, no less, had told the Government of the United Kingdom that they would supply a plane and it was certainly not the position of some junior civil servant to tell us that there never would be a plane. It would also have hurt him to be the cause of my disillusionment, when it was clear to him as I turned up at his office each day with my suitcase packed yet again that I still had faith in the system. Far better that I should draw my own conclusions and leave him with a clear conscience.

'Do you think that you could sort of make your own way to Xavantina?' enquired Iain. I was a little startled. My efforts at the Portuguese language were largely confined to ordering beer and breakfast. For the rest I trailed round behind Iain as we jumped in and out of taxis – a mode of transport I had never previously used – ferrying us between the offices of the British Council, the Central Brazil Foundation, the Embassy and the University whose role in the thing was not entirely clear to me – nor, it seemed, to them. Then back to the Hotel Nacional or one of the splendid restaurants nearby for a magnificent lunch.

It was sitting one day over such a meal that I came to learn about 'Industria Brasileira' – 'made in Brazil'. We had been joined by the local head of the British Council and it was somewhere between the excellent cold soup and a gargantuan steak that he noted a small thread on the shoulder of his shirt. It clearly offended him and so he attempted to pick it off; as he picked more thread appeared and the more he picked the longer the thread became, until in a final savage movement he reached the end of the thread and deposited the sleeve of the shirt on the table.

'Industria bloody Brasileira' he expostulated; the expression was to become an expedition byword for all the locally manufactured things that didn't do what they were supposed to do.

Ian's question hung in the air, could I really make my own way to Xanvantina? Undoubtedly I was getting bored and my figure, fashioned by four years at university during which I had majored on beer, was, under the influence of large lunches, the local beer and larger dinners becoming, to say the least, rotund. When you stand five foot five you can't really afford too much excess poundage.

'Don't see why not,' I said.

The journey would involve two flights, two overnight stops and a bus journey – didn't sound too bad. And so I was put on a plane to Goiania, the capital of the state of Goias, armed with a huge array of letters bearing lots of stamps and seals and saying goodness knows what in Portuguese, that I was to wave under the noses of anyone that I needed to help me.

My third ever flight was my first encounter with the DC3.

Where the VC10 had the flowing lines of a racing car, the DC3 had more the lines of a dumper truck. It sat on the tarmac at an alarming angle, perhaps so that it had a head start in becoming airborne on short runways. The impression of slope was even more profound once you got on it. My seat was at the front and, carrying an enormous quantity of hand luggage, not to mention the excessive poundage that was testimony to my week in Brasilia, I found the incline quite daunting. By the time I reached my seat at the top of the slope, I was breathing heavily. Over the years I have made many flights on the DC3 which was the veritable flying workhorse of the developing world. While the VC10 with all its beauty was to have a short life, so the DC3 was to serve for more than 50 years, with some 13,000 aircraft being produced since the prototype first flew in 1935.

My instructions were that on arrival at Goiania I was to proceed straight to the airline office, wave a selection of my letters under the nose of the official there who would promptly issue me with a ticket for the flight next day to Aragarças. The official was a mournful-looking individual with an enormous moustache; etched into his wrinkled face was all the sadness that was his burden for having spent so many years forced to disappoint would-be travellers. In clear and slowly enunciated English, I explained that I required a seat on tomorrow's flight to Aragarcas and presented him with my letters. He read carefully through them, consulted a slip of paper pinned to a wall behind him, gazed sadly at me, and with a little shrug and an upturning of the palms intoned:

'Lotação esgotada.' My approach to communication in the Portuguese language was still very much at the stage of: speak slowly and clearly in English; if at first you have not been understood, repeat a little louder and even more slowly but without showing any sign of impatience. I applied the approach. The booking clerk returned to his surveillance of my letters then with another shrug repeated:

'Lotação esgotada.' I repeated my request yet again, a little more loudly, a little more slowly. Although I was studiously avoiding any signs of impatience, the level of my voice was by now attracting considerable attention. A small crowd of airport officials, porters, intending passengers and the families and friends of arriving or departing passengers had gathered round the ticket office, and the clerk was having an animated discussion with them. I was just opening my mouth to repeat my request when the ticket clerk held up his hand to silence me, pointed to the eight on the large clock behind him and said:

'Amanhã.' That was a word already learned, and with a sense of relief I understood that I was to report at 8.00 am tomorrow, presumably to be issued with my ticket, though the flight was not due to leave until 1.30 pm. The assembled crowd seemed pleased at the outcome, perhaps having feared that an impasse might be reached, and there was a lot of happy chatter, hand slapping with the ticket clerk and cheery smiles and waves for me. The ticket clerk and most of the crowd accompanied me outside to the taxi rank and helped load me and my baggage into a taxi.

Prompt 8 o'clock I was standing at the airline desk and prompt 8.43 the ticket clerk from the evening before appeared. He was about to open his mouth when, with a huge shrug, he took my passport from my hand and proceeded to write out my ticket for the 1.30 flight to Aragarças. I was later to learn that 'lotação esgotada' meant 'sold out', and that most internal flights in Brazil were 'lotação esgotada', despite the fact that when you eventually got on one it was invariably half empty. Seat occupancy rate had little to do with the relationship between the number of seats on the aircraft and the number of people wanting to travel, but reflected the ability or willingness of potential passengers to bribe the ticket clerk. My flight was no exception and was not much over half full as we started to taxi promptly at 1.30 – an impressive display of efficiency by VASP, the Brazilian domestic carrier.

We reached the end of the runway, at which point the plane turned round and went back to the apron; the steps were brought back to the plane and my friend the ticket clerk boarded the aircraft carrying a cardboard box, which he took up to the flight deck. It might have been the black box, but looked suspiciously like a lunch box and very probably was. The clerk then proceeded to issue what were obviously detailed instructions to the occupant of the seat next to mine as to what needed to be done with the 'Inglesa' when we got to Aragarças. I had been kindly placed in the care of a guardian; no matter that he spoke not a word of English nor me a word of Portuguese, I felt an overwhelming sense of confidence that my guardian would do whatever it was that the ticket clerk had instructed. Perhaps the clerk was carried away with a sense of his own virtue in releasing a ticket to me without my shelling out the requisite bribe and determined that, having facilitated my passage thus far, he should do what he could to make the rest of the journey go according to plan.

After two hours of buffeting through the low level tropical turbulence and a stop at a tiny village called Epaula in the middle of nowhere, coming in to land at Aragarças is a fabulous sight, and not just for the relief at coming near to the end of a deeply uncomfortable journey. The town lies at the junction of two rivers. The waters of the Araguaia are brilliant green and those of the Garças deep brown. A hugely impressive bridge crosses the two rivers just before their confluence, after which the rivers run side by side in the single bed until gradually they mix to a dull greyish colour as the now much mightier Araguaia continues its journey to the Amazon.

In fact there are two towns. Aragarças was a rather formal development of the Central Brazil Foundation in the 1940s, built as the gateway to the Mato Grosso, boasting wide streets with lights. Mirroring it on the opposite bank of the river was Barra do Garças; the mirror however was a distorting one for where Aragarças was neat and orderly Barra do Garças was higgledy-piggledy and reminded me of towns in old films about the wild west; there were horses hitched to rails and you expected that at any minute people might burst from the swinging doors of a saloon and start a gunfight. Importantly, however, Barra do Garças was the only place to shop. A Metro Centre it was not, but it boasted an array of small shops. Most of these sold exactly the same things, but rarely at the same time. As I was to come to learn, shopping in Barra do Garças was an exercise in patience. You start at one end of the town with your shopping list and rattle off the first item.

'Não tem, que mais?' was the answer you came to expect. ('Don't have it. What else?') The tone often seemed to imply that you were asking a ridiculous question or making an outrageous request, and yet you knew that the shop had stocked the item the last time you were there. So you work your way through the list and move onto the next shop where you continue the process. If you are lucky, by the time you reach the other end of the town and the last shop, you have located the majority of the items on the list.

My guardian led me first to the offices of the Central Brazil Foundation; I clutched in my hand a letter addressed to the head of the station. He was in São Paulo and the radio wasn't working so they couldn't call up to Xavantina to advise of my arrival. Next came the bus station where with remarkable ease I was able to book a bus for the following day to Xavantina.

Obviously bus passengers were not in a position to bribe the ticket clerks so occupancy of the bus did directly relate to how many seats it had and how many people wished to travel. I was told I had been fortunate, as there remained only two seats.

The Kanaxue was not the only hotel in town, but was the only one regarded as being fit for habitation by anyone other than the hardiest of locals. At this, my first encounter with a hotel away from the big cities, it seemed at best basic, if not to say primitive. It took time and a few months at base camp to come to appreciate its charms, built as it was around a courtyard shaded by some leafy trees and with pots of bougainvillea bushes; the beds had mattresses and mosquito nets, and the toilets sort of functioned. It had only one room available and so my guardian and I would have to share it. Strange that even at this point we never got to exchange names. It seemed as if he had willingly, or unwillingly, accepted an important task; he went about it efficiently and conscientiously, but made no attempt to turn his role from the guardianship that he had undertaken to companionship, but then even if we had exchanged names the language barrier would have anyway brought any expansion of the relationship to a rapid end.

Contact with CBF – done; bus to Xavantina – booked; accommodation for the night – done. You could almost see him mentally ticking off the list of duties to which he had been assigned. He pointed to his mouth – the final duty, to get something to eat.

The best restaurant in town was the Vera Cruz, a charming open-air place overlooking the confluence of the rivers. The food was consistently good; certainly it was consistent, and that first night I had an excellent meal of rice, beans, fried banana, chicken legs and steak – as indeed I had every other time that I ate there. If that first meal seemed excellent, the ones that came after a few months in camp were Michelin four stars.

I had repaired to the restaurant with my guardian and we had not been there long when a small noisy phalanx appeared at the entrance. At its centre was a tall elegantly dressed man probably in his early thirties, who, it transpired, was a lawyer from São Paulo, and he spoke excellent English. Now, what a smooth São Paulo lawyer was doing in Aragarças was something that I never asked and he never volunteered. Apparently, shortly after my arrival, runners had been sent scurrying around Aragarças to locate someone who spoke English and could provide some companionship to this lonely Inglesa. They were like that, the Brazilians; gregarious themselves, they couldn't imagine someone being at least for a while quite happy with his own company. As goes with the trade, the lawyer clearly enjoyed the sound of his own voice and spoke at length about Brazilian politics, the opening up of the interior and the problem with the Indians. He believed that the North Americans, he told me to my horror, had dealt with the problem much better – they annihilated them.

As suddenly as he had arrived, he announced it was time to go. An appointment apparently in the red light district, which my guide decided he would join. A red light district in this little backwater? It would not be long before I came to learn that no matter how small, how isolated or how poor a village was, it would always have a church, a football field and at least one house with a red light at its door. It was explained to me that not all the girls you would find behind the red-lit door were true professionals. Many were part-timers using the trade as a little income supplement and it was by no means unknown for marriages in the church up the road to have been prematurely consummated in the glow of the red light. '*Going to bed with women,*' says George Mikes, '*is almost a national hobby with Brazilians; it is rather like cricket in England.*'

I met someone on a bus once, travelling from Goiania back to Aragarças who explained to me:

'In these small towns, there are no dance halls, women are not welcomed in the bar and there is no cinema to take a girl to. In the red light district you can get to meet a girl, she makes a bit of much needed money, you have some fun and who knows, you may both fall in love.' As Mikes put it: *'According to Victorian novels these girls ought to be desperately unhappy; but they do not read Victorian novels and they are quite content.'*

I did not feel quite ready for bed and I hadn't been invited to join the lawyer and my guide – perhaps they thought I looked too young, or maybe it was simply not on the list of services that my guardian had been allocated. The restaurant was still busy, mainly with youngsters who seemed to be neither eating nor drinking, but there was an air of hopeful anticipation hanging over the place. Hopeful anticipation was a near permanent state in Brazil. Usually it was anticipation of the occurrence of a particular event or happening, but sometimes it is just unspecified anticipation. It's a bit like my mother; she was always worried. With five children, their spouses and sixteen grandchildren she had plenty to worry about, but sometimes she would admit that she had nothing specific to worry about, she was just worried.

The anticipation that pervaded the restaurant turned out to be well founded, as shortly a small band arrived and set itself up on a makeshift stage. The notice in front of them and the emblazonment on the bass drum announced them to be The Comets – drums, bass guitar, lead guitar and rhythm guitar. It was effectively the identical line-up to The Invaders – the pop group with which I had sung for two years around the clubs and dancehalls of Tyneside. The similarity did not end with the line-up as the band struck up with a selection of English and American pop songs of the late fifties and early sixties.

Some they sang in English, some in Portuguese and some in a random mix of the two; it didn't matter which language they sang them in, I was word perfect in the English version of them all. How seriously bizarre to be sitting in a small town in Mato Grosso watching this musical reincarnation of my youth.

To the disappointment of the restaurant's clientele, I decided it was time to go to bed. Numbers had swelled considerably and some of them were even buying beers, cokes and 'cafesinhos'. While The Comets had attracted much attention, they were obviously a regular turn whereas I was not and the fun they had just watching this strange little Inglesa had the edge on the performance of The Comets.

I had been in bed less than 20 minutes, my guardian had not yet returned from the red lights, when in my semiconscious state I thought I heard English voices, very English voices, in the courtyard and then my name being called.

The advance party of the expedition comprised a doctor, Phil Rees, a botanist, Jim Ratter, a forester, David Gifford and a soil scientist from the same faculty as me, Roy Montgomery. I emerged from my room to the dimly lit courtyard. David was tall, quite broad with a ramrod back and a generally military bearing. He wore thick-rimmed spectacles and sported a very South American moustache and had quickly earned the nickname Jânio Quadros because of the remarkable resemblance he bore to a Brazilian president who had held office some six years previously. Although Jânio Quadros – the real one that is – had remained in office only about 200 days, he was well imprinted on the minds of the Brazilians (admittedly his successor lasted less than two weeks so maybe 200 days wasn't bad at the time). Perhaps his lasting fame had less to do with his brief struggle to combat inflation and more to do with his radical legislation to outlaw gambling and to ban women from wearing bikinis on the beach – I assume meaning that they must wear more concealing beach attire rather than nothing at all. However, the fact that he hailed originally from Mato Grosso perhaps lent credence to the possibility that he might be seen on the streets of Aragarças or some other central Brazilian town. Certainly to walk with David along the street was to attract somewhat nervous attention and to be aware of the name Jânio Quadros being whispered behind cupped hands.

Jim Ratter was tall, lean and largely bald. He made up in the follicle department by sporting the most enormous red beard. Of all the small advance team he had made the most attempt to learn a little Portuguese.

It was David and Jim who now stood in the courtyard of the Kanaxue calling out my name. I was very short and fairly stocky and I wore my hair in the style of my musical heroes, the Beatles. It would be an exaggeration to say that I was clean-shaven since I hardly needed to shave at all. The shortness, the hairstyle, the beard-free face – I looked about fifteen, and David and Jim were obviously taken aback at this new addition to the expedition.

They had come down to Aragarças so that Jim could take the flight the next day to Goiania, and on arrival had learned that a new Inglesa was occupying the only room that had been available in the hotel. It was decided that David and I would depart right away for Xavantina in the Rural (pronounced with the accent on the 'al' – the four-wheel-drive land vehicle which, together with the pick-up version, the Jeep, totally dominated the vehicles of the interior) and Jim would take over my bed. The mail that I was carrying was sorted and distributed and David and I set off at around midnight on the long trek to Xavantina, a journey of 90 miles and a large number of bridges. The road was little more than a dirt track and the term 'jolly sporting' had been coined by the advance party to describe these bridges, with the sport coming in trying to align the wheels of the Rural with the two planks that constituted the bridge. 'Ponte esportivo' became one of the expedition's stock phrases used by English and Brazilians alike as a wonderful understatement of one of the greatest perils that we faced, with any slight misalignment of the wheels potentially hurtling you down into the chasm below.

It is not difficult to imagine the consternation of my guardian when he returned from the red light district to discover that in the space of a few hours I had lost most of my hair, grown a foot longer and sprouted a huge red beard. It took all of Jim's few words of Portuguese and a great deal of gesticulation to convince my guardian that he was not witnessing some black magic, or 'macumba', as the Brazilians called the particular brand of pagan ritual that had been brought to Brazil from central Africa. After all it was in these rivers that macumba led to the transforming of the 'boto' or giant freshwater porpoise into a variety of shapes including the human male form, in which guise the 'boto' would prey on young women.

As it happened the whole pantomime was a waste of time. About forty-five minutes out of Aragarças the road was blocked by a lorry that had broken down in the middle of it, making it quite impassable. So, David and I turned round and headed back to Aragarças and a small hotel that made the Kanaxue look like the Ritz. Next morning we went to the airport to put Jim on his flight only to find that inevitably it was 'lotação esgotada' so with a collective shrug we all returned to Xavantina.

# CHAPTER 4

# BY THE BANKS OF THE RIVER OF THE DEATHS

Perhaps taking inspiration from its evocative name, the Rio das Mortes became the last great frontier for the Xavante and other Indian tribes inhabiting the Xingu region of central Mato Grosso. Driven relentlessly from the south, the Indians finally stopped on the northern bank of the Rio das Mortes and held a firm defensive line so that even into the middle of the twentieth century those who crossed it, like Fawcett and the many subsequent expeditions, were unlikely to return.

Xavantina had been built by the Central Brazil Foundation on the banks of the Rio das Mortes, following the virtual demise of the previously unconquerable Xavante Indians, in whose honour the village had been named. But there was little honour for the small remaining rump of a once-proud tribe; from their settlement a few miles away they would appear regularly in the village that bore their name, not as its masters but as pathetic beggars. The village had two distinctly different parts to it. Built by the government was a micro Brasilia with a neat grid of houses, a small hospital offering virtually no facilities and certainly no doctor, a small air force base with a dirt runway, a church and a football field, though being a government enterprise, no red light district. But as in Brasilia spontaneous development was quick to follow and a sprawl of thatched huts, including a few with red lights, extended well beyond the village road system.

For centuries the Rio das Mortes had been the frontier at which foundered all attempts to penetrate further into the interior. Mineral prospectors, explorers, government expeditions, none got much further than the Rio das Mortes and those that did stayed either briefly on the other side or simply never returned. Like all these predecessors the Xavantina/Cachimbo Expedition had ground to a halt on the southern bank of the Rio das Mortes, not, however, because of fierce Indian tribes, wild animals or terrible tropical diseases but because of the even more unconquerable Brazilian customs officials.

Stuck on the docks in Rio de Janeiro was all the equipment that a modern expedition needed from water purifiers to microscopes, from mist nets for catching birds to safari camp beds, from botanical books to boxes of survival rations, from a prefabricated laboratory to a comprehensive medical kit. To be fair to the Brazilian customs they were faced with a bewildering variety of items, many of which were entirely alien to them and all of which had to be checked against dozens of pages of roster, and the Brazilian customs service was grossly understaffed. But putting aside fairness, the fact was that someone was waiting to be paid a big bribe and neither the academics of the Royal Society nor the cultural envoys of the British Council were geared to passing large bribes to customs officials.

So the expedition sat in Xavantina, in a charming bungalow provided to us by the Central Brazil Foundation, with a wide veranda and a cashew tree, and looking directly down at the Rio das Mortes. Unable to reach the intended base for the expedition some 160 miles further north, the advance party had set about a rigorous scientific investigation of some relatively unspoiled country a short drive from Xavantina. It seemed a far cry from the adventure for which I was geared and I found it difficult to get myself enthused by it. After porridge – for which we used to take turns preparing as this was too early for the cook – we would leave the house in Xavantina at 6.45 in the morning and drive the few miles to the path that led to the area that had been chosen for investigation, returning to the house at 11.00. We would have a swim, lunch, then write notes or have a kip in the hammock, returning to the site around 3.30pm for a couple of hours. Although I would turn out dutifully each day with my new colleagues my heart was never there, though it did have the major plus point that it started to get me used to working in temperatures that I had hitherto never imagined, let alone worked in. There was, however, much else that did interest me.

Strangely, the formal settlement of Xavantina had no shops and no bar, a deficiency fortunately rectified by the shantytown that now merged with it. My colleagues were somewhat past their student days and after the evening meal, consisting with monotonous regularity of rice, beans, macaroni and some meat of dubious origins, they were content to get on with writing up their notes or their letters home, trying to coax a small radio to produce a static-filled BBC World Service, or simply going to bed. So, after a few nights of conforming to the system, once the meal was over I picked up my Portuguese dictionary, my cigarettes, a fistful of Cruzeiro Novo (the currency had recently been revised so that the New Cruzeiro equated to 1,000 old Cruzeiros which gave some idea of the level of inflation that Jânio Quadro had tried to tackle, along of course with outlawing gambling and bikinis) and thus armed went off to find the bar.

The shop and the bar were one and the same establishment, the designation 'bar', as proclaimed on the front of the small thatched wooden building, based on it being equipped with a kerosene refrigerator, three plank tables and some plastic chairs. Three men of indeterminate age – at least indeterminate in the dim lighting of kerosene lamps – occupied one table and I took up position on the adjacent one and ordered a beer. I soon made friends with the three men who introduced me first to 'cachaça', according to my dictionary 'a strong spirit made from sugar cane and drunk either neat or as a 'batida' with a lime squeezed into it. 'Firewater' was probably the most apposite description and I decided that it was a drink I would gladly avoid in the future, though at times when beer ran out it could develop a certain appeal. Suitably plied with 'cachaça' the men soon became my language teachers until my head swam with Portuguese vocabulary and strong liquor.

Over the course of the next six weeks I would go most evenings to the bar. The number of 'teachers' did swell somewhat and the 'cachaça' bill soared but at a few pence for a shot of 'cachaça' lessons were still working out at a lot less than a Linguaphone course, though I had a sneaky suspicion that the Royal Society would not feel inclined to reimburse the money to me. The bar had windows, though not of the variety that had glass, and at them would gather those too young, too poor or of the wrong sex to be able to go into the bar. This did not prevent them from making their contributions to my education through the window, and from time to time I felt it incumbent upon me to extend the round with bottles of Coca Cola and 'cachaças' dispensed to those outside.

We progressed from single words to short sentences. They would tell me something and I would look up each word in my dictionary. I became aware that compared to my 'Teach Yourself Portuguese', they were constructing the language in a much more simplified fashion. At first I thought they were doing it for my sake, but as my comprehension of the language grew I realised that they spoke to each other in exactly the same way. After a couple of weeks the local schoolteacher joined the group; he spoke a bit of English and undoubtedly this helped things along. There was many an evening when, for at least part of the time, the roles would be reversed and I would find myself teaching them a few key English words and phrases – though I still paid for the 'cachaça'!

I was young, my brain receptive and I had always had some facility for languages. By the time I moved on to base camp my Portuguese had become quite passable. I use the word 'Portuguese' in the loosest possible sense. As spoken in central Mato Grosso, the language was to Portuguese what Geordie is to English. In each case there is an undeniable association between the root language and the dialect, but the pronunciation and the use of peculiarly regional words and expressions can make it difficult to see that association. Both dialects had in common a certain abruptness, a certain economy of effort; there is no room for pronunciation that prolongs the word, hence for example the short 'a' used in the northeast. Go to São Paulo and declare something to be very bad; 'muito ruim' you will say, and pronounce it 'mweeto rueem' with a slight rolling of the 'r'. In Mato Grosso they favour putting the 'very' after the word and 'muito ruim' becomes 'hoy moont'. As there were many very bad things about the expedition, 'hoy moont' became probably the most frequently used words in its three-year duration.

Six months later I was to be on a bus travelling from Brasilia and fell into a conversation with the man in the seat next to me. After a short time he said to me:

'I know where you come from.'

'Where?' I responded.

'You are a Matogrossoense,' he declared triumphantly.

'Good try,' I said. 'In fact I'm a Geordie, but it's a mistake that anyone could have made.'

Since well before my arrival the bungalow had become a gathering place for the local population. Total strangers would come and sit on our veranda or in our living room quite simply to watch us or to study intently some of the equipment that we used, or botanical specimens that we had collected. Meal times were peak viewing and it would not be uncommon for the five of us to sit to dinner with a dozen or more people looking on. They were not there because they wanted anything, these were not poor people, mostly they were employed by the Central Brazil Foundation, though doing what, was not apparent. They were not on the scrounge, like the sad rump of the Xavante Indians, they were simply curious. They listened intently to our conversations without understanding a word. Some would claim a right to be there on the basis of kinship with the cook, some were village worthies giving an air of being there as a sort of civic duty, but others offered no justification for their presence, they were just curious. In a village with no television and no pre-packaged entertainment, and without the sort of cultural heritage that might be found in more natural settlements, the 'Inglesas' were the entertainment gift from heaven.

The arrival of a young, presumed to be single, male with a Beatles haircut brought, however, a new influx. These were the pubescent, some probably prepubescent, girls of the village. They were shy at first and unlike their seniors they sat around some short distance from the house just quietly watching. But this didn't last for long. On my second Saturday in Xavantina it was decreed that we would have a day off and David, who was one of those people that seemed to be able to turn his hand to anything, decided to fix up the old record player that we had found in the bungalow. Our young entourage closely observed the process and the prettiest of them, inevitably called Maria, came up to me and indicated that she had records and would like to bring them. Her collection comprised three '45s', of which one was an advertisement for Kolynos toothpaste, but it's amazing how you can get a good bop going on a Saturday afternoon with two Brazilian pop songs and a toothpaste advert. Thereafter the girls felt no inhibitions and wandered freely around the bungalow observing us eat, work or even sleep.

Our daily ablutions were a particular highlight for them. Although the bungalow boasted a shower of sorts, most of us preferred to use the river where we could combine a swim with a bath and doing our laundry. My departure from the bungalow with my towel would usually ensure a hasty gathering of girls on the riverbank. The bank down to the river from the bungalow was a bit of a scramble and the girls would generally gather at a rough ledge halfway down. At the worst of times my antics provided much amusement, but sometimes I really excelled. One day I came without my soap. No point in not making use of my audience, so I shouted out that I needed soap from the bungalow. This caused great hilarity because in the local dialect there were two words for soap. There was a coarse green soap – 'sabao' – that came in huge blocks and was used exclusively for doing laundry; the soap that you washed yourself with was 'sabonette', and I asked for the wrong one. Why the idea of me washing myself in laundry soap was quite such a source of hilarity I couldn't fathom, but once they had milked the idea for all the mirth it could provide, the faithful Maria went and fetched the 'sabonette'.

By the time I came to return to the bungalow, I was in such a state of confusion that just as I reached the ledge where the girls assembled I tripped over my flip-flops and slid back down the slope, getting covered in red earth. I had no choice but to return to the river. It had been a particularly good day for them – well worth missing school or chores or whatever they were supposed to be doing.

The daily routine did offer its moments of excitement. One day as we arrived at the study area we realised that a massive bush fire was sweeping towards it. The team was horrified; the idea had been that this area would be protected so that the bushes and trees could be monitored over the life of the expedition as people transited through Xavantina. Plants that had not been in flower or fruit and were therefore difficult to identify would be collected, and possibly the Brazilian academics who were supposed ultimately to be part of the expedition would adopt it as a key research site. Our traverse started at the top of a ridge and the only way to prevent it being burned to the ground was to back-burn the opposite ridge slope down which the fire would soon sweep. This was David Gifford territory and he soon had us organised with military precision into a fire-fighting machine. So we set fire to the vegetation at the bottom of the adjoining ridge and chased it up the ridge to meet the oncoming fire from the other direction. It was over 90 degrees – without the benefit of the fire – and by 6.30 in the evening we were all totally exhausted, filthy and parched but we had succeeded in creating a firebreak between our ridge and the oncoming fire. We all agreed that the Royal Society owed us a drink and so on our way home we stopped off at my local. Of all nights for it to happen the bar had run out of beer. But it had lots of gin and limes and a fridge full of ice and a reasonable supply of

tonic water, and so I was introduced to 'gin-tonico', a drink
that was to play an important part in my life.

We employed in Xavantina a small labour force, the majority
of whom would ultimately move with us to base camp and
mostly stay for the duration of the expedition. One of these
was Raimundo Aselino de Castro, almost universally known
as Taituba, after the town of Itaituba in the state of Para where
he had been born, though he would often introduce himself
by his full name and rather liked being called Raimundo,
which he seemed to feel accorded him a greater status. Unlike
the rest of the labour force, Taituba had been seconded to the
expedition by the Central Brazil Foundation. He had a laugh
that could crack mirrors and would send chickens and dogs
scurrying for cover; he had a serious weakness for 'cachaça'
and would disappear sometimes for days on end on some sort
of blinder. He was effectively illiterate and had no sense of
hierarchy; every member of the expedition was accorded a
nickname by Taituba, often related to some animal or plant,
and it was Taituba who had so accurately identified the striking
similarity between David and Jânio Quadros. However,
despite being described by one of the advance team as the
'ultimate in non-companions', he had a heart of gold and on
the occasion of my birthday just a few days after my reaching
Xavantina, he bought me the most enormous tin of local
sweets that he presented to me with great pride. But it was not
for his heart of gold that he was a lynchpin of the expedition;
Taituba was a naturalist in a class of his own. He had spent
many years living with an Indian tribe and seemed to know
every tree, bush, flower, insect, bird and mammal. Not only

did he know them all by their Brazilian and often a number of Indian names, but he had a fundamental understanding of the relationships between species. One of the expedition's senior botanists is quoted as saying that his taxonomic judgement would do credit to a professor of plant taxonomy. He was also a very good organiser of parties.

We were going backwards. A few weeks earlier there had been great excitement at the news that our goods had been released by customs and the expedition's newly acquired lorry arrived loaded in Xavantina. There was barely half of the expedition's goods on board; whoever had ultimately done the necessary with the customs officers had obviously got their sums wrong. So now it was time for most of the advance party to pack up and return home to their academic institutions, as the beginning of the second wave led by Professor Paul Richards and his postgraduate student, George Argent, arrived. Like so many expeditions before them our expedition had failed to get beyond the banks of the Rio das Mortes. It marked the end of the first frustrating phase of the expedition, but for Taituba it was still an occasion for a fiesta and he organised it in grand style.

On the evening before their departure there appeared a three-piece band comprising an accordion, cymbals and a triangle; we had seen none of the musicians before – certainly they were not part of the onlookers who sat around the bungalow – and never saw them again. The music was remarkably good and we suspected that Taituba had 'imported' them from Aragarças. The booze flowed and the place filled up. There were the Inglesas and the usual onlookers; all our labour force was there and a good number of my tutors from the bar in the shantytown. And of course there were the girls. Amongst, yet clearly not a real part of, the onlookers was the man I had dubbed the quiet man. He was always there, somehow uncomfortably placed between the onlookers and the girls. I learned that night that my 'quiet man' was Maria's father and came to realise that whenever Maria was within touching range of the young Inglesa, father was there too. Bit of a bummer.

Uninvited, for surely not even Taituba could have stage-managed that, were two men who had just paddled for twelve hours down the Rio das Mortes carrying a couple of dozen eggs to sell. For reasons that I never understood it was inordinately difficult to buy eggs, so their wares were enthusiastically purchased from them. They then faced a two to three day return trip to wherever they had come from and I boggled at the notion that they had made a three-day trip to sell a few eggs. Mind you, they stayed for the duration of the party and clearly enjoyed themselves, so maybe Taituba was somehow behind it all.

No good party is complete without a party bore, though we never knew whether Taituba had arranged one specially or it just happened of its own accord. He had the look of an enormous bullfrog with massively protuberant eyes; he was severely under the influence of 'cachaça' and worked his way round all the Inglesas mournfully recounting to each of us, in largely incomprehensible Portuguese, what I took to be his tale of woe, and inviting us to go back to his house where the party might be continued. At regular intervals his young son appeared, clearly bearing a message from mother that his father was to accompany him home, an instruction that he totally ignored. He must have copped it when he did eventually get home.

A couple of days before their departure, a decision had been reached that the only way of getting Jim's large collection of botanical specimens shipped back to England was for them to be driven down to Brasilia, where he would personally organise their despatch. Phil was the only one of the advance party not to be leaving, as he still wanted to see the establishment of base camp and hopefully set up the medical facilities there, so he and I were deputed to drive the Rural loaded to its roof with the botanical collection. So now, instead of crossing the Rio das Mortes and forging into unexplored territory I was in retreat to Brasilia.

From Xavantina to Brasilia by road was around 700 miles and the stretch from Xavantina to Aragarças with its jolly sporting bridges turned out to be one of the better bits. We had left Xavantina at about 5.30 pm and fortified ourselves with a meal at the Vera Cruz in Aragarças. What followed was an 'estrada ruim'. The dictionary strictly defines 'ruim' as 'bad, evil, wicked, or wretched'. Pronounced the local way – 'estrada hoy moont' – it conveyed exactly somehow the horrors. The road was ferociously corrugated so that most of the journey it was like driving over corrugated iron, but with the subtle difference that rather than being rounded, the corrugations are sharply pointed. The road was dissected at frequent intervals by gullies that could be two feet deep and if you failed to spot them in time could break your axle. Next came the sand drifts which occurred in isolated patches for no discernible reason; hitting one of these was very much like hitting sheet ice, as the Rural would slide uncontrollably through them, and you just had to hope that it wouldn't slide into anything too unyielding. Then, of course there were the sporting bridges. The sport provided by the bridges on the road between Aragarças and Xavantina paled to local harrier level compared to the positively Olympian heights reached on the road to Goiania. Planks were frequently missing or broken and extended detours were required to get round them, manageable only because this was the dry season, not that there was ever any warning of these hazards so you might be halfway across a bridge when you discovered that one of the two planks came to an end before the far side was reached.

Phil and I took turns driving, doing an hour to an hour-and-a-half at a stretch, which was about as long as the intense concentration required could be held and arms retain the strength to do battle with the steering wheel. 'Off duty', we would retire to the back seat of the Rural and try to get forty winks. Every now and then we would drive through a raging bush fire, a fantastic sight lighting up the sky for many miles around.

We reached Jatai at cockcrow – to be precise at 4 o'clock in the morning – but the thing I came to learn about Jatai was that it was perpetually cockcrow. Nicknamed 'Bee City', it would have been much more appropriate had it been nicknamed 'Cockerel City'. For reasons that nobody could ever explain to me, Jatai had more, and more vociferous, cockerels than any other town in Brazil, a situation compounded by the fact that the bloody things hadn't a clue that they were only supposed to crow at dawn. To spend a night in Jatai was to try to sleep through eight hours of a perpetual dawn as hundreds of confused cockerels heralded every quarter of an hour of the night. Jatai marked more or less the halfway point to Goiania and after a couple of reviving 'cafesinhos' we continued our journey on an ever-improving road. Thirteen hours after leaving Xavantina we had covered the four hundred or so miles to Goiania with no mishaps greater than a blow out, the cessation of any functionality of the speedometer and a steady drip of oil from the engine. We headed directly to the Bandeirante – the best hotel in town – and we arrived there very bleary-eyed and covered in orange-red dust mixed with liberal sprinklings of dirty oil. In response to our request that we might be directed to somewhere where we could clean up a little, the manager was summoned, who provided to us at no charge the facilities of an en-suite bedroom from which we emerged clean and refreshed and ready for a well-earned 'gin-tonico'.

The onward journey to Brasilia was tame by comparison, though passed through some magnificent scenery. The land was deeply dissected and often rather barren, reminding me a little of some of my native moorland, but in the valleys there was tall forest and every now and then there would be a tree flowering in magnificent reds or purples or oranges. Brasilia itself was the usual gloomy scene. The balance of our equipment had been released by customs but had gone missing somewhere between Rio de Janeiro and Brasilia, the expedition was going broke because the transfers of money from England were not getting through and more people were scheduled to arrive, but with the expedition still stuck on the south bank of the Rio das Mortes. Still, on the positive side negotiations to purchase a much-needed new Jeep seemed to be nearing completion.

After two days in Brasilia it was a relief to be headed back to the more cheerful atmosphere of Xavantina and despite some rain, making driving even trickier if somewhat less dusty, we made it back in good time. What we didn't know was that less than 24 hours behind us was our brand new Jeep bringing Iain, Angie and the second long-termer Tony Matthews, a forester who would be working under the guidance of David Gifford, and who had just arrived in Brazil. Suddenly it looked as if we might be on the move, a decision having been made on high that we should move north even in the absence of half of our equipment.

The little following party arrived at the bungalow the next day just as I was changing for my evening ablutions and parked the car next to the old Rural. It made quite a contrast as despite its journey from Brasilia it still had the sheen of a brand new car and looked very smart in its blue livery. Tony and Iain went to change quickly so that they could join me for ablutions in the river. Angie declined to join us and sat on the veranda with a cold drink.

There was a rumbling sound a bit like rolling logs, a piercing scream and a tremendous crash; briefly silence and then a further rumble, a further scream, followed by another crash. We ran from the house to see the beautiful brand new blue Jeep wrapped round a tree half way down the riverbank. En route down it had demolished one tree, but fortunately its descent had been arrested by the next one about ten metres further down, where it now rested somewhat precariously. Had it made it past that tree, then it would have had a clear run straight into the torrential waters of the Rio das Mortes. The explanation for the disaster was that this brand new Jeep had suddenly suffered a spontaneous failure of its handbrake and simultaneously jumped out of gear. The other possible explanation was that our Team Leader, who had been driving the Jeep, had forgotten to apply the handbrake and had not left it in gear. We didn't have sufficient confidence in the handbrake failure and jumping out of gear theory to make a decision to sue the manufacturers of the Jeep. The next day our lorry appeared loaded with supplies for the move north and succeeded in pulling the Jeep back up the riverbank. Damage was assessed and it was concluded that the Jeep could be repaired – just about.

In preparation for our forthcoming departure I accompanied the lorry back into Aragarças to obtain further supplies and to deal with the mail. Realising that outbound mail, once we had moved north, would be rather less regular, or aware perhaps that many an expedition had crossed the Rio das Mortes never to be seen again, everybody had moved into frantic letter-writing mode so I had quite a heap of mail.

The process in the post office in Aragarças was a lengthy one. Each letter had to be weighed and the value of stamps required computed. The post office in Aragarças was not at that time geared to overseas mail and indeed never became geared to it in the two years that the expedition coursed its mail through that post office – obviously not quick learners. Or perhaps it was a fear that suddenly the Inglesas would up sticks and disappear leaving the postmaster with an embarrassment of international stamps for which there would never be any further demand. The post office accordingly kept only stamps essentially intended for the local postal system. Every letter required a vast number of these low denomination stamps and fitting them onto the envelope was a process requiring a high degree of spatial awareness combined with considerable manual dexterity – neither of which are skills that I have ever demonstrated.

In time we all learned how best to position the address on the envelope to facilitate the fixing of the stamps. The stamps of course were not gummed and each one had to have glue applied to it with a brush, from a large pot of a foul smelling semi-coagulated liquid. It is one of the differences that I have observed between people and flies. While that glue to us seemed potentially noxious, it was highly attractive to flies, and part of the art of dealing with the outgoing mail was to minimise the number of flies per stamp for a surfeit of flies under any one stamp meant that it didn't lie properly and risked being lifted off by the franking machine. Once all the mail was stamped up the postmaster would frank it while you watched just so that all parties were happy with the process and any fly laden stamps that came unstuck on the machine could be replaced – at your cost of course. That day I spent two-and-a-half hours in the post office.

# CHAPTER 5

# IN FAWCETT'S FOOTSTEPS

The adventure had begun. The cosy drive to our transect just outside the village, the comfort of the bungalow, the civilisation of the local bar, all this was surely now behind us. We were on our way to Fawcett country.

When you are young you live in the certainty that nothing awful is ever going to happen to you. I recall one day when we were working in the research area near Xavantina. We had a routine whereby we were dropped at the beginning of the path by the doctor, who then returned to Xavantina, picking us up at an appointed time. There was a contingency plan that if anything happened that required us to be pulled out of the area early, the doctor would come to the beginning of the path and blast the horn. In that quiet and desolate area sound travelled far. One day we were just settled in the area to be surveyed that day when we all distinctly heard the blast of the Rural's horn. After a brief discussion it was decided that we must all return to the vehicle without delay. We marched in silence along the track. I understand now that my colleagues walked in the silence of fear; they had wives and children and they knew that things went wrong in life. We had been summoned from our work. The omens were bad. I walked thinking only that it seemed a good skive off work and maybe there was something exciting happening. We got to the road to find nothing – no vehicle, no message, nothing. At the appointed time the vehicle rolled up and nobody was ever able to explain how we had heard the sound of a Rural's horn.

So for me it was without trepidation that on Friday 29th September 1967 we departed from Xavantina to head north. We started off at 8.00am; George and I crossed the river by canoe so that we could photograph the arrival of the lorry on the other side. Passage across the river, we were to come to learn, was always fraught and always took an extraordinarily long time. No matter how many times we made that crossing, no matter how often that pontoon had ferried vehicles across the river, it was as if every time was the first time and you knew that something would always go wrong. The pontoon reached the north bank and the planks were put in place to allow the lorry to come off it. There was a tremendous cracking sound; the driver, Joachim, accelerated furiously and the lorry shot onto the bank as the broken plank disappeared down the Rio das Mortes – a narrow squeak.

George and I had not wasted our time while awaiting the arrival of the lorry on the north bank, but had discovered that there was a little stall rejoicing in the name Bar Gloria selling 'cafesinhos', and we had filled the time usefully supporting local enterprise. It was time to depart. Overall I was excited to be on the move because that, after all, was what I had come out to do, but I felt a tinge of regret at leaving our bungalow with its cashew tree and fabulous view over the river, my evenings in the little bar in the shanty town, and who knows, one day Maria's father may have been called away on urgent business to Goiania or Brasilia or São Paulo or somewhere else a long way away. Angie and Professor Richards joined Joachim in the cab and the remaining six of us balanced ourselves a little precariously on top of the lorry's load together with a cock and a hen. A gang of Brasileiros (the collective name by which we always referred to our labour force, just as the scientists were always simply the Inglesas) led by Taituba had travelled north ten days before to get some basic facilities in place so we knew that base camp was the first turn on the right, approximately 160 miles to the north.

The road passed through largely monotonous vegetation of fairly open bushes and small trees known in Brazil as 'cerrado' or in its slightly higher and denser form as 'cerradão' (pronounced 'cerradon'). It was, however, punctuated by sudden beautiful sweeps of grassland and occasional high ridges breaking up the otherwise gently rolling relief. We saw quite a few deer, and colourful parrots and macaws screeched overhead, flying usually in pairs or sometimes bigger family groups. Thousands of locusts flew into or past the lorry; at rest they were a dull brown but in flight revealed brilliant blue underwings and bright red bodies. At about the midway point of our journey we came across a small fazenda. We had passed a few such establishments, mud huts with palm-thatched roofs and hammocks slung inside or on a sort of veranda. Cooking pots were stacked up at the side of the house and a few pigs, chickens, occasionally a cow and always a number of small children scratched about in the bare earth surrounding the hut. The number of these little fazendas would grow alarmingly during the time that the expedition was on the ground. Some were simply landless people coming to take their chance of being left alone to scratch an existence out of a small plot of land. Others were the functionaries of big landowners who had staked claim to vast areas of this virgin land but wanted to do nothing to it at present other than keep others off it.

It was the fairly large number of chickens at this fazenda that attracted us to stop, in the hope that we might be able to make a purchase to supplement our single cock and hen which, even if they got down to it quickly, would not be providing us with a reasonable supply of fresh meat and eggs for a long time. The 'fazendeiro' was a man by the name of Geraldão, short and squat with a huge potbelly, which he took great pride in displaying for all to admire. He was in his hammock when we arrived, a place, as we came to learn, where he spent a large amount of his day. He greeted us affably and inevitably offered us a 'cafesinho' which, alongside the adrenalin rush provided by the high caffeine content, also left you with a mouthful of coarse grounds to chew on, as he had no way of filtering his coffee. It was entirely possible to be still chewing on these grounds or picking them from your teeth when you arrived at base camp.

Despite the affability, he was adamant that he could not sell us the dozen or so chickens that we tried to purchase from him. Then with that wonderful gesture that we came to know so characterised the rural Brazilians he made us a present of two chickens. He had disappointed us in our attempted purchase, but delighted us in the kindness of his gift. The fazenda of Geraldão became a regular stopping place for the people travelling to and from the base camp; it marked more or less the midway point of the journey and coffee that you could still be chewing some hours later became quite addictive. Whoever stopped there could be assured of a 'cafesinho' and not once would Geraldão accept any payment for it. Of course we would make little gifts to him like the heavy gauge plastic bags that were a much sought-after product of the expedition.

Without warning, without a road sign or a roundabout, we arrived at the first turning on the right and drove down a narrow track for a mile to what was to become home for much of the next twelve months. We had travelled 160 miles from the bank of the Rio das Mortes. While most of that journey had been made through the cerrado we had come with shuddering abruptness to the forest. Seen from the air or on the air photos, the boundary between the cerrado and the forest was for mile after countless mile as sharp as a blade and without any obvious reason for this dramatic change of vegetation. Base camp was situated almost exactly on this junction.

Our camp was built on the site of a former road builder's camp that had been identified for us by Taituba during a previous reconnaissance mission. Ahead of us an advance group of our Brazilian labour force had started the process of building our new campsite. They knew what they were doing, those road builders, and the location had been well chosen at the junction of two relatively small but clearly perennial streams. One stream was to provide our water supply, with water being pumped up to a large tank located on top of a wooden tower at a height of around six metres. Funny how people get allocated to the most inappropriate jobs. Despite all our efforts the outlet from the water tank blocked at frequent intervals; not only am I exceptionally short but I have a very poor head for heights, so I suppose that it was inevitable that to me should be allocated the job of unblocking the outlet. Every time it blocked I would be dispatched to shin up to the top of the tower to unblock it. Rats were the most frequent cause of blockage, though occasionally I would find more interesting wildlife like a bird or a snake or sometimes simply an accumulation of vegetation. Depending on the precise nature of the blockage, I may have been able to sort it out simply by leaning into the tank, but at other times I would have to clamber into it, and peering over the edge of the tank did induce a giddiness that was mild vertigo. Access to the upper reach of the larger stream was totally prohibited and notices in English and Portuguese, with graphic illustration for those who could cope with neither language, made it clear that pissing or worse was a capital offence. Downstream of the barrier was free access and was where Inglesas and Brasileiros alike could do their ablutions, wash their clothes and wash the dishes. The other stream we would come to dam in order to create a swimming pool. A characteristic of the local landscape was that alongside all streams there was a band of tall forest known as the 'gallery forest', and it was in a clearing of this that base camp was to be established. This provided a degree of shade to the campsite, though there had been sufficient clearing of this forest that it was still light and during much of the day quite sunny.

The camp was in two parts. On one side of the streams were the living and working quarters. One fifty-foot long hut housed the Brasileiros with their hammocks slung at one end and cooking facilities at the other. Another similar hut provided the dining, storage and general sitting-around area for the Inglesas with their kitchen at one end. A somewhat smaller hut was to be built as the 'dirty' laboratory, and when eventually found, a prefabricated aluminium hut was to be the 'clean' laboratory. On the other side of the streams was the Inglesas' sleeping quarters, comprising a little individual hut for each person known somewhat optimistically as our 'casa'– a house or home – although as pressure of numbers built up later on, we had to construct a sort of terrace row of sleeping quarters for the very short stay people. With the exception of the 'clean laboratory' and the Bishops' sleeping quarters, all fabrication was done in the traditional way of the region with the poles that underpinned the construction cut from the forest, the roofs made from the 'buriti' palm fronds, and walls, for those who wanted more privacy in their 'casa', constructed from smaller branches. Personally I never went for the wall but left my buriti thatch long so it overhung the roof and gave a feeling of privacy without reducing the breeze through the hut, though it did of course mean that passers-by were treated to the awesome view of my hairy legs if I was changing in my 'casa'.

If Taituba was the undisputed cognoscente of the area's natural history, Arjimeiro was the craftsman par excellence. He was older than the other members of the expedition's labour force with a high proportion of European in him and a face like wrinkled leather. He was always calm, never flustered and never beaten by any task. In Portuguese there is a word 'jeito'; as used locally it really had no direct translation but simply meant 'a way of doing something', and Arjimeiro always had a 'jeito' for everything. Whatever technical task might be getting the better of us someone would eventually say:

'Let's call Arjimeiro, he'll have a 'jeito'. And he always did. One day I was trying to mend the lid of the little aluminium box in which I kept tobacco and failing abysmally. (Despite the assurances of my benefactor at São Paulo airport, I still liked to roll my own sometimes, though I had also developed something of a weakness for the Brazilian 'cheroots' which cost all of four old pence each). Arjimeiro had been watching my struggles. Aside from the practical function of the box for keeping my tobacco from drying out, it also had a sentimental value. I gave up and passed the box over to Arjimeiro, who within the space of a few minutes had restored the box to its former glory.

While the construction of the traditional buildings was left to the Brasileiros, Iain decreed that the Inglesas should do the assembly of the aluminium huts. The Brasileiros were deemed to be fine with a hammer and nails, but the greater refinement of nuts, bolts, washers and braces was a job for the Inglesas. While asking me regularly to shin up to the top of a six metre tower was wholly inappropriate, asking me to participate in the construction of a prefabricated building was like asking a pig to dance the minuet. One Christmas my parents purchased for me a Meccano set to try to encourage some technical skills, but the only person who ever used it was my youngest sister.

Undeterred I joined Iain in the great construction. With a little help from the Brasileiros who would hold panels in place while we bolted them, unbelievably the aluminium house came together. The only problem was that there was no way that the door would come anywhere near to closing, and since the whole point of the 'clean' laboratory was that it was a place where microscopes and other fragile equipment, as well as the more delicate specimens, could be kept without getting covered in the dust that infiltrated every corner of base camp, having a door with a six inch gap rendered the building a little pointless. Arjimeiro would have a 'jeito'.

He spent a long time studying the nearly completed aluminium hut from every angle. Finally picking his spot he stepped back about ten yards then took a run at the building, hitting the selected spot in a solid shoulder charge. He was not the strongest or sturdiest of men but as he hit it the aluminium frame gave an ear-splitting crack and the door popped neatly into place; it never gave us any further trouble. Arjimeiro had a 'jeito' for everything.

The first contribution from Anthony Smith appeared in The Times on 21st October, before he had visited Mato Grosso, under the headline: '*Mato Grosso expedition sets up base camp with no name.*' Never believe everything you read in the newspaper, not even The Times; I had already named the camp 'Fim d'Estrada' – end of the road.

Strictly it was not in fact at the end of the road that, in ever deteriorating condition, extended a further 140 miles and then ground to a halt. Just as the advance party of the expedition was setting out for Brazil there had been a change of government, a change of heart, a general disillusionment as the going – so easy through the cerrado – became slower or more difficult through increasingly dense forest. In true Brazilian fashion they just abandoned it, leaving machinery rotting and rusting at the roadside. When I returned to Brazil in 1971, attention had been turned to the Trans-Amazonas highway, and the VW Beetles that choked the streets of Rio, São Paulo or Brasilia were covered in rear window stickers declaring that 'we are all going to the Amazon.' Funny, I had never seen a single car with a rear windscreen sticker declaring that they were all going to Mato Grosso; the Amazon sounded much more glamorous and anyway it was two fingers to the international community that was trying to persuade the Brazilian government not to open the way to the rape and destruction of the Amazonian forest. Not of course that any of the drivers of those Beetles had the slightest intention of leaving their big cities.

Given the enforced abandonment of the concept that the expedition would work just ahead of an advancing road which was no longer advancing, it made little sense to go further north. From a practical point of view our current location could, for a lot of the year, be reached within a day from Xavantina, and from a scientific point of view it was ideally placed to study two major vegetation types and perhaps unravel one of the great ecological mysteries of what, in the absence of human interference, caused this abrupt transition from cerrado to forest. From base camp we could continue further north, go east towards the headwaters of the Rio das Mortes or strike to the west to Colonel Fawcett's Dead Horse Camp in the headwaters of the Xingu. Dead Horse Camp II did not seem like a very catchy name for our own camp. So, okay, Fim d'Estrada was stretching it a bit, but I was less concerned with scientific or geographical accuracy than I was about giving camp a name that could be fitted into the Grammy-winning comedy song by Allan Sherman. Set to the tune of Ponchielli's 'Dance of the Hours' and based on supposed letters sent from a child complaining about his summer camp, 'Hello Muddah, Hello Fadduh' was highly apposite. Its opening verse goes:

> 'Hello Muddah Hello Faddah,
> here I am at Camp Granada,
> it is very entertaining
> and they say we'll have some fun when it stops raining.

> It did not require a genius lyricist to convert this to:
> Hello Muddah Hello Faddah,
> here I am at Fim d'Estrada,
> it is very entertaining
> and they say we'll have some fun when it starts raining'.

Members of the expedition could then be fitted at will into further verses:

> Iain Bishop is our leader,
> He is such a hopeless bleeder
> He keeps running out of money,
> And when the beer dries up it may not seem so funny.

# CHAPTER 6

# NOT LIKE IT IS ON THE TELE

The expedition settled quickly into a routine at base camp. The day always started with porridge, a tradition carried on from our days in Xavantina. It was a popularly held belief that the porridge was laced with bromide. This was denied, but then generations of British servicemen firmly believed that 'the authorities' routinely put bromide in the NAFFI tea in order to damp down the troops' sexual urges, something that the authorities also denied. Suffice it to say that of the fifty or so British members of the expedition the only one who never ate the porridge was Iain – despite being a Scot.

The pattern of movement of scientists in and out of the expedition started. Paul Richards and George Argent departed, Brian Freeman arrived and a botanist, David Philcox, from the Royal Botanic Gardens at Kew. David had only half a lung but that didn't deter him from smoking like a chimney. He was the third David on the expedition; David Gifford aka Jânio Quadros was always known as 'David', Philcox became 'Dave' and because of my diminutive stature I was christened 'Davidinho' – the little David, frequently just shortened to 'Dinho'. My tutor, Peter Askew, and The Times' Anthony Smith made the first of their visits and a replacement doctor arrived in the form of the lanky John Guillebaud.

If there was a total monotony to breakfasts the same could not be said about the evening meal. Indeed this came in three varieties: 'Salchisas Tipo Vienna' with rice and/or macaroni and beans; 'Kitut de Boi' with rice and/or macaroni and beans; and sardines with rice and/or macaroni and beans. For a change you could have just rice and/or macaroni and beans. 'Salchisas Tipo Vienna' was a vile tinned sausage, and if it was indeed the good people of Vienna who had invented this adulteration of the sausage then they had a lot to answer for; certainly I have never felt any desire since then to visit Vienna. Marginally less revolting was the tinned 'spam of ox' which while barely recognisable as some form of beef was, at least by comparison to the 'salchisas', reasonably bland. The sardines should have been the best, and occasionally we could buy tins that were just sardines in an oil, but all too often they were in a concoction that had distinct undertones of 'Salchisas Tipo Vienna' and I wondered if the Viennese had also had some part to play in these. As expedition supplies gradually trickled out of Brazilian customs, we were able occasionally to raid containers of trek rations which came in ten-man-day boxes and consisted mostly of dehydrated vegetables and protein mixes, but bizarrely also included a tinned Dundee cake. Any special occasion would be marked by a raid on the trek boxes for one of these.

In a major concerted Inglesa/Brasileiro venture over a weekend, we had dammed the second stream and cleared an area about 20 yards by 20 yards to create a swimming pool. After a couple of weeks the swimming pool had filled sufficiently for us to take our maiden swims – though sadly without maidens. Brian decided on the spectacular approach. Tall trees, from most of which hung long trailing lianas, surrounded the pool, and naked as the day he was born Brian took a run at the pool, grabbed a liana and swung himself over the pool. There was an almighty crack and Brian landed arse first in the pool. His injuries were mercifully minor but nobody after that tried the Tarzan act.

Today we would have been expected, in the isolation and hardship of life in the middle of the jungle, to have torn one another apart. I have never personally watched a reality TV show but that I understand is the general pattern of things until one member of the party after another manages to be more obnoxious than the others and is dispatched from the jungle; I believe it is something like that anyway. However, in the evenings we would, like Sir Arthur's knights, sit at the large round table that Arjimeiro had constructed and discuss great matters of science or philosophy.

In his book 'Mato Grosso'[4], Anthony Smith writes:

> *'Of course everyone had to specialise in that wilderness, but the mealtime conversations helped to break down these artificial barriers as the ornithologist asked about Hymenoptera, or the hydrologist asked about the fish'.*

However, he didn't always see it quite like this. We had our first visit from Anthony Smith a couple of months after the establishment of base camp. At the end of the first evening his comment as he rose from table was:

'Do you realise that for the last two hours your conversation has not risen above the level of your navels?' And I suppose it was true that discussion of food, drink, stomach upsets and sex did dominate conversation, presumably the effect of the bromide having worn off by that time of evening.

Not all of the people that arrived at base camp were expected, and perhaps the least expected was the French cyclist. We had been at the camp for only a few weeks. Iain and Angie had gone back to Brasilia to continue the ceaseless search for the expedition's equipment and perhaps, at least for

---

4    Mato Grosso by Anthony Smith, 1971, designed and produced by George Rainbird Ltd.

Angie, to escape from the camp, so I had been left in charge. The lorry had just rolled up with much-needed supplies, most importantly rice, which we had been eking out for over a week, and which was leading the labour force to the brink of revolution. They were a good bunch, our labour force, and put up cheerily with all sorts of inconveniences, but deprive a Brasileiro of his rice or his coffee and you have disaster in the making. Given the Brazilian proclivity for revolution, I had felt some concern that my first spell as stand-in Team Leader could end ignominiously with my being deposed, perhaps to be replaced by Taituba. My only consolation was that Brazilian coups tended to be largely bloodless affairs so I didn't feel too physically threatened although, like all great leaders, Iain obviously knew when it was best to leave things in the hands of his deputy.

Such was the excitement at the arrival of the lorry, and such was our eagerness to unload the rice, that it was quite some time before I noticed that shortly after its arrival somebody came cycling into the camp, propped his bike up against the end of the long hut and stood quietly watching the frantic unloading of the lorry. It was one of the labourers that eventually gave me a nudge and nodded his head with a quizzical look in the direction of the cyclist. I could hardly just ignore him so I went to find out what we might do to assist him.

His name was Jean Pierre Vuillomenet and, as perhaps one might have guessed of a cyclist in the middle of Mato Grosso, he was cycling round the world. It was not for the first time either as he had already done it once between 1960 and 1963, spending the intervening years as a merchant seaman to save up enough money to do it again. This time he planned to take in the Mexico Olympics while he was at it. Certainly it made our existence seem rather mollycoddled with our comfortable 'casas' and a lorry ferrying in supplies to us. He was an engaging bloke, with an encyclopaedic knowledge of the world that I suppose you get by seeing it by the sweat of your own brow. He stayed a few days and then set off up the track that led back to the road.

There was of course another possible explanation for his appearance – he was a French spy. We all know that the French are not to be trusted in these matters. They have never quite got over their failure to establish any major French colonies in South America. I regard Surinam as being a borderline case when it comes to the real South America. Likewise France's sneaky occupation from 1555 to 1567 of an island in Guanabara Bay facing the city that is now Rio de Janeiro and which they cheekily called 'France Antarctique' doesn't really count. So you can imagine that the French would have been none too pleased to discover that the Brits were now exploring the very heart of Brazil and potentially driving onwards to the Amazon, and all of this in cahoots with the British Council. Knowing the French, it was entirely feasible therefore that Alliance Française had been brought into play – the French equivalent of the British Council but thought by some to be a branch of the Direction Générale de la Securité Extériure, part of the French spying system. This organ of government openly admitted to including in its remit industrial espionage, so why not ecological espionage alongside this?

It seems a not unreasonable hypothesis that the Direction Générale de la Securité Extériure had assigned an articulate, English speaking young man with a wide knowledge of the world and flown him into Xavantina. Here he had made contact with our lorry driver who had been bribed or threatened to carry him and his bike to base camp. Consider the following facts: our French cyclist arrived on the day that the lorry arrived and left on the day it returned to Xavantina; he never did offer any explanation for what he intended to do when he reached the final end of the road another hundred or so miles further on; he couldn't have gone on and certainly if he simply returned on the same road, why did he not call into base camp? He had showed an inordinate interest in what we were doing and spent much time mooching round our stores and laboratory. The whole thing had a strong whiff of subterfuge, though I would have to admit that there is a book by someone of the same name entitled 'La Planète a Vélo' (the planet by bike) but then the French are very thorough in their espionage.

Money, or more precisely lack of it, was a constant problem for the expedition and for this the blame lay probably 50-50 between Iain and the Royal Society accounts department. Iain hadn't a clue about keeping orderly accounts, in fact nobody on the expedition seemed capable of adding a column of figures. He seemed just to 'lose' money, presumably because he simply didn't keep a proper note of what he was spending. I had been taught to wrap up money in a piece of paper and every time I made a payment I would note it down on the paper in which the money was wrapped. Iain seemed to have no such system and tended to assume that unaccounted–for money had been stolen. The Royal Society accountants took a quite personal umbrage at Iain's very casual approach to account-keeping. Ledger entries like 'not sure – £27' or 'lost, presumed stolen – £100', do not go down well with trained accountants, who would nitpick through the accounts refusing to replenish the expedition bank account until everything was explained to their satisfaction. The gulf that existed between the expedition and the accountants was beautifully illustrated when the accounts department refused to sign off one set of accounts 'because all the receipts are in Portuguese'.

Never was our cash-flow problem felt as acutely as in the run-up to our first Christmas at base camp. Early in December the lorry had been dispatched to Brasilia carrying a long shopping list with money firmly at the top of it and instructions to the driver not to come back till he had the money in his hand. The first crunch point was that Peter Askew was due to start his journey back to the UK on the 15th but the lorry had still not returned, which meant that we not only had no money but no petrol either. As a dedicated family man with three children soon to become four, his non-appearance at Christmas would not have gone down well. In the end we scraped together every drop of petrol on site; the drum was drained, requiring us to filter the last gallon which was more like sludge than petrol, the last drop of petrol was siphoned out of the Rural – which didn't travel far these days – and a couple of small cans were found lying around. It just filled the tank, which would give enough petrol to get the Jeep to Xavantina as long as there were no problems.

Iain had accompanied Peter in the hope that en route they would meet the lorry, but three days later he was back and still no lorry and still no money. However, he had begged credit off some of the shopkeepers in Barro da Garças and so returned with some cans of petrol, crates of beer and other essentials.

It had been agreed that all the Brasileiros could return home to celebrate Christmas, but with the continuing financial crisis they could not be paid and so 'celebrate' might have been putting it a little strongly. Without a lorry we were also obliged to ferry the labourers back to Xavantina and Aragarças in two batches. Iain and Dave took the first batch on the 22nd and went round Aragarças begging tick for all our Brasileiros which was most graciously granted, though the shopkeepers must have thought it a pretty rum do when the great Expedicão Inglesa had no money. They returned the next day to base camp and the second batch was taken down by Tony and John; it seemed strange waving off the last of the Brasileiros – six of them jammed into the back of the Jeep with a large bottle of wine that we had given them to ease the journey and each smoking one of my precious Brasilia cheroots.

A strange silence descended on the camp as we started the somewhat anxious wait for the return of the Jeep the next day. At the best of times there was little traffic on the road but you would hear a vehicle on the road maybe four or five times a week, probably from the big Fazenda Suià Missu at the end of the road; we always reckoned that if you got stuck another vehicle would probably come by within twenty-four hours. However, after what was probably a pre-Christmas rush of six lorries a few days ago we had heard not a single vehicle, and if Tony and John did have any trouble they would be pretty much stuck.

Happily they rolled into camp about seven o'clock on Christmas Eve, with tales of fallen bridges and meeting a crocodile in the middle of the road; the rainy season was starting to take its toll. The six of us got out the beer and the cheroots and got stuck in. There was a temporary lifting of the ban on anyone consuming more than one beer per evening – an essential rule to spin out our limited stocks of beer given the propensity of some members, like me, to take the 'live for today' approach and just drink the beer till it was gone. We talked and sang Christmas Carols – the Tyne seemed a long way away.

The unaccustomed intake of the three of four beers of the night before had left me with a distinct hangover and I wasn't the only one feeling a little queasy. We had decided that

Christmas would be celebrated in as near to traditional style as possible, and in the absence of goose or turkey that meant turning to our own poultry. As we sat round our round table nursing our hangovers, the suggestion was made that perhaps we should just settle for a nice tin of 'Kitut de Boi' with maybe a sprig of thorny palm sticking out of it, as it was clear that nobody really had the stomach to deal with the poultry. But hangover or no hangover, I am a traditionalist and my foot came firmly down. I undertook to slaughter, pluck and gut the birds if someone else would do the cooking. It was a deal, even though I had never in my life dealt with poultry that required anything more than eating. Amazing what you can do if you have to, and others shrugged off their hangovers and joined in the spirit of the thing. Our birds were not what you would call plump and it would need two to feed the six of us. By unanimous consent the cockerel was the first to go; I always suspected that he must have come from Jatai as he certainly crowed at quite random times of day and night. John played an important part when it came to carving; he had after all already completed the first part of his Fellowship of the Royal College of Surgeons and his knowledge of the anatomy of a cockerel proved most valuable, if not totally accurate. I made a mental note to make sure that I never ended up on his operating table, a mental note that was in the event unnecessary since he ultimately became a gynaecologist.

Preparation of our Christmas dinner took us most of the day and somewhat belatedly I felt some sympathy with my mother. However, it was all accompanied by suitable fortifying liquid intake and by the time we came to eat it – trimmings and all – it tasted most excellent. We had made some coloured lights, found a sheet to use as a tablecloth, and Angie had written out menus that she put in everybody's glass. All in all it might not have been home but it was a good night.

# CHAPTER 7

# THE BEAUTIFUL GAME

Inevitably the Brasileiros were all football fanatics but few could match my passion and I blessed the day that my life of solitary journeys in my little green car changed forever.

It was March 1950 when we moved to Whitley Bay, a somewhat second-rate seaside resort just a stone's throw from the mouth of the Tyne, with pretensions to being the Blackpool of the northeast – we even had illuminations, though not quite on Blackpool's scale. However, the miles of glorious sandy beach are hard to match anywhere. I was five-and-a-half years old and had never attended school. A combination of my supposed delicate constitution, a soft-hearted mother who, as a qualified infant teacher, claimed to be teaching me herself, and an excessively sympathetic truancy inspector, had kept me out of the classroom, leaving me largely free to pursue my solitary existence pedalling my little green car up and down the lane. This tranquil life was about to change.

In front of our new house was a patch of bare land about the size of four football pitches that was euphemistically called 'The Green'. Its limited verdure came from a few hardy weeds which pushed their way through the stones and rubble that made up most of its surface and in the summer it was used as a coach park. Across The Green and almost immediately opposite the house into which we were moving there lived two small boys, one of them much the same age as me. They had been hanging over their gate most of the morning watching us move in. Having satisfied themselves that there was a potential playmate they presented themselves on our doorstep to invite me to go out to play. I overheard the conversation between my mother and the boys. She was naturally delighted that potential playmates had materialised so quickly; she worried about the rather solitary, make-believe life that I had led in Rowlands Gill and of course immediately accepted the invitation. I was off like a shot, up two flights of stairs to the attic and under the bed that had just been installed there.

And there I stayed. My mother called me, but getting no response told the boys she would bring me over to their house when she found me. At first she was not too concerned, I had to be somewhere in the house or garden. But after a pretty thorough search had failed to find me, panic set in. Not unreasonably, nobody had contemplated looking under the beds. Now my mother pictured me wandering lost around the streets of Whitley Bay; I must have slipped out of the front door as the removal men came and went and, having absolutely no knowledge of the area, had immediately got lost. There was no choice but to call the police. I was horrified when I heard the arrival of the policeman and decided that my interests would be best served by awaiting his departure before making my prodigal return. The family over the road was called Polglase, and Philip was to become my greatest friend through childhood and teenage years, my goalkeeper and the drummer in the band.

Truancy Inspectors carried out checks on parents who did not send their children to school regularly. The countless hours spent pedalling my little green car out of doors had given me a healthy complexion, now further freshened with the sea air, which made it difficult to sustain the 'delicate constitution' argument, and the Truancy Inspector in Whitley Bay lacked the kind heart of the one in Rowlands Gill. So, within a couple of months of moving to Whitley Bay I became a pupil at St Edwards R.C. School. While I found it difficult to muster enthusiasm for the three 'Rs', that first school introduced me to the most enduring love of my life.

My fellow pupils did not have pedal cars or teddy bears that travelled to South Africa, but what they did was play football. The toll of the hand-bell that signalled each break was immediately followed by the mass exodus of the boys to their playground (the girls had a quite separate playground – it was all so much more sensible in those days) where a game of football would immediately ensue. There were no sides as such; alliances were temporary depending on who you might pass to that would quickly return the favour, or what move might conjure a goal by hitting the wall between two chalk marks.

There was only one thing that was allowed to interrupt the game that went on before the bell that marked the start of the school day and that was the appearance of Frank Brennan. Standing 6 ft 3 inches (at a time when the average height of a north-eastern man was not much over five-and-a-half feet), weighing 14 stone and wearing size 11 boots, Brennan was a giant of a man known as the Rock of Tyneside. As Newcastle United's central defender for a ten-year period from 1946, his simple mantra was 'thou shalt not pass', and if he couldn't get the ball then for sure he would get the man. It was our great fortune that his daughters attended St. Edwards and as soon as his car appeared there would be a rush to the railings and we would hang there in the hope of getting a good sight of him. In my last year at primary we had a school outing up the north Northumberland coast and to our delight Frank Brennan was one of the accompanying parents. Needless to say, the moment we arrived the boys set up a game of football. The

73

game lasted most of the day and I never flagged. Despite a near heat wave – a rare occurrence on the north Northumberland coast – I raced from one end of the pitch to the other, was involved in every bit of action and scored lots of goals. My face burned and my legs ached but I was sure that at the end the 'Rock' would come over to me and confide that he would be recommending me to Newcastle United. He didn't.

Although the bus fare from school to home was only tuppence, except in the most extreme of weather conditions Phil Polglase and I would walk the mile or so between home and school, always with a stone that we would kick between us all the way. 'The Green' was much too rough a surface for playing football but just fifty yards from our doorsteps was the Links where you could have fitted a hundred football pitches. And beyond the links the promenade, and beyond the promenade a wide expanse of golden sands that stretched almost unbroken for nearly ten miles from the rather genteel residential small town of Tynemouth north to the industrial conurbation of Blyth. We would get home, change from our school clothes to our football kits and be on the links within minutes.

We had acquired two old cricket stumps that we guarded jealously and these were put in place to mark the goal. Phil was tall and thin and I was short but beginning to fill out a bit; not surprisingly we were universally known as 'the long and the short of it'. Phil wanted to be a goalkeeper, I wanted to be a centre forward, and so the relationship was entirely mutually satisfactory. Phil's father came from Cornwall (by pol-, tre- and pen-, you will know the Cornishmen) and knew absolutely nothing about football. He judged how well Phil had been playing by how muddy he was and so Phil would throw himself around with gusto, ensuring that he returned home covered in mud from head to foot – for it was rarely that the Links was not soaked by rain or sea frets. Sometimes we would be joined by a boy who lived round the corner and then we could play 'three pots in', the two outfield players battling to be the first to score three goals and win the privilege of going in goal. The flaw to the game was that only Phil actually wanted to be in goal so when the other two of us were playing outfield the challenge was to score two goals as quickly as possible to demonstrate your superiority but then try to make sure that it was your opponent who got to three first. And there we would stay until we were called to our suppers or it was simply too dark to see the ball any longer.

Our usual 'pitch' was situated close to the Panama Dip, barely 100 yards from our homes, a circular arena surrounded by three tiers of park benches and flower beds and with a fountain (usually not working) at one end. This location had the advantage that when the goalkeeper missed the ball it came to a halt at the hedge that surrounded the Dip and saved the considerable time involved in chasing the ball halfway across the Links. On a Sunday afternoon a Scottish marching band used to play in the Dip and a group of kilted girls danced Scottish jigs. The band marched in splendid order led by a man with a mace which he used to direct the band when to start, when to stop and which way to turn, and he would sometimes throw the mace extravagantly in the air and catch it again, to the tumultuous applause of the spectators. Behind the man with the mace came the bagpipes, followed by the side drummers, and bringing up the rear the man with the huge base drum suspended on his chest.

The first time was a genuine accident; an outrageously hit shot that flew above Phil's outstretched arms, over the hedge, bounced down two tiers of the Panama Dip and right into the path of the band. It is amazing what a football in the path of a marching band can do and we watched at first with horror and then with glee as the precision marching of bagpipe players and drummers disintegrated into chaos as they tried to skirt the football. Thereafter it was entirely contrived and indeed we would spend some time in the week practicing wellying the ball over the hedge and into the Dip. Mostly the ball would lodge somewhere amongst the benches or flower beds on one of the upper tiers, but when we did get the ball into the path of the marching band or into the midst of twirling girls it was enormously satisfying.

In the summer we would gravitate from the Links to the beach. Here it was piles of coats or towels that formed the goal posts. The game might start with just the two of us but others quickly joined in; there was no formality to it, if you wanted to play football you simply got assigned to a side and away you went. As the numbers outgrew the pitch the coats or towels were moved to expand it and on you would go. Of course when the tide came in the game would get compressed into an ever-decreasing area so that it became more a collision of bodies than a game of football.

That could well signal the point at which we took to the sea. I visit that northeast coast frequently these days and gaze in wonder at that cold grey sea in which I spent so many hundreds of my childhood hours. If you are a seaside resort blessed with an icy cold sea then you might as well make the most of it and a 1909 guide to the town proudly proclaimed that 'the sharp bite of the saline waters at Whitley Bay is one of the utmost value in all classes of debility and especially for the jaded businessman'. Nothing these days would drag me into those freezing waters, but in those days we could stay in the water for half the morning, though at extreme low tides there was something that could drive us out which the numbing temperatures didn't. Turds – human turds. The problem was simple; in those less rigorously legislated days sewage was discharged into the sea through pipes that just weren't long enough, so at very low tides and with unfavourable currents the effluent would slosh around the low water mark.

It was when I graduated to the grammar school in Newcastle that football took on a new dimension. The education committee in their bountiful munificence had provided me with a train pass to go to school, but which I could use at the weekend. By then I was a supporter of Whitley Bay Athletic and faithfully attended their home games, paying thruppence to get in and another sixpence on bus fares, as the ground was located at the outskirts of the town. They played in splendid shirts of large blue and white squares with buttons and collars and long sleeves. I embarked on my support just after one of their most successful spells saw them winning league and cups in the early fifties, only to go into a period of near terminal decline during the years of my faithful attendance – a pattern that I was to repeat with my next football team. On a rainy day there was the comfort of a small covered area but almost whatever the weather I took up my position standing at the railing which surrounded the pitch, at the end towards which they were kicking, as close as possible to my heroes.

But in 1957, armed with my education committee train pass and having finally persuaded my mother that it was perfectly safe, she gave me two shillings and I set off to St James Park, the home of Newcastle United. It cost me one shilling and sixpence to get into the ground and sixpence for a bag of peanuts. These were dispensed by white-coated men who walked round the edge of the pitch carrying massive baskets of peanuts wrapped in newspaper cones and calling 'peanuts, tanner a bag.' The ploy was to throw your sixpence to them, in return for which they would throw to you your cone of peanuts, doing this with remarkable accuracy deep into the serried ranks of the crowd. Not that their throwing prowess was required in my case, for in those days small boys were allowed to sit around the edge of the pitch, though you had to get there early to secure such a desirable slot, providing as it did a boot-level view of the action. I virtually always did; the turnstiles would open at 1 o'clock but I would have been queuing for at least half an hour before that to be sure of my pitch-side seat. Children were always given precedence at the front of the terraces. On those rare occasions when a train failure or some other calamity made for a late arrival at the ground, I would make my way to the back of the crowded terrace and wait for someone to spot me. I would then be lifted and passed down over the heads of the spectators to the front.

I had every reason to be optimistic that bright September day in 1957 as I watched the marching band that provided the pre-kick-off entertainment. Newcastle had already won the FA cup three times in the 1950s, most recently just two seasons ago, and they were still regarded as the FA Cup kings, being the first team to get to ten cup finals, to win six FA Cups in the twentieth century and with the most wins at Wembley. But in fact I was setting out on a journey that is best described by the title of a recently published book: 'Newcastle United – Fifty Years of Hurt'. I was hooked from the start; from the moment the black and white shirts were greeted by the roar of 30,000 spectators, from first witnessing the rock hard combative Jimmy Scoular, the marvellous goal scoring feats of Len White and the silky skills of George Eastham, Whitley Bay Athletic were forgotten and my blood turned black and white.

It is now well over 50 years since Newcastle won a domestic competition, their only trophy during that time coming in what in the 1960s was called the Inter-Cities Fairs Cup – a second tier European competition subsequently known as the UEFA Cup and most recently the UEFA Europa League.

They won the Fairs Cup in 1969, having gained entry to it through a back door opened by a bizarre regulation that only teams from cities that did not have representation in one of the other European competitions were eligible. This eliminated Everton, Spurs and Arsenal, all of whom had finished above tenth-placed Newcastle in the league. Throughout these years my support has never wavered and, although most of my adult life has been spent far from Tyneside, I have missed no opportunity to take my place in St James Park even when it meant a 420–mile round trip every other Saturday. If asked whether I class myself as an optimist or a pessimist I need only point to Newcastle United – you have to be the ultimate optimist to go on believing that this season maybe they will win something.

So now in the middle of Mato Grosso my passion for kicking a football could continue unabated. Almost every evening that I spent at base camp when work was finished, we would play football. Our football field was just off the road opposite to the entrance to the camp. We had located it on what had been one of a number of attempts by the road builders to construct an airstrip. The soil had been well compacted, but was quite sandy so that even after heavy rain it quickly drained. During the dry season it did get a bit dusty and a scuffed shot would be accompanied by clouds of red dust, bringing hoots of derision from the opposing team. The teams would normally be mixed, but just occasionally we had enough football-playing Inglesas to play an 'international', which of course Brazil always won. There is a lovely Portuguese word 'saudade'; it doesn't translate quite directly but it's a sort of longing, a yearning for something that has passed, a fond remembrance. These days as I push my complaining body up hills or through its daily exercises it is with 'saudade' that I look back at the time when after a day pounding through the bush I could return in the evening, change walking boots for football boots and play football for anything up to a couple of hours.

The football field also served a valuable social purpose. Brazil is a highly egalitarian society, but the reality of camp was that for most of the time the Inglesas were the bosses and the Brasileiros were the workers. Football, to make a bad pun, produced a level playing field. If my captain of the day wanted me to play on the left rather than the right I played on the left, even though my left leg had always been strictly for standing on. If I held the ball when I should have passed I would get bollocked by my Brazilian team-mates. It all helped to produce the sort of harmony that for the most part characterised life in camp.

But that is not to say that we didn't have our problems, and they had a knack of arising when Iain was away and I was left in charge of camp. The problems fell into two broad categories – argument between two or more Brasileiros, and arguments with us. Mostly they occurred on evenings after the lorry had returned from Aragarças and it wasn't difficult to understand why. 'Cachaça' was strictly forbidden in base camp but there was no doubt that the driver or more probably the driver's mate succumbed to pressure and would smuggle in a bottle or two. The result sometimes was nothing other than a more boisterous singsong than usual but at times it could turn nasty. On one occasion an argument broke out between the cook and one of the labourers; as it became increasingly heated the labourer went and fetched his machete and proceeded to menace the cook with it. For the most part we left the Brasileiros to sort out their own problems but we certainly couldn't risk the cook and so I was volunteered to try to restore peace. Given the size and strength of the labourer I wasn't going to try brute force but the offer of one of my cheroots all round while we sat and discussed the problem did the trick – a veritable cheroot of peace.

On another evening the deputy cook went on strike; he had been press-ganged into the job when the previous incumbent deserted us and had never really been happy about it. Suddenly about half way through his dinner preparations and obviously having been swigging the 'cachaça' bottle as he prepared, he downed utensils, marched up to Angie – the only person in the living 'casa' at the time – and announced that cooking was women's work, he would do it no longer, and Angie should take over. I was quickly summoned and there followed a major confrontation, culminating in my dismissing him. Angie did indeed finish the cooking and long into the night we could hear what sounded like fomenting revolution amongst the Brasileiros. I came down nervously to breakfast the next morning, half expecting to be met by the strike committee. There was the unwilling cook making the porridge. He smiled at me sheepishly; there was no need for further discussion, but as soon as we were able to recruit another deputy cook we did.

Perhaps the most unnerving experience was the evening when Taituba roared into the living 'casa' waving a revolver around his head. He was shouting incomprehensibly but the word 'Inglesas' appeared frequently. Like 'cachaça', revolvers were strictly forbidden in base camp, but we knew that a number of the Brasileiros had them. Taituba let off a couple of shots in the air and disappeared off over the bridge that led to the Inglesa sleeping quarters. It was clear that he couldn't be left running amok around the camp so I set off in pursuit. I knew well all the paths around camp and, with a little light from a torch, I started to search the paths for evidence of him. He had gone ominously quiet and it was pretty frightening walking in near total darkness knowing that somewhere out there was a very drunken Taituba with a loaded revolver, so I simply kept calling his name. I needn't have bothered calling;

a short distance from the last of the sleeping 'casas' the alcohol had finally taken over and there was Taituba slumped against a tree, the revolver on the ground beside him. I took the revolver back to camp, rounded up a couple of the Brasileiros and we carried him back.

Most times these bust-ups would be followed by deep penitence and often some little gift. I used to run a 'canteen' for the Brasileiros, all very simple, mainly so they could buy beer on the same footing as the Inglesas did, along with cigarettes, toothpaste, soap and other bits and pieces. One day one of the Brasileiros came to me to purchase four packets of cigarettes, handed over his money and then handed two of the packets to me – for absolutely no reason other than just a kind gesture; they were like that.

The numbers at camp were set to rise dramatically during February and early March and the first problem that this presented was our dining table. Like King Arthur's knights we had all fitted comfortably around our large round table but with about fifteen people expected to be in camp by early March we simply wouldn't all fit. Arjimeiro examined the situation in his thoughtful way. Building a larger round table wouldn't work, so we either constructed an additional table or we attached extensions to the existing table. With Iain away I was as usual in charge of the camp, so this momentous decision lay at my door. Two tables, I felt, could be divisive – younger members/ older members, sober members/drinking members, curfew adherents/curfew breakers, long-termers /short-termers. No, the principle of all-inclusive scientific debate, not to mention all-inclusive bawdy jokes sessions, booze-ups and singsongs, round the dining table had to be maintained, and so the round table was fitted with wings. It was probably the oddest-looking table that ever existed; however, six people could be seated around the segments of the original table that didn't have appendages and a further five on each wing. If numbers rose above that – which they did later on – then we would just have to make sure that a proportion of them were out at sub-camps. The seats on the original round table were of course the most coveted; Iain and Angie had reserved places but for the rest there were some unseemly scrambles down from the sleeping area when the dinner gong went, to try to grab one of the prime seats.

The influx started with Iain and Angie returning to camp with Professor Owain Richards and his wife Maud. A few days later somewhat unexpectedly, the lorry rolled into camp bringing the returning Brian Freeman – a most welcome addition to the team as he was a fund of hilarious anecdotes, mostly revolving round his somewhat colourful love life. He had arrived back ahead of schedule and by pure chance encountered the lorry in Aragarças.

Supplying the camp was becoming quite problematical and we had not seen the lorry for some time. While the store of rice and beans was sufficient for a while, we were rapidly running out of tinned meat; even the vile 'salchisas' were becoming a mouth-watering prospect. On the bush telegraph, Iain had heard that there was a small fazenda on the road to Xavantina that might sell us a cow so the day after returning from our trek a small butchering party set off in two vehicles to try to find it. About 50 miles south of camp was the Rio Turvo. The bad news was that the bridge had been swept away; the good news was that the fazenda was not far the other side of it. There was a ropey old wagon sitting at the other side of the river. A small raft was constructed onto which we piled our clothes and the butchering equipment and we swam across the Rio Turvo. Quite what the wagon was doing sitting on the other side we never fully comprehended; was it something to do with the fazenda that somehow divined our coming, was it waiting on the off-chance of offering a taxi service, or was he in good Brazilian fashion just waiting and hoping that someone would come along and fix the bridge. The lorry was commissioned to take us to the fazenda where with a lot of haggling a deal was struck and for £20 we became the proud owners of a 200 kg cow. A single and extremely accurate blow on the head with the back of the axe felled the cow and its throat was cut. Speed was of the essence as the majority of the fly population of the Mato Grosso was making its way to the fazenda, so in what seemed like no time at all it had been butchered with remarkable skill by one of our Brasileiros. The fazenda owner served up rice and beans and a little of the freshly butchered meat was roasted to go with it. We could hardly ferry a 200 kg butchered cow across the river on our little raft and so some trees were felled which didn't constitute a bridge but formed a sort of hand rail, clinging on to which we propelled ourselves across the Rio Turvo with hunks of meat over our shoulders.

That night we had a barbecue. A fire was built in the middle of the campsite and we roasted huge hunks of meat on it. Inglesas and Brasileiros all joined together in an orgy of meat eating washed down with what were virtually the remains of our dwindling beer supply. Those who could play guitars played, those who could sing sang and those whose feet were not too sore danced.

The limited fridge capacity was packed with meat and the rest was salted and hung out to dry. A few days later we returned to the Rio Turvo in the hope that our lorry might be on the other side and sure enough it was. Some rather more substantial trees had been felled across the stream and our intrepid lorry driver decided that rather than a massive exercise of transferring the contents of the lorry across the river and into the two vehicles, he would try his luck at getting across it. The gap between the wheels was carefully measured and the trees adjusted to the same width. He came over very slowly at first but as one of the trunks started to roll and the lorry tilted to an alarming angle he put his foot down hard and shot off the end of the bridge – our beer supply was safe.

People came and people went. The next long term soil scientist Pete Searl arrived in late March. He had just completed his PhD at Newcastle and was now a research fellow. He had red hair and a huge red beard. Because of his fair complexion he turned bright red in the sun and Taituba nicknamed him 'porco rosa' – pink pig, almost as bad as 'saraway'. My powers of observation were sorely tested after Pete had been at camp for about a month. I realised one evening when he came down to dinner that there was something different about him, but just couldn't put my finger on it. Was it a new haircut? Had he got a new shirt on? Was he wearing different spectacles? In the end I gave in; shaving off his enormous great red beard, he explained, was in fact the reason for his change of appearance. Well, fancy not noticing that.

Ro McConnell, an internationally renowned fish biologist, arrived at about the same time and was one of the great characters of the expedition, with the endearing habit of always referring to fish in the plural as 'fishes'. Despite being that much older than the 'young brigade', she was very much one of us and when after her all too short stay I drove her down to Aragarças it was a close call as to whether she would get on the plane, announcing at the last minute that perhaps she could stay another month. While I would have welcomed her staying on I realised that it just wasn't a runner and more or less dragged her onto the plane.

# CHAPTER 8

# ALL CREATURES SMALL...

Play a word association game with any of the fifty or so Brits who eventually participated in the expedition:

'I say Mato Grosso, you say the first word that comes into your mind.'

'Insects' would almost certainly be the instantaneous response of virtually all of them. Insects assailed our every sense and sensibility. All had a time and place, and nature, as manifested in Mato Grosso, decreed that as the time and the place of one assailant passed, so the new time or place would be the perfect environment for the next assailant. There was virtually no time, no place, that didn't harbour insects intent on drawing their nutrient requirements from your body. We were a pre-packed food supply. Sweat bees would swarm all over these sweating Inglesas and the tastiest bits seemed to be in the ears and up the nostrils. To crush them was to release an odour sufficiently unpleasant that you would prefer to brush them off rather than annihilate them, which is what you really wanted to do. So numerous, so all pervasive could they be that the less image-conscious members of the expedition took to wearing beekeeper's headgear – of course I never did. The nets would anyway not protect you from the 'pium', a minute blood sucker that carried an anti-coagulant so powerful that in no time at all your every fleshy exposure would come up in huge red blotches. Their place was in the sun and escape could be effected by finding shade, but finding shade invariably meant finding mosquitoes. These came in a variety of shapes and sizes from a swept-back-wing version relying on speed of attack to gets its fill of blood, but with so unsubtle a bite that you knew instantaneously of its attack, to a magnificent iridescent blue one that seemed to just float for ages patiently awaiting the time that your guard came down, and then gently alight. Such a gentle touch did it have that invariably it was already filling up on your blood before you knew it. There was much debate as to whether, once a mosquito had started to engorge, it was best to let it continue on the grounds that it might also suck out some of the anticoagulant that caused continued itching for hours, or was it best just to splatter it as soon as you spotted it and thereby hang on to as much of your own blood as you could. Sunset at least saw the retreat of the 'pium', only for it to be replaced by the 'maruim', an irritant on a par with the worst of Scottish midges.

In 1956 Brazilian scientists had imported southern African bees as part of an attempt to breed a honey bee better adapted to the South American tropics. Inevitably, and probably during their keeper's 'cafesinho' break, some of these bees escaped quarantine and began breeding with local Brazilian honey bees. The resultant Africanised Honey Bees multiplied at an unbelievable speed extending throughout South and Central America at a rate greater than 200 miles per year. They acquired the name killer bees because they would viciously attack people and animals that unwittingly strayed into their territory, often resulting in serious injury or death. Bizarrely they were known locally as the 'Europa' which seemed a little unfair on Europe, which was neither the source of the bees nor in any way responsible for its escape and subsequent proliferation. Forget the snakes that crossed my path, forget the jaguar with which I once came face to face, the most terrifying sight in Mato Grosso was a swarm of 'Europas.' They could literally blacken the sky, and the sound of an approaching swarm could be heard when they were still a mile away. Then you just stood and prayed that they wouldn't take umbrage at what you were wearing or where you were standing and decide to attack. Only once did I see a swarm descend and fortunately it was not a large one. I was in the Jeep, which just the day before had been used for carrying a carcass and had not been properly cleaned out. The swarm had clearly detected it and were, as they say, making a beeline for it. The driver and I disappeared at a rate of knots into the bush. The swarm descended on the Jeep, almost entirely covering it; there they stayed for nearly half an hour, and then as suddenly as they had arrived they left and we felt safe to emerge from the bush.

So although nobody was ever attacked by a swarm, the individual 'Europas' were a significant part of the misery caused to us by the insect life. Like the sweat bees they were attracted to our moister parts, but while the sweat bees packed nothing stronger than a stench if you squashed them, the 'Europa' packed a powerful sting. The problem was that you were often unaware that they were there and might for example lower your arm, only to discover painfully that a bee had been quietly feeding in your armpit; or sitting cross-legged you might give your flip-flop a flick to find that a bee had taken up its position on the sole of your foot.

Not all our assailants came to us on the wing and one of the most hated of them was the tick. The ticks came in a variety of sizes from the very large – big enough to cover a sixpence – to those that wouldn't have covered a pinhead. The larger ones were generally the less problematical because you could often see them coming or were at least aware of them as they started to burrow into your skin. But every now and then, perhaps because bees or piums or mosquitoes distracted you, one would get itself embedded and that spelled trouble. Once in they were extremely difficult to dig out, with the risk that in trying to extract them they left behind their mouthparts. I have one place from which I extracted a well-embedded tick minus its mouthparts, that to this day can flare up into an itchy lump. Hand-rolled fags did come into their own in persuading a reluctant tick to give up its grip; the manufactured variety was rather too large a diameter and in trying to burn out ticks you risked branding yourself. My hand-rolled jobs were much thinner and were used by smokers and non-smokers alike to persuade reluctant ticks that they were not welcome. More insidious were the pinheads. These formed clusters of hundreds of individuals that hung on leaves of grass and, as you brushed by, would detach themselves from the grass and transfer to your person. It was entirely possible for half a dozen of you to walk in file along a path and for five of the six to return without a tick to be seen, while the sixth was covered in them. Once they had made their transfer to your body they scattered in all directions. Far too tiny even for my hand-rolled cigarettes, the only course of action was to spend the evening picking off these minute arthropods before they reached the parts that insects couldn't reach – and nor could you.

On the hatred scale the 'tabanids' took some beating. It wasn't that they generally caused long-term problems of continuous itching or vectored disease, it was almost more the sheer effrontery of them combined with their ugliness. A bit like a giant version of the clegs that I knew well from my Northumberland moors. Their attacks lacked any subtlety. They detected you, they went for you; they had a saw-like proboscis and could be through your trousers and into your skin in no time. The violence of penetration, designed for much thicker-skinned animals than an Inglesa expeditionary, never failed to cause an extremely painful shock.

Our whole irritation with the insect world was well summed up by an incident that happened one day as a party of us were out exploring some of the country away from camp. We had hacked our way through the bush all morning covered in sweat bees, being bitten by 'piums' as we crossed open country and by mosquitoes in the forest and had been assailed by ticks of every size. We had stopped for a short break to catch breath and take stock when a tabanid landed on Iain's thigh. The anger, the frustration, the total hatred that we felt towards the insect world welled up in Iain and he dealt the 'tabanid' a vicious blow with the flat of his machete. He mustn't have had it quite flat for he had scythed a three-inch gash in his thigh which positively spouted blood and could have been extremely serious had it not been for his heavy duty trousers and the fact that we Inglesas really didn't know how to keep our machetes sharp. He limped his way painfully back to camp where the resident doctor was able to sew him up – but at least there was one less 'tabanid' to attack us.

Was there not, you may wonder, some defence against this entomological onslaught and of course the answer is 'yes' – there was 'repellente' (pronounced 'repelenchi'). This local insect repellent was certainly effective, but had the major disadvantage that it rotted anything with which it came into contact. Plastic biros were particularly soluble in this thick greasy liquid. Any attempts therefore to apply 'repellente' and then settle down to write notes was out of the question as your hand and your biro rapidly coalesced into one. Applied to the forehead and allowed to be carried in sweat down to the vicinity of the eyes was almost certain to carry the risk of partial blindness, and inadvertently touching the private parts with hands that had been used to apply 'repellente' was to render the bromide in the porridge quite unnecessary for at least a week. So most of us just settled for the insects, though newcomers would go through an initial phase of applying 'repellente' until perhaps they began to wonder what something that would so rapidly dissolve biros might be doing to their skin. In the end you just got used to the insects. During his first visit Anthony Smith was left in no doubt that the insects were the real trial faced by the expedition and in his Times article 'Mato Grosso: the first dispatch' he wonders why Mato Grosso is known as the green hell rather than the biting hell. During his second visit he asked me whether the insects were as bad as ever.

'No,' I responded, 'they are nothing like as bad as they were during your first visit; in fact I hardly notice them.'

'And yet,' he observed, 'for the hour that we have been sitting here you have done nothing but scratch and pick ticks off yourself.'

For some, of course, the insects were the very reason for their being there. Brian Freeman was the first entomologist to spend time with the expedition. His arrival did nothing to lessen the constant attacks, but at least he could give us the names of all the things that attacked us. Brian had arrived in Brazil without the sort of stout boots and protective leggings that were essential for working in the bush. As far as possible Brian amassed his entomological collection from whatever flew by as he sat in some cool shady spot – he felt quite strongly about the virtue of not breaking sweat and had a maxim that went something like: never stand if you can sit, never be in the sun if you can be in the shade, never walk if you could just stand and never hurry unless it is to the sanctuary of the shade. However, forays to the bush were an inevitable part of life and, by chance, Brian had crossed in Brasilia with the departing doctor, Phil Rees. With no likelihood of returning and weighed down by souvenirs of Mato Grosso, Phil had donated his locally purchased knee-length boots to the Expedition and told Brian that he could have them. Enter Jonas, one of two brothers who had been early recruits to our labour force. The elder brother had just quit the Expedition with some garbled story of family woes, unreturned loans, unrequited love and the state of the political economy of Brazil.

Jonas had espied the boots lying around camp and found them to be a perfect fit, so by the time that Brian arrived at base camp possession favoured Jonas with nine points of the law. On the other hand Phil had specifically told Brian that he could have them. In the absence of Iain I was again in charge of the camp and nominated to broker a deal. After a little persuasion Jonas agreed that he would give up the boots. But there was a snag – Jonas's own footwear had been taken by his brother to Xavantina for repair and refurbishment. Brian was the proud owner of a very new, very smart pair of Hush Puppies, considered in their day to be the height of chic. It was agreed that pending the return of his own footwear Jonas could have the temporary use of Brian's Hush Puppies, as he was at the time assigned to camp-based duties. It seemed like a fair deal. We never saw Jonas or the Hush Puppies again. There were stories of him having been seen on the road waiting in the hope of some passing vehicle but whatever, it seemed like a rather extreme step for the sake of a pair of Hush Puppies, no matter how chic they were considered to be in the 1960s. I was touched when Taituba came to me that evening and assured me that none of this was my fault but that Jonas was just a bad man, and pledged the unwavering support of the remainder of the Brasileiros.

Of greater entomological eminence was Professor Owain Richards, Fellow of the Royal Society, the man who had rewritten the acknowledged bible of the entomological world, brother of the botanist Paul, and accompanied on one of his two visits by his wife Maud, an eminent entomologist in her own right. They say that you grow like the people you live with and perhaps this can be extended to growing like the things that you study. So you didn't have to look at him twice to know for certain that Professor Owain Richards was the world's greatest authority on wasps. He was as thin as a lath with sharp indisputably waspish features, while it also took little imagination to guess that his wife was a senior figure at the Locust Research Centre. Professor Richards collected prodigiously, discovering an incredible number of species hitherto unknown to science.

His collection technique was relatively simple. As he concentrated mainly in the cerrado, most nests could be reached with a pair of long-handled loppers. Having spotted the nest, one of the labourers would wield the loppers and snip off the branch or twig to which the nest was attached. Professor Richards would be standing underneath, holding what looked like a vast fine-meshed butterfly net. This was equipped with a drawstring and, as the nest fell into the net, the drawstring was pulled rapidly closed just as the swarm of angry wasps came pouring out of the nest. Bingo, you had an intact nest and the entirety of its inhabitants. The technique foundered, however, when nests were discovered that were out of reach of the long-handled loppers.

It was difficult to live in this rarefied scientific atmosphere without feeling some aspiration to the academic life. Before my departure for Brazil this was a career that had never entered my thinking but here, surrounded by Dr This, Professor That, and those with the illustrious FRS after their name, academia seemed very glamorous. I decided that I should set my sights on academic achievement but realised that to reap its benefits while I was young enough to enjoy them I would have to do it on the fast track. What I did know was that it was not just what you know but who you know that determines what you achieve, particularly if you are looking to achieve it in overdrive. I made certain therefore that when the more eminent members of the expedition needed a helping hand I was always there, confident that the good word would later be put in for me at Oxford or Cambridge or in the hallowed precincts of the Royal Society.

So, when Professor Richards announced that he had spotted a wasp nest of potentially great significance that was out of reach of the loppers, I was the first to volunteer my services. We departed the camp just before dusk and walked the short distance to the site of the nest. Dusk was the preferred time to capture nests as by then the wasps had all returned from their day's labours collecting pollen or whatever, which meant that you would capture the entire population of the nest and also be at less risk of a foraging wasp spotting your evil intentions. We were accompanied by a couple of labourers and a few other members of the expedition who had proffered help or were just plain curious. I carried a ladder, but we knew that to place the ladder against the tree would for certain disturb the wasps, leading to some measure of exodus from the nest. This would reduce the scientific integrity of the collection and, perhaps, to me more importantly, bring a significant risk of wasps, angered at being disturbed in their evening, delivering their stings. The game plan was simple. I would hold the ladder close to but not touching the tree; Professor Richards, who didn't weigh more than a pinch of snuff, would ascend the ladder with the loppers, snip the branch that it was built on and one of our labourers, standing just to the side of the ladder would catch it in the drawstring net.

All went according to plan, except that the damned fool labourer missed the nest, which instead landed on my left foot. I had a perfectly simple choice to make as the wasps started to pour out of the nest – drop the ladder and run like hell, depositing Professor Owain Richards FRS on his face amidst a swarm of angry wasps, or stand my ground and get stung to bits. The Brazilian labourers and onlooker members of the expedition were already to be seen scattering in all directions. They say that at the moment of death your past life flashes in front of you. Well at that moment it was the future that flashed through my mind: aspirations to academic recognition in overdrive seemed significantly less likely, were I to deposit Professor Richards FRS on his face amidst a swarm of wasps. So I stood my ground. Professor Richards shinned down the ladder and with a turn of speed remarkable for one of his age joined the mass exodus from the area.

It was difficult to count the number of stings that I received as in places they coagulated into single great lumps. I never made any progress in academia, and the nearest I got to the Royal Society was a cocktails evening for members of the expedition some time after it finished. But Professor Richards bought me two beers and our Team Leader a third, and this at a time when we were supposed to limit our nightly intake to one to try to make the limited stocks in our little 'canteen' last, so it was not a totally wasted bit of suffering.

Attacks on our personages were not confined to the insect world; vegetation could turn pretty nasty too. Getting through the cerrado was generally not too difficult, but the real challenge lay in the gallery forests that formed dense, almost impenetrable bands alongside the frequent streams that ran through the area. Through these you would have to hack your way with machetes. Lianas were everywhere and seemed to reach out to entangle you in their sinewy strands. Vicious thorny palms could lacerate the skin, and an individual thorn could embed so deeply that the only remedy was to stop and have one of your party separate the thorn from the tree, then your hand from the thorn. In the dry forest the going was often easier, but the ground could be criss-crossed with shallow roots and trailers within which your feet got frequently entangled. It was entirely possible on, say, an eight hour march through the dry forest to split those eight hours roughly equally between the horizontal and the vertical position.

My tutor, Peter Askew, had sight in only one eye, the other having suffered a tubercular attack in his childhood. Battling one day through the bush and possibly disadvantaged by the lack of perspective vision that comes with being monocular, he stumbled into a bush and a razor-sharp leaf lacerated his one functional eye. The resident doctor of the time had just set off in the company of Ro McConnell on a trip to the Suià Missu to examine the fish of that river. It was not that this exercise was seen as likely to result in the need for medical attention, even though Ro was at the somewhat older end of the expedition's age spectrum, but rather that the doctor was a keen fisherman. A vehicle was dispatched in hot pursuit and a reluctant doctor was dragged back from his fishing trip, reaching camp at about six in the evening. To the relief of all he pronounced that the cornea was not damaged, stitched up the outer membrane, shot some antibiotics into it and fixed Peter up with a large piratical patch. For a few days Peter had to keep the patch over his eye and I had to lead him like a blind man around the campsite.

# CHAPTER 9

# TALK ABOUT GIRLS

As part of my Leverhulme scholarship there was provision for me to get out of camp and spend time in some relevant activity. It had been agreed that the first such stint should be spent with the Brazilian Soil Survey, who were in the early stages of a massive survey of the much more highly-developed southern part of Mato Grosso, which would later be hived off to the separate state of Mato Grosso do Sul. So, on the day after Boxing Day, almost exactly three months since I arrived in base camp, I was headed back to the Rio das Mortes. I sat in the back of the Jeep. In the cab were Iain and Angie on their way to Brasilia, ostensibly to sort out money and other administrative matters but probably as a Christmas break, and Dave driving who was hoping to bring back the Jeep with at least a core of our key Brasileiros – like the cook.

I was looking forward to spending time with fellow-professionals and being able to discuss some of the issues that I faced in understanding the soils of our study area. I was looking forward to seeing an agriculturally developed area as, perhaps, a portent of what would happen in our area in the next ten to twenty years. Most of all I was looking forward to seeing girls. For three months the only female forms that I had laid eyes on were Angie and the capybara. Not that Angie was unattractive, indeed she was a very good-looking girl, but she was the Team Leader's wife, and the capybara later turned out to be a male (notoriously difficult to sex young rodents was our leader-cum-chief mammalogist's excuse).

After all the recent rain it was a glorious day and, once it had warmed up a bit, sitting in the sun in the back of the Jeep was delightful. About 70 miles down the road there appeared at the side of the road a lady with a baby and three other small children; they came, she said, from a fazenda not far from there and had to get to Xavantina. We continued the journey with the mother and baby replacing Iain in the front, and the rest of the children in the back of the Jeep with Iain and myself. We hadn't gone far when for no apparent reason the Jeep swung violently off to the right, ploughed through some bushes and as it was about to plunge down a 20 foot drop to a small river Dave managed to heave the car back onto the road. The collective sigh of relief had reached little more than that initial pursing of the lips when we realised that he had overcompensated, and we were now heading to the even sharper drop to the river on the other side of the road. As we crested this, the driver's door flew open and Dave shot out of the cab. Heading sideways now down the slope the Jeep started to roll, when miraculously one of the rear wheels got wedged against some boulders and it ground to a halt. Funny how at the time I felt no particular fear; it was like I was watching it all happen to someone else, but as I stood in the back of the Jeep and looked down the ravine into which we were about to plunge, the closeness of the miss really came home to me.

We faced a dilemma. If we tried to shift the car we risked it continuing its descent to the river, so that when eventually we encountered another vehicle it would have little chance of hauling us out. However we knew that we could wait for days for that other vehicle to materialise. We decided to give it a go. Iain sat in the passenger's seat, from where he could just reach the pedals and steering wheel, but should be able to hurl himself out of the passenger door if the Jeep continued its roll. Dave and I stood in the passenger door, leaning backwards as far as we could like we were the crew on a racing yacht. The Jeep started to come away from the boulders and inch forward, until with throttle full on it shot at an alarming angle back onto the road. We sat and said little and smoked a couple of cigarettes before resuming our journey. I peered more carefully at the lady; she and the children sat apparently impassively a little way from us. She didn't look like a Christmas angel, but for sure someone had been looking after us.

A few miles further on we met our lorry. The money had never arrived from the UK, but in the end the spirit of Christmas had seized the British Council which had loaned some, and so with great nobility the lorry driver and his mate had set off on Christmas eve on the long trek back to base camp. So now we were back in funds and I was looking forward to the next few weeks. Our little misadventure on the road and a ferry crew who seemed still to be celebrating Christmas meant that we didn't get to Xavantina till late and, having to leave early the next morning, there wasn't even time for the expedition groupies to muster themselves.

I didn't, however, have to wait long for my first encounter with the opposite sex. Iain, Angie and I were on an early flight out of Aragarças which unbelievably was not 'lotação esgotada' and ran, by Brazilian standards, to time – about an hour late. From Goiania we were continuing by bus to Brasilia and, as I organised myself in my seat in preparation for the long journey, realised that a girl diagonally across from me was staring at me intently. I gave her a little smile. It was all the invitation that she needed and within a minute she had decamped from her own seat and came to sit next to me. Brazilians come in all shades and hues. Our labour force ranged from Julinho who was lighter-skinned than I was, to Leonardo who was probably pure African. This girl came in-between – a glorious olive colour – and had long flowing black hair; her name was Aninha. I judged her to be about eight years old but learned that she was actually eight-and-a-half.

'Are you a soldier? she asked. I was still wearing my bush clothes – dark green cotton trousers, a khaki shirt with epaulettes, and heavy boots. I could sympathise with her question. I started to explain where I had come from and what we were doing there. A look of sheer horror started to spread across her face; perhaps I was over-embellishing it a bit. At one point the awfulness of it all seemed too much for her and she held up a small hand to stop me going further.

'Your accent,' she said, 'is terrible.'

'Sorry,' I replied, 'but that is how we speak where I am living.'

'Then I must teach you to speak properly; we don't have much time'. So for the next four hours she converted my 'hoys' to 'ruims', my 'moontos' to 'muitos' and my 'brigads' to 'obrigados'. She told me that it was impolite to call your elders 'you' to their faces but they must be 'o senhor' or 'a senhora'. It seemed that there were indeed a few little refinements to the language that my friends in the bar in Xavantina had sort of missed out on. In the days before most buses provided on-board entertainment, this one just had. Passengers who were too far away to hear properly what was being said moved closer so that three or sometimes four people might be squeezed into a seat made for two, but nobody seemed to mind, nobody wanted to miss the fun, and there was often lively discussion on some of the finer points of pronunciation.

I was to visit her house in Brasilia, Aninha insisted as, to my intense embarrassment and the delight of my fellow passengers, she kissed me goodbye first on the bus and then again at the taxi stand. Well, it was a start to my reintroduction to a world more than half populated by the opposite sex. What I needed now was to meet her older cousins.

The following evening I continued my journey to Rio de Janeiro. It was a pretty typical Brazilian flight. First I was told that the flight was full, then it set off two hours late but having reached the end of the runway turned round and returned to the terminal apparently to unload a passenger who had taken ill – dying of boredom perhaps? – and finally having to be diverted from the domestic airport of Santos Dumont to Galeão, the international airport, on account of fog. Somewhere around 3.00am I eventually got checked into the Hotel Gloria.

The next day I made my way by bus to the famous Copacabana beach, two and a half miles of great curving bay. As vast sandy bays go it bore certain comparisons to Whitley Bay; indeed, the sand at Whitley Bay was probably cleaner and brighter, and Whitley Bay did not suffer from the slight haze of pollution that hung over the Copacabana. Thereafter, even for someone brought up not 200 yards from its beachfront and whose early childhood years were spent supporting its football team, one had to concede that Whitley Bay did rather lose out to the Copacabana. Behind the bay the mountains rose majestically and, although the lower slopes were scarred by the slum dwellings – the 'favelas' – the mountains were still magnificent, coming to a crescendo at the Corcovado with its awe inspiring figure of Christ, recently named one of the New Seven Wonders of the World, gazing down over the city. Mirroring the mountain backdrop are the hills rising out of the ocean, most strikingly the sharp peak of the Sugar Loaf Mountain.

But never mind the mountains, the beach as far as the eye could see was filled with girls. Jânio Quadros may have failed in getting through the legislation that banned bikinis from the beach, but he had obviously come mighty close because some of the bikinis were virtually non-existent. The girls were all uniformly bronzed, long-limbed and lithe; they lay topping their tans, played volley ball on one of the numerous courts along the edge of the bay, or strolled languidly up and down the beach, occasionally leaping into the sea to cool off. After three months at base camp it was like dying and waking up in heaven. I set up my little pitch; it really didn't matter where as the view everywhere was quite spectacular, and I am not talking about the mountains. I had 'borrowed' a towel from the Gloria and made a neat pile of my clothes, tucking the little bit of money that I had brought into my shoe, and launched myself into the mass of humanity in the ocean. There was another difference between the Copacabana and Whitley Bay; entering the North Sea is done by slowly painful degrees, letting the near freezing water inch up your legs until, with the water just a whisker away from your private parts there is no option but to go for broke and submerge the whole torso. From the Copacabana you just run into the water and hurl yourself gratefully into the ocean's slightly cooling waters.

Funny how we look our nationality. After five months in Brazil and working much of the time out of doors I looked as dark-skinned as many a Brazilian, and yet within a few minutes of entering the water people were calling 'Inglesa' to me. I played about in the water for nearly an hour, getting involved in an impromptu game of football being played in the water. Some of the tackling was vigorous, to say the least, and I couldn't help but feel that at any level the Brazilians still missed no opportunity to exact some little further revenge for England stealing 'their' World Cup the year before. Still, it was largely good-humoured and I eventually made my way back to my 'pitch' to rest and dry off in the warm sun. Trouble was that all that was left of my 'pitch' was the faint imprint of a Hotel Gloria towel – no clothes, no shoes, no towel, no money.

On the beach you could wear just as little as you liked, but an entirely different morality applied on the street where it was strictly illegal to step off the beach in swimwear; fines could be instantaneous and to an impoverished student, substantial. I had a dilemma. The bus was out of the question – I had no money for the fare and they almost certainly would not have let me on in my undressed state; I couldn't attempt to walk back to the hotel without for sure being stopped by the local police. The only option that I was left with was to stand at the beach edge and try to hail a cruising taxi. They studiously ignored me. Eventually a passer-by took pity on me. He went to the road edge and stopped a taxi; a very Brazilian discussion took place, involving significantly raised voices and a great deal of gesticulating and pointing mainly towards me. It was clear that the taxi driver was not happy at carrying a passenger who clearly had no money and might hop out and disappear once near enough to home. I was eventually called over; I sprinted across the promenade and into the back of the taxi where I was told to tuck myself as far into the corner of the seat as I could. This alternative morality that applied once off the beach included it being offensive to sit shirtless in the back of a taxi. The driver enquired of me my destination and quoted the fare which the passer-by paid despite all my protestations. That was Brazil; one Brazilian steals your clothes, another pays for your taxi home.

It was New Years Eve and the time had come, I felt, to move from interested spectator of the other 50% of the population to something a little more interactive. After dinner I headed back to the Copacabana, making sure that my wallet was well tucked away and my trouser belt securely fastened. The beach was busy, with small groups of people clearly participating in some sort of strange ritual which seemed to centre on a large model boat. I watched for a while, but my primary focus was to ensure that before midnight I was suitably ensconced in some cosy nightclub and set to take part in the anticipated rituals there, which I assumed would include a great deal of interactivity. There were myriad little nightclub type places along the Copacabana and choosing one was largely a matter of tossing a coin, though I was influenced by the music that pounded through half-open doors. I made my choice, paid my money and marched into the throbbing music. The place was deserted. I went to the bar and ordered the 'gin-tonico' that came as part of the entry price, feeling pretty downcast. I had blown most of the money that I had available and certainly would not have been able to afford entry to another nightclub. I observed to the barman that it seemed a little quiet.

'You are too early,' he told me. 'Most people like to watch the 'macumba' – the black magic – on the beach and see in the New Year there. Take a pass-out and come back a bit after midnight and the place will be jumping.'

I returned to the beach and certainly the pace was hotting up. Now all over the beach you could see that little hollows had been dug in the sand and filled with burning candles. In places the candles were laid out in the form of giant crosses, around which Negro women dressed in long white robes danced and chanted to the accompaniment of drums. A bowl was passed from woman to woman, each of whom drank deeply from it. The centrepiece of the ceremony was the model boat that was slowly being filled with white lilies. The dancing became more impassioned and from time to time one of the women would break from the circle and throw herself convulsively around or lie prostrated on the sand. As midnight approached the singing and dancing became more frenzied and the boat filled up with flowers, until at a few minutes to midnight a group of people who were obviously the chieftains picked up the boat and set off to the sea, behind them a long procession carrying candles and more lilies. On the stroke of midnight the little boat was launched into the sea, against a backdrop of what seemed like millions of fireworks filling the night sky. There was something profoundly moving about this juxtaposition of the ancient 'macumba' and the much more modern firework display, and I stood for a long time watching as the crowds started to disperse from the beach.

Time for me also to disperse and discover to my delight that the barman had not lied to me – the little nightclub in which I had invested my funds for the night was indeed jumping. I pushed my way through the swaying crowds of dancers to the bar and ordered myself a 'gin-tonico'. Once served I edged into a position at the end of the bar which would give me a good view of what was going on and hopefully be able to spot the available talent. The dawning came relatively slowly.

This was the first day of 1968 and it was only in 1967 that the Sexual Offences Act in England had partially legalised homosexuality, and 13 years before it would be decriminalised in Scotland. For me and most people like me, homosexuality was something that you had heard of, probably cracked jokes about, but had never had any sort of contact with. The concept of a whole nightclub devoted to homosexuals was beyond contemplation, but what was dawning on me was that the entire clientele was male – and that they were dancing with each other. I froze; a bloke came up to me and invited me to dance. No 'gin-tonico' has probably ever been downed so fast and, given the incredible sum of money that I had paid for it, there was no doubt that the cost per second of consumption well exceeded anything that went before, or that I have consumed since. I fled. Back on the street there were still throngs of people and no shortage of bars and nightclubs, presumably mostly with a heterosexual clientele and which would no doubt be open for hours to come. Trouble is I had gone and blown my limited funds. I had just enough money for a beer at a pavement café and a bus – remarkably still running – back to the Gloria. My first real night out after three months deprived of female company could not have gone worse.

After my experience of losing my clothes on the beach I was a bit nervous about returning there, so I spent New Year's Day at the hotel pool. I had no desire to engage in conversation with the predominantly American and German tourists who constituted my fellow guests, so I just got on with writing up my diaries, letters and reports and addressed the waiters and poolside staff only in Portuguese, which acted as enough of a deterrent to possible would-be holiday friendship seekers. But they say it takes one to know one, and the girl from the British Embassy simply marched up to me late that afternoon and demanded to know what it was that I had been writing all day. She was a newly arrived secretary at the Embassy waiting for her long-term accommodation and in the meantime billeted in the Gloria – not exactly roughing it then. She had been there for six weeks. She was long in the body, and in the tooth, and very upper class. She had not wholly embraced Brazil, her major complaint being its serious dearth of eligible males – a situation which she clearly did not see me ameliorating to any significant extent. However, a male was a male and so she invited herself to dinner with me. The next day when I returned from my first meeting with the Brazilian Soil Survey I found my slightly faded English rose had rounded up two further Embassy secretaries and it was proposed that we should all go to dinner and the cinema together. So although I didn't fall into the category of eligible male I concluded that I had a certain curiosity value: 'I have found this cute little Englishman; strange northern accent and lives in the middle of Mato Grosso; you really ought to come and take a look at him.'

And so they did, and I put on my most Geordie demeanour which delighted them, and we all had a good laugh at the film which was called 'Two for the Road'. I no doubt reinforced their prejudices that north of Watford Gap was a strange and alien world, and for my part I concluded that the diplomatic secretary selection process placed a lot more emphasis on accent than on looks. I, on the other hand, have always placed more emphasis on looks than on accent, other I suppose than having a certain preference for girls with a Geordie accent – very clearly not a selection criterion for diplomatic secretaries.

So I decided that whatever the risk of losing my clothes again, I needed to return to where the looks were, so headed once more to the lithesome young bodies on the Copacabana. I toyed with the idea of burying my clothes when I went for a swim but decided that the better strategy would be to identify an honest-looking family and entrust my clothes to them. I didn't need to do either. I had hardly been on the beach for ten minutes when a girl approached me and asked if I was American. There we go again – why did I stand out as so foreign? Maybe you would never get a local on his own on the Copacabana. I admitted to being English and she informed me that she and her friend were studying English and would like to talk to me. At a stroke I had sorted everything – someone to look after my clothes when I went into the sea, and looks that left the Embassy secretaries at the starting line, even if the accents would not have got them jobs in the diplomatic service, particularly since their English teacher was obviously American.

The girls were horrified that I had done so little sightseeing in Rio and determined that this should be rectified. So after a swim (we left all the clothes unattended on the beach – apparently a pile of three lots of clothing are less likely to be filched than a pile of one) I was whisked away. One of the girls had a car, which she drove at high speed through the streets of Rio; first stop the Corcovado, a 700 metre high mountain lying within the city limits. At the top is the magnificent 30 metre statue of Christ placed on an 8 metre high platform which houses its own church. We queued for the rack railway and then climbed the 222 steps that took us from the railway terminus to the foot of the figure of Christ. We were blessed with a clear day and the view over the city was utterly spectacular. But we couldn't linger so back down the 222 steps, back down the rack railway and back to a high-speed dash across the city to the Sugar Loaf Mountain.

Time was short, explained the girl who was driving, as she went through another red light, though her constant transgression of traffic regulations brought little more than cheerful leers from the male motorists that she cut or pedestrians that she caused to scatter to safety. Driving in Mato Grosso could be nerve-wracking, but it never matched the levels of terror reached during these drives across Rio. Our objective was the Sugar Loaf Mountain and we screeched to a halt close to the starting point for the cable car that would, in two stages, take us to the top of the mountain. From the speed of the journey across the city we now faced the crawl to the cable car. At times the queue moved imperceptibly slowly, a situation not helped by the fact that the operator took frequent breaks for a 'cafesinho' or a cigarette, leaving cars swinging gently in the breeze, yet nobody seemed to mind. We made the halfway stage, but the queues for the continuation of the journey were enormous and my companions suggested that we settled for this halfway point if we were not to spend half the night there. Even at this halfway level the views out to the ocean and back to the city were quite superb.

The evening was decreed to be a visit to the Camecão, one of the city's most popular dance spots – and entirely heterosexual. I was to be picked up at the hotel at 9.30pm and was torn between disappointment and relief when I found that it was not one of the girls driving but her father; nice girls in Brazil were still chaperoned. However, the prospect of another race through Rio – this time in the dark – had been causing me a certain amount of anxiety, and the greater chance of returning from the night out in one piece undoubtedly had appeal. The father may not have been in line for a green cross code badge, but probably travelled at half the speed of his daughter. The Camecão lived up fully to its reputation. The bands changed at regular intervals from pop to ballroom to carnival. I danced with the girls alternately and since neither was prepared to sit out more than one dance at a stretch I was kept going without a break for some hours. I use the word 'dance' in the loosest possible sense as, despite my mother's attempts, I had never learned to dance properly. The difference between my movements for a fast beat rock number and those for a waltz were entirely a matter of speed, the concept of a disciplined sequence of steps being entirely alien to me; if my mother had had her way, what rich entertainment the clientele of the Camecão would have missed that night. When it came to the carnival band my style of dance came fully into its own; all idea of dance partners disappeared and I was able to dance with both girls at the same time, indeed with half the girls on the dance floor. The diligent father picked us up at around 3.00am – probably on his way from the home of his mistress. As George Mikes explains:

> 'I should not like to give the impression that Brazilians are lax in their moral attitude. Every paterfamilias would insist on his daughter being properly chaperoned while out with a young man; lack of strict and proper arrangements would worry him so much that he would not be able to sleep in peace with his mistress.'

They bade me a somewhat tearful goodbye but I assured them I would be back and, one day, who knows, I may be. But for now the somewhat delayed departure of the soil survey to southern Mato Grosso was approaching.

At breakfast the next morning it was hard to say whose surprise was the greatest – mine to discover Iain and Angie sitting there when they should have been en route back to camp, or theirs to see me still in the Gloria when I should have been away with the soil survey. It transpired that they had been summoned to Rio to meet a high powered Fellow of the Royal Society who had come, ostensibly, to 'do some liaison work with the Brazilian authorities,' but in practice had come to see why the expedition was having so many problems. At the same time it provided an opportunity to try to get some money out of the bank, as the expedition was still stony broke and now deeply in debt to the British Council. There seemed to be some idea that by going to the bank's headquarters we might find that there was indeed some money in the expedition's account. My being there was a bonus, because in theory a separate fund of money had been transferred in my name to cover my own costs to the expedition and pay for my trips out of camp, and this could be used to bail out the expedition.

No, there was no money in the expedition account but yes, there was money deposited in my name. Unfortunately I couldn't draw it out as this would be my first withdrawal and they needed to go through a reference and identity checking process that would take about a week. The girl who was dealing with us had stepped straight from the Copacabana.

She was stunningly beautiful, olive-skinned with enormous brown eyes and jet-black hair down to her shoulders.

I gazed into her dark brown eyes.

'What are we going to do?' I asked her. 'We have no money, we have nothing to eat, we will starve to death.' Her brow puckered in consternation but then quickly cleared and her glorious smile returned.

'You must all come and have dinner at my house tonight,' she said – and she meant it.

Then the damned, fool, interfering, busy-body Bank Manager burst onto the scene and announced that there was, after all, money in the expedition account, but it hadn't been converted from Sterling to Cruzeiros. One might imagine that such an operation would be pretty straightforward for a bank, but under normal circumstances this would apparently take some days. However, especially for these Inglesas he would fast track the process and we could make an immediate withdrawal. Blast the man; I was looking forward to dining at the teller's home.

# CHAPTER 10

# WARMING UP FOR CARNIVAL

Southern Mato Grosso had been earmarked as an area for agricultural intensification and as a first step there was to be a detailed survey of its soils. A team of twenty-one soil surveyors was being mustered for the initial phase of the task, accompanied by a significant group of camp followers comprising technicians, labourers, some wives, a few girlfriends and even two babies. By now I had seen enough of the Brazilian way to know that organisation was not a national forte. We were already a week behind the intended departure, something that appeared to cause not the slightest surprise or concern to my Brazilian colleagues, indeed the fact we were running so late was never even mentioned. It did not augur well and when at last the convoy rolled out of Rio I felt a deep sense of foreboding. How wrong I was; we had a marvellous time.

We drove the 1,000 km from Rio to Campo Grande, stopping overnight in a grim industrial town called Sorocaba on the way; its airport code of SOD pretty much said it all. We stayed in a hotel which made the Kanaxue in Aragarças look like the Hilton. Three of us shared a room, which at least meant that the mosquitoes were not giving me their undivided attention all night, but three people strained the failing toilet system to the point of total collapse. Leaving early the next morning was not difficult to do. Crossing the Parana River took us from the state of São Paulo to the state of Mato Grosso and immediately the tarmac gave way to dirt or, given that it was raining torrentially, to mud and floods. Water got into the engine and it took some time to get it going again, and the silencer fell off, making our entry to Campo Grande spectacularly noisy – this in a two month old Rural; Industria bloody Brasileira.

Campo Grande was a biggish town with aspirations to be the next great growth centre, and driving round the town you were regularly confronted with promotional banners with declarations such as: 'You have the luck to live in Campo Grande – you are living at the crossroads of progress.' It has turned out to be a not unreasonable prediction; Campo Grande was made the capital of Mato Grosso do Sul when that became a separate state, and the city has grown from around 100,000 at that time to not far off a million today, with a unique culture derived from an influx of Japanese from the island of Okinawa, and Arabs from the Lebanon adding to the usual Brazilian ethnic mix.

I could never decide conclusively how much was owed to top-notch Brazilian planning and how much was just chance, but the first evening in Campo Grande, which was to be the base for the forthcoming survey, more or less set the tone. We dined at the ten-pin bowling alley, and occupying the adjacent lane was a large party of girls. Two single-sex lanes rapidly became two mixed-sex lanes. More or less the first question that a girl would ask was if you were married. The bachelors would proudly declare their bachelorhood and hold up pristine wedding ring fingers. The married men had two ready responses. The first was:

'Married? Sure I am married there in Rio but not here in Campo Grande; here I am single.'

The Portuguese word for married is 'casado' and so the alternative response was:

'Sure I am 'casado' but not 'castrado'.

The answers seemed to satisfy, and the subject of marital status never arose again.

The girls aside, the bowling alley differed significantly from the few I had ever been into at home in another respect. In my limited experience of bowling alleys, you knocked down the skittles and from above the end of the lane a sort of grab dropped down which collected the skittles together and repositioned them for the next player. Here, instead of a grab, a pair of brown legs appeared followed by the remaining parts of a small boy in dirty white shorts and shirt and at remarkable speed he had the pins all in position again, though I got a distinct impression that a measure of sport was seen in getting the ball down so fast that the small boy had to scramble out of its way. How the boys must have blessed me, for I knocked down very few skittles. For those of us brought up in a more economically advanced society, the idea that it was cheaper to use small boys rather than invest in a relatively simple bit of machinery was difficult to accept, but then it did also offer a little much-needed employment.

The Carnival in Brazil lasts for the four days leading up to Ash Wednesday, but the build-up starts before the Christmas decorations are down. The day after our arrival in Campo Grande was a Saturday, and I was told that a table had been booked at the Radio Clube. Good luck or good management I just couldn't say, but the table next to ours was populated entirely by girls; I wondered if some of them were the same girls that we had met at the bowling alley the night before, but the Radio Clube was relatively dimly lit and I just couldn't be sure. This was to be my first of three themed Carnival dances and the theme of this one was Carnival Hawaii. Many of the participants were dressed in accordance with the theme, the girls in vivid Hawaiian costumes and huge garlands of flowers,

115

which they would use to ensnare boys of their fancy. There would be groups of five or six girls all in identical costume and looking quite spectacular; it seemed to me that they must spend most of the week preparing their Saturday costumes. In the afternoon my Brazilian colleagues had insisted on taking me to the shops to acquire a shirt which presented a less drab image than the one they felt that I projected. In fact the shops had been closed, but one of our group who knew Campo Grande well simply knocked up the shopkeepers.

At the third shop we found something sufficiently bright for their wild tastes but still conservative enough for mine. I realised that the Brazilian male was a great deal more interested in clothes than the average male Geordie, and men's clothes shops considerably outnumbered those for women. Dancing Carnival-style made my own freestyle version of dancing look like ballroom; as far as I could make out it consisted of jumping around and waving your arms in the air to the accompaniment of very loud music and a lot of shouting, with changes in tempo each being heralded by the blast of a whistle. It was interesting that the one member of our group who came from German origins could never quite reach the levels of exhibition that the rest of the Brazilians – or indeed a well-fuelled Geordie – could. I barely needed to find fancy dress for the next Saturday when the theme was Carnival Hippy – pronounced 'eepee'. Much to my amusement I discovered that the 'eepee' image was clearly seen as a British thing and the girls' matching costumes were heavily dominated by Union Jacks, pictures of the Tower of London or of course Beatles or Stones. Just being British pretty much seemed to qualify me as being appropriately attired in the 'eepee' theme, and I came close to winning the best costume prize but this was much more deservingly won by a group of girls in English football kits, which happily in those days involved very short shorts.

If a first question to you was about your marital status, the next was probably where you would be spending Carnival. I was met by nothing but total incredulity when I told people that I would be spending Carnival in a base camp in the middle of Mato Grosso. Offers of accommodation in Campo Grande so that I could spend Carnival there abounded, and as Carnival 'eepee' drew to a close at around 4.00am I did wonder if the Leverhulme Trust might be persuaded that a return to Campo Grande, happily coincident with Carnival, to see how the survey was progressing was a good use of my scholarship. Given, however, that all the Soil Surveyors would have tailed it back to the real Mecca of the Carnival, my case would have been a thin one. And so, Carnival Cowboy was to be my last taste of the Carnival. No prizes for guessing how the fancy dress looked with nearly everyone toting a revolver. What was somewhat disconcerting was that I reckoned that half the revolvers were real. I had to be up early the next morning to catch my flight out of Campo Grande and decided that a strategic early withdrawal from the Radio Clube was appropriate.

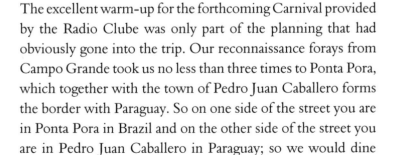

The excellent warm-up for the forthcoming Carnival provided by the Radio Clube was only part of the planning that had obviously gone into the trip. Our reconnaissance forays from Campo Grande took us no less than three times to Ponta Pora, which together with the town of Pedro Juan Caballero forms the border with Paraguay. So on one side of the street you are in Ponta Pora in Brazil and on the other side of the street you are in Pedro Juan Caballero in Paraguay; so we would dine in Paraguay to the accompaniment of Spanish music played

117

on a harp and two guitars, and sleep in Brazil in the company of mosquitoes. Since Paraguay had almost no import tax, the whole of the front street of Pedro Juan Caballero was made up of shops selling whisky, imported cigarettes, perfumes, radios, toys and anything else that was heavily taxed in Brazil.

'Is there not a lot of smuggling?' I enquired of my colleagues.

They assured me that there wasn't and then proceeded to load up the back of the Rural with whisky:

'For Carnival,' they explained.

Other members of the team took their turns to look at the soils and land use of the area around Ponta Pora, and of course load up with whisky.

As for work, well of course the planning was fundamentally flawed in the first place because trying to carry out the first phase of a soil survey – usually involving covering a large area as quickly as possible – at the height of the rainy season really doesn't make a lot of sense, so we could hardly be expected to achieve much. The kind of planning – if planning it was – that ensured that we never dined, drank or played bowls without female company had simply not featured in setting the work programme. Of course it has to be borne in mind that leaving it till the rains eased up could possibly have encroached on Carnival, which could obviously not be contemplated. We did travel quite extensively throughout the area and stayed in some quite fascinating places, though usually unintentionally. But it was simply the process of getting from point A to point B that became the purpose of the day, and there was little time for looking at soils. The roads were often waist deep in water, and although the Brazilians roundly cursed the Rural I felt that driving it through feet of water was a bit much to expect and we spent as much time pushing it, trying to dry it out or sitting in garages with it as we did travelling in it.

One day typified the progress of the survey. We had left the town of Rio Verde at 7.00am and made good progress, despite the torrential rain. We stopped at a small roadside café for a lunch of bread, cheese and sardines and when we came to continue our journey found that the Rural wouldn't start. Eventually we got it going by pushing it. Half-an-hour later we were sliding almost sideways down a steep hill to a bridge at the bottom, when the guy driving realised that the bridge was short of an important component part, namely the planks that you crossed it on. He managed to stop the vehicle, but in so doing stalled it and of course it wouldn't start again. Our only option was to get it back up the hill, or at least far enough up it to get it push-started. To do this we had to dig foot-holes, push the Rural up for as far as we could stretch from our foot-holes, wedge it then dig a new set of foot-holes. It was a slow business. Then we had to find enough of the planks to rebuild the bridge. We launched the vehicle down the hill, the engine fired, we shot across the planks which fell back off the bridge behind us, and up the other side. What stops we made thereafter were kept short, and one of the party sat with his foot well down on the accelerator so that the engine didn't have any opportunity of stalling on us. As soon as we reached our destination of the small town of Dourados, we took the vehicle directly to the garage. One had to say that at least all these little towns did have a garage and you didn't have to book the car in a week ahead. The mechanic had been working on the engine for nearly two hours without success when a passer-by stopped to enquire what the problem was. He took a look at the engine, fiddled around with a few things and started up the vehicle. He shook us by the hand and continued on his way. Nobody knew who he was; he asked for no money, nothing. He just did the job and went on his way.

Our travels did at least give me a preview of what would undoubtedly happen to the expedition's currently virgin lands as we watched the forests being felled and rice, maize and coffee take its place. The better land had gone to big landowners, while poorer land was a patchwork of small fazendas. All over, small towns were springing up as the commerce centres for the fazendas, and my Brazilian colleagues assured me that these were real boomtowns. This was progress but it was hard not to feel sad, knowing that it was only a matter of time before the rolling cerrado, the huge expanses of dry forest, the galleries of forest along the streams and their populations of birds, animals and, yes, even insects would disappear from where the expedition currently sat.

One day we visited the Campo Grande Experimental Farm; it was a quite delightful location and beautifully laid out with neat rows of staff houses and well equipped laboratories.

'And what work are they doing here?' I enquired of my guide. The question seemed to surprise him.

'None,' he said. 'There are no scientists here; it is much too far from Rio.' That rather summed it all up; they had such good intentions but didn't really expect to see the intentions become reality, because basically nobody wanted to leave Rio. It was a bit like the expedition which was supposed to be a joint Anglo-Brazilian venture. Around sixty scientists ultimately participated in it, but only a dozen of these were Brazilian and of nearly 22 man-years of scientific input, barely one man-year came from the Brazilians. But then the north of Mato Grosso is a hell of a long way from Rio. So we had a swim in the semi-natural pool – a bit reminiscent of the one at base camp – and were back in time to go to Campo Grande's other 'Clube', but which turned out not to be as good as our usual haunt.

From Campo Grande I flew to Cuiabà, at that time the capital of the whole of Mato Grosso. I had enjoyed my three weeks in the south, but the strain of communicating almost entirely in Portuguese was telling a bit and I looked forward to speaking my own language again. Cuiabà was an old city founded almost 250 years ago and retaining some delightful old buildings. Most impressive was the large Government House, in front of which was a park with a spectacular fountain constantly changing patterns and colours. The streets were thronged with people who appeared just to be strolling around on that warm Sunday evening, the park forming a major focus of their perambulations. There was music playing and the passage of the people looked a bit like a dance being performed in a castle. I spent only fourteen hours in Cuiabà but found it enchanting. Perhaps it was the fact that about 80% of the strolling population were young and most of these were girls; even on the Copacabana I don't think that there was such a density of young women. The contrast between this and my imminent return to base camp with the team leader's wife and the capybara (which was yet to be diagnosed as male) being the only female elements seemed particularly poignant. Still, at least the blokes all spoke English, as of course did the Team Leader's wife, though not the capybara.

From Cuiabà I was able to fly directly to Aragarças, an uncomfortable flight as a heavy storm raged, and when, already pretty buffeted, we arrived at Aragarças we circled for half an hour, getting slightly lower on each circuit before finally coming in to land. Lunch at the Vera Cruz seemed less spectacularly good; maybe it was a bit of queasiness after the flight but probably it was just that five weeks of city dwelling had raised my gastronomic expectations. Still, I tucked heartily into my barbecued steak that evening, knowing that it would be the last fresh meat that I was likely to see for some time.

The girls in Aragarças were not as numerous as those in Cuiabà or Campo Grande, nor as smart as the girls in Rio, but they were a lot cheekier. On finishing my meal I set off to have a stroll around the town before going to bed, only to find myself corralled by a gang of girls who insisted that I would not be released until I sang them some English pop songs.

# CHAPTER 11

# THERE IS NO SUCH THING AS WASTED EXPERIENCE

So there I was surrounded by Aragarças girls demanding a performance which might have fazed some, but fortunately there had always been within me the desire to be on stage. An early manifestation of this was my ambition to become an altar boy.

Although we were in the same school year, my great friend Phil Polglase was nine months older than me and had enrolled to become an altar boy. A degree of piety backed by strongly religious parents were undoubtedly the driving factors for Phil, but I had a somewhat different take on it, for it seemed to me that being on the altar was the next best thing to being on the stage. Of course the 'audience' in those days saw relatively little except your back, because the mass was conducted in Latin with the priest and servers facing the altar away from the congregation. Still, it was a sort of stage and anyway I had heard that the altar boys had a Christmas party. So I made representation to the Parish Priest to be trained as an altar boy – no mean undertaking as it involved learning by heart some significant chunks of Latin. But first, I had to pass the critical test. In those days the server had to move the 'Book' twice during the course of the mass from the epistle side of the altar to the gospel side early on in the mass and back to the epistle side towards the end. The 'Book' was a massive tome resting on a very solid wooden cradle and I had to prove to the Parish Priest that I was able to move it. The book was heavy, the altar was high and I was small, and there was no way that I could manhandle it off the altar and back on at the other end. I was bitterly disappointed and, mistaking my disappointment for religious fervour, the priest determined that something would have to be done to enable me to serve at mass. So, two hassocks were fetched and one placed at either end of the altar. Standing on the hassocks I was able to get just enough purchase on the wooden cradle that I could get the book off and onto the altar.

After that it was relatively easy. I have always been quite good at learning lines, so memorising passages of totally meaningless Latin I did not find difficult. Soon I was part of a rota that served at seven o'clock mass every other week and one or more masses on a Sunday. There were times as I kicked my stone along the fifteen-minute walk to church on a bitterly cold January morning that I wondered if it was all worth it. The 'audience' on such days was pretty sparse, but then the Sunday masses were always well attended.

In 1955 I moved on to the Catholic grammar school, having scraped through the 11+ by the tightest of margins. In those days borderline cases were referred to an interview and it was into that category that I fell. The cost of failure was high because the alternative in those days was the Secondary Modern, schools that were the sump into which the 11+ failures sank, to be provided with a relatively rudimentary education aspiring only to get them through the low-grade 'Certificate of Secondary Education', with virtually no possibility of proceeding to a higher education. Not only that but the Secondary Modern was quite local and I had already set my heart on getting to the big city of Newcastle. The interview was not going swimmingly well and we were getting to the end of my allotted ten minutes – not a long time to determine one's future. The interviewer posed his next question – what was Switzerland famous for making? I knew it was famous for its mountains and people who could yodel, but you couldn't say it made them. I was struggling, then I saw the interviewer look at his watch. I will never know whether he was taking pity on me and dropping the broadest of hints or simply looking to see how much longer he had. 'Watches,' I said, and three months later I was on my way to the Grammar School.

There was nearly a last minute hitch when my mother – still concerned that my diminutive size indicated a delicate constitution – decided that perhaps the travelling was more than I could be expected to cope with. It was a significant journey to the west end of Newcastle – a twenty-minute walk to the station, a half-hour train ride and finally fifteen minutes on a trolley bus. Perhaps, concluded my mother, we should forsake the catholicity of my secondary education and I could attend a more local grammar school. The problem was solved with digestive biscuits. Daily, I was sent to school with four digestive biscuits covered thickly with butter, which had ceased to be rationed the year before, and these I would consume at mid-morning break to replace the energy expended on my long journey. Sadly my great friend Phil Polglase did not accompany me on that journey; he had decided that his calling in life was to become a missionary priest and he had gone off to a Dominican Seminary. Happily he was to rejoin me a few years later, when the discovery of sex during a summer vacation led him to abandon his vocation.

My school career started auspiciously enough, being presented with 'Hornblower Goes to Sea' at the annual prize-giving in the City Hall as my reward for coming third in the end of year exams. I also got to sing solo in front of a large audience in a place that I would come to in later years to watch my musical idols. I didn't get the solo slot that I really wanted. There were two up for grabs; the first was 'Panis Angelicus', a hauntingly beautiful piece in which the soloist sang, with the choir repeating each line just out of phase with him to great effect, but my voice was deemed not quite good enough to be the soloist. Instead I got 'Joe the Carrier Lad' – a song which lacked the moving quality of 'Panis Angelicus' but was rather jolly.

From thereon my relationship with my 'alma mater' deteriorated fairly rapidly, settling finally into one of mutual aversion. I struggled with some of my subjects, particularly maths, with the teachers quite unable to understand why someone who was actually quick with figures, which I was, could so totally fail to grasp the basic principles of algebra, geometry and trigonometry. It was therefore assumed that I was just being bloody-minded. These days there is probably a name for the condition, and if there isn't I will gladly offer mine, for there is no doubt that my inability to cope with those subjects led to a more general disillusionment with most of my studies so that in the end it was only English – that I loved – and French – for which I had a natural aptitude – that provided any respite from the grinding tedium of learning.

But it was in the fulfilment of my self-appointed role as class jester that I really incurred the wrath of the school. I was an excellent mimic and my playground performances of my various teachers went down well with the pupils but unfortunately not with the staff. Nor did my coaching of my fellow pupils in an alternative tune to the school song enhance my stock with authority. I felt that I couldn't be blamed for the fact that the lyrics of the revered school song just happened to fit perfectly into a much more upbeat popular song of the day but this, it was felt, was disrespectful to the saints that figured prominently in the school song. Personally I am not so sure that old Saint Cuthbert wouldn't have rather liked the more upbeat version to tap his feet to as he sat in his cave on the Farne Islands.

The long journeys to and from school that my mother had so feared would tire me out became some of the better parts of the day. A few of us travelled from Whitley Bay and more joined the train at stops en route. We would all gather at one end of the back carriage and play silly games, while the anoraks would spend the journeys with faces pressed up against the windows and spot trains, where our branch line ran beside the main lines or we passed through the bigger stations or alongside railway sheds. They would religiously record their numbers in their train-spotting bibles, becoming feverishly excited if they saw a 'streak', the sleekest and fastest trains of the day, or even a 'blinker' with its protruding smoke deflectors. But it wasn't for me, it all seemed like too much hard work, and anyway there were too many days when the train journey had to be used to do the homework that I should have been doing when instead I had my ear pressed up against my late grandfather's floor-standing radio, listening through the crackles and whistles to the latest pop music beamed out through the pirate station Radio Luxembourg.

The train journey for me was all too short and, despite our prayers for lengthy breakdowns or forests-full of leaves on the line, the Whitley Bay branch line for the most part bucked the British Railways trend and ran remarkably on time. So it was on the trolley buses that we had to pin most of our hopes of avoiding assembly and these were much more obliging. Powered as they were from overhead electric wires through spring-loaded trolley poles, they enjoyed the in-built design weakness that, particularly going round corners, the poles would become detached from the overhead wires. The conductor would jump off the bus and take a long rod carried on the side of the bus with which he would reattach the trolley poles to the wires. Some conductors were adept at this and we would be on our way again in no time. But others were less skilled, or the crossover switch was in poor condition, and then the hold-up could be long enough to ensure that we were too late to go into assembly.

Such occurrences were pleasingly frequent, because it was not just your own trolley bus that might derail but another somewhere on your route and, since Newcastle had at the time the biggest trolley bus network in Britain, there was ample scope for delays. As long as you arrived late as one of a sufficiently large group then you were not deemed to be late through your own fault, and instead of sitting through assembly you were banished to the changing rooms, which was much more fun. Delays on the way home were somewhat less welcome, although I was not always sorry to miss the normal train, because then I would fill in the available time by walking through to the main part of the Central Station, from where the long-distance trains departed. I would watch fascinated as people boarded trains for exotic destinations like London or Edinburgh or Bradford or Brighton. It all seemed such a far-off world and perhaps deep down there was a developing urge to travel.

While I didn't get to travel to any of these exotic destinations, a little bit of that great outside world did come to me, for during the last two weeks of July the character of Whitley Bay dramatically changed. In a custom dating back to the twelfth century the businesses and industries of Glasgow closed down for those two weeks, and in their tens of thousands the marauding Scots poured into Whitley Bay. Suddenly your Geordie accent seemed foreign amongst the unintelligible voices of the Gorbals. At Whitley Bay station the holidaymakers were greeted by pipe bands, while the buses that discharged their loads on 'The Green' were greeted not by pipe bands but by me and like-minded friends.

By the time I was about seven, despite still being small for my age, I had outgrown my little green car; my parents could never have afforded to buy me the bike I craved, but my Uncle Ernest made me a bogie. For the sake of those who associate bogies with the nasal passages, let me explain that the bogie of my childhood was a contraption based on four pram wheels with a wooden central axis to which were attached the rear wheels and which provided the platform to sit on. Attached by a rotating pin was the crosspiece that carried the front wheels and provided the resting place for the feet that also steered the bogie, though this could alternatively be done using the rope attached to the crosspiece. It was a splendid piece of transport – at least for going downhill – and explained why so many babies could be found marooned on the streets of Whitley Bay in wheel-less prams.

The coaches disgorged their 'bus-lagged' passengers – it was a six hour journey from Glasgow to Whitley Bay in those days – and we were there with our bogies waiting to transport their bags to their boarding houses. Sixpence was our asking rate, but these were canny Scots and many a time it would be a threepenny bit that you got for your efforts. Just sometimes you hit lucky and served someone who had maybe had a nip too many from his hip flask on the journey and, filled with a sense of goodwill to all men, would give you a shilling. It was important to move fast, as the buses poured in at a great rate and your earnings depended on making as many trips as possible in a short space of time. Not all your customers welcomed being led through the seafront streets at a trot. You learned to target customers with care. Old folk and mothers with babes in arms were to be avoided, which displayed a certain lack of social awareness, but then this was business.

Right royally were the Glaswegian hordes entertained, for in their honour Whitley Bay laid on its carnival. There were children's sports on the beach and on the links – sack races, egg and spoon races, three-legged races and their ilk. There were treasure hunts and sand castle competitions and singsongs and beauty parades and bonny baby competitions. Results were always rigged so that the local children never won anything; when we did come first, some infringement would have been spotted and the best placed Glaswegian would be declared the winner. For a spectacle there was nothing to compare with the Miss Marilyn Monroe contest. It was held on the beach and consisted of three plywood cut-outs, one tall, one medium and one small, proportionately shaped to the vital statistics of Marilyn Monroe. The swim-suited girls would take up their positions in the cut-outs and the winner would be the one that was finally adjudged to most exactly fit the shape. The organisers of the carnival in Rio never thought of that one. Big name bands would play at the Empire ballroom and the carnival would culminate in a great parade of floats through the streets of the town.

For me, however, the focal point of the fortnight was the 'go-as-you-please'. A large stage was set up in front of the fountain in the Panama Dip with a proper microphone and cumbersome crackly speakers at either side. The Dip was filled with deckchairs and, weather permitting, it was usually packed every afternoon. This great extravaganza was compèred by a tall thin man in a morning coat and top hat, who had a non-stop line of patter and was one of the funniest men I had ever seen. Spying him once behind the stage having a cigarette I tried to engage him in witty conversation, only to be told to 'bugger off he was on his break'; they say there is a dark side to all comedians. The role of the compère was to persuade members of the audience to come onto the stage and perform their party pieces. It wasn't difficult; they lined up in their droves. They recited poems, told jokes, danced jigs and juggled tennis balls. They played semblances of tunes on the mouth organ – often passed from one to another – and gave painful renditions on the bagpipes. But mostly they sang, and mostly they sang 'I Belong to Glasgow'. I won't pen the words here though even after all these years I could do it without thinking I heard it so many times, albeit that many of the performers could only manage the chorus.

Every afternoon we would join the queue of aspiring entertainers – Phil Polglase with a couple of drums precariously balanced on home-made stands, a boy from the neighbourhood who had a 'double bass' made in the best skiffle traditions from a tea chest and a piece of string, and I was the singer. To the tuneless backing of the drums and tea chest bass, I treated audiences to skiffle music and the early rock and roll of Tommy Steele and Lonny Donegan, until the compère would more or less forcibly remove us from the stage. We never won a prize but this we attributed, not to the quality of our performance, but to the fact that we were not Glaswegian and did not sing 'I belong to Glasgow'. It was one rendition or another of this which would usually be voted the winner on the basis of the level of audience applause. The process lacked the sophistication of Hughie Green's 'clapometer' that made or destroyed potential stars in the TV programme 'Opportunity Knocks'. The compère was the sole arbiter of the level of the applause so that even on the days that we packed the Dip with family and friends, clapping and cheering till they nearly exploded, we still wouldn't win.

Despite my relationship with the school, I scraped through enough O-levels for them to accept me reluctantly into the sixth form. It was all relatively straightforward in those days. You either went into 'arts' or 'science'; if you went into science you probably did maths, physics and chemistry with a view to becoming an engineer, a career to which most boys aspired. If you were no good at maths you did biology, physics and chemistry probably as the route to doing medicine. Despite the fact that I was stronger on the arts side than the sciences, I could visualise no future following on from studying English, French and History, so I opted for Biology, Physics and Chemistry.

In that era, even in a fairly large grammar school like St Cuthbert's, it was still very much the minority who went on to the sixth form. When you did, it was automatic that you became a school prefect and were entitled to wear a different blazer to distinguish you from the masses and to establish your position of authority. Well, nearly automatic, as the school decided that it was appropriate to make an exception of me. And so, in my non-prefect blazer, I stood out amongst my peers, which simply served to enhance my notoriety, something that quite pleased me. There seemed to be little benefit to being a prefect, except that prefects were allowed to pass break times in the school gardens. These were a recent addition to the school grounds and had been attractively laid out with paths winding through them and benches on which you could take your well-deserved ease. So masters and prefects could stroll through the gardens at break times, whilst I was obliged to pass them in the school yard.

As if my studies were not challenge enough, as if my popularity with authority was not at a low enough ebb, I now embarked on a supplementary career as a pop singer. Building on our acclaimed success in the Panama Dip – acclaimed by us if not by anyone else – we now took a quantum leap as a pop band. The boy with the tea chest was given the boot; skiffle was fine but it was not where we wanted to be. The world of pop was now being populated by Buddy Holly, the Everly brothers, Little Richard, Freddy Cannon, Roy Orbison, Del Shannon and a whole host of one or two-hit wonders. But it was on Cliff Richard and the Shadows that we styled ourselves. A boy in school heard that I was forming a band and presented himself as a lead guitarist. He turned out not only to be a highly accomplished musician, but to have a mother rich enough to fund the expensive equipment now required by a band, in the form not only of a top of the range Fender Stratocaster electric guitar (as played by Hank Marvin, lead guitarist of the Shadows) but all of the amplifiers, echo chambers and other paraphernalia needed if we were to sound like Cliff and the Shadows.

Over the fence at the bottom of my garden lived a rather older boy who had shunned continuing education and worked for an insurance company in Newcastle. I knew he played the piano because I had heard him on summer evenings playing all the pop songs of the day. I invited him to join us, and discovered that he was both pianist and guitarist and was already making something of a local name for himself playing in pubs and clubs. And Phil Polglase bought himself a 'new' set of drums, which he painted red and emblazoned on the front an adopted stage name of Red Shelly in honour of his drumming hero of the day – Shelly Manne.

I now spent even more hours in my attic bedroom glued to my floor-standing radio, absorbing every new release. As with the Latin mass I had no difficulty in learning the words; in two or three hearings I could be word perfect, bedevilled only by the erratic reception of Radio Luxembourg, which could result in some slightly odd words appearing in my lyrics. So, usually within days of a record being released, I had the words, and the equally diligent members of the band had also been glued to Radio Luxembourg learning their parts. So it was a couple of rehearsals and we were belting out the hits even before they were the hits.

The record companies should have employed me, for I could have saved them millions that they spent issuing records that flopped. I knew a hit when I heard one and usually on the first hearing. For that era I had the common touch – if I liked it, as sure as hell so would enough others to guarantee it a place in the Top Twenty.

In their turn the record companies could have saved me a few bob if they had made it clearer that the replacement of the large unwieldy 78rpm records by the small, light and highly portable 45rpm discs was an irreversible process. Personally I couldn't see that these flimsy things could ever oust the sturdy '78' which had survived for generations. At home we had a wind-up gramophone that had belonged to my father's father which had with it a fantastic collection of records going back to the great Enrico Caruso produced at the beginning of the 1900s. Nobody was going to tell me that these magnificent records would become obsolete. I was quite probably the last person in England to buy a pop record on a 78rpm disc; it was Kathy's Clown by the Everly Brothers in 1960. I was the only person who couldn't bring his record collection to a party in its neat little slotted bag, barely the size of a lady's evening purse, and it cost me a lot of money to try ultimately to replace my favourite 78s with 45s.

We started at the local youth club, held in my old primary school hall under a mutually beneficial arrangement. We weren't very good and got paid accordingly – nothing, but then neither was the decrepit gramophone playing its worn, scratched and largely out-of-date records. At least we were bang up-to-date and for a while afforded a certain novelty value. We performed against a background of the pinging and ponging of table tennis balls – table tennis being one of the youth club's major attractions – and a constant hubbub of conversation, this being the other major attraction for a group of kids that was too young to go to the pub and too poor to sit in a late night coffee place. Usually, however, we would manage to attract a gang of girls that would dance together in front of the stage – our own groupies.

It was through one of the pianist's contacts that we got our first regular booking – a Saturday night at the Silver Swing in Byker. Built in the east of the city to provide housing for labourers in the industries that lined the Tyne, the suburb of Byker declined as the industries died, and by the beginning of the sixties was generally recognised as one of the most deprived areas of Tyneside. In the mid-1970s it became a target for the social engineers with the building of the Byker Wall, a largely failed attempt to retain the communities that had existed in the original densely packed terraces by building a vast futuristic agglomeration of maisonettes housing some 9,500 people. Its probably greater claim to fame was the children's TV series Byker Grove, which ran for nearly 20 years from 1989, and trailed many of the social issues faced by the young in deprived areas. Not that Byker Grove was filmed in Byker, which was deemed to be just too squalid for people to find credible, but rather in the more genteel suburbs at the west end of the city, with occasional forays into the badlands of Byker for some 'atmosphere' shots and backdrops. A blogger on a site discussing the Byker Wall put the area in perspective, saying that he wouldn't mind living there if it wasn't for the people. Well, the Silver Swing was a bit like that. It was a reasonable venue with a small stage, quite good acoustics and cosy lighting – the problem was the people.

Strictly the Silver Swing was not licensed and had only a soft drinks bar, but a blind eye was turned to people bringing in their bottles of Brown Ale, which was all the customers seemed to drink. By then we had become a more polished act and, generally speaking, evenings at the Silver Swing started well and we got an enthusiastic response, but as the level of consumption of Brown Ale rose it could rapidly turn ugly, with fights breaking out occasioned usually by disputes over girls. We were expected to keep playing no matter what mayhem was breaking loose, on the basis that if the music stopped then there wasn't much else to do but fight and everybody would join in. We did our best, but unfortunately we would all too often become the object of the aggression, usually because somebody decided that the girl he was with or just wished he was with, was making eyes at one or more members of the band. It was at the Silver Swing that we all learned the art of appearing to smile at the audience but without ever looking at one of them, though it wasn't easy when a high proportion of the audience was made up of pretty girls, dressed in accordance with the regional tradition – that is wearing next to nothing whatever the weather.

Then the bottles would start flying, and the bouncers would hustle us off into a back room and lock the door till the ringleaders were sorted out and thrown out and we could resume our place on the stage. There was no concept of a break, so that other than those occasions when we were forced off the stage we would perform non-stop from 7.30 till 11.30, all again on the basis that if the band stopped the fighting commenced. Exits from the Silver Swing could also be perilous, as those who felt that one of the band had stolen the affections of his lass would lurk at the bottom of the stairs waiting for us to emerge. After a couple of close shaves, arrangements were made for us to make our exit down a fire escape to the waiting beat-up old van, returning for the equipment the next day.

It had been a great experience and we had learned much, not just in terms of making a presentable sound but in handling audiences, be they adoring or aggressive. Still, none of us was sorry when we were offered a regular Thursday slot at the Black and White Club. With one secured booking per week we could afford to part company with the Silver Swing and seek new venues for Saturday nights. Byker Bridge spanned the Ouseburn over a distance of about 380 yards and that was about how far we were to travel, but that 380 yards took us into a new world. This wasn't the posh suburb of Gosforth or Jesmond, but somehow the journey across that bridge seemed to leave behind the grimness of a decaying industrial dormitory and offer a less deprived existence to its inhabitants. To add to its allure, the dance hall was within a spit of the newly created Tyne Tees Television studios – one of the early steps in bringing a new face to the abandoned riverside warehouses. It was about as near as we would get to a TV studio, though later we did have two failed auditions with Tyne Tees. A further tangible benefit to crossing the bridge was the Tanners Arms, where you could have a drink without the risk of getting your head kicked in because somebody didn't like the style of your shoes or the colour of your shirt. It also boasted myopic barmaids who seemed not to notice that, while most of the band looked or even were 18, I was still not 17, had not started shaving, still stood not a lot over five foot, and had such a baby face that conductors never quibbled when I paid the under 14s fare on the buses. The Tanners became a favoured drinking venue for some years, certainly till well after I no longer had to depend on the failing eyesight of the bar staff to be served.

The Black and White Club was in a proper dance hall. It had an integral sound system, not just speakers flanking the stage so for the first time I didn't have to belt out the songs at top volume to avoid being drowned by the drummer. A huge rotating glass globe showered the place with ever changing colours of light and the dance floor was sprung. When the place was full and the music was rocking, from the stage I could see the motion of the dance floor, and since I was very prone to seasickness it could make me feel quite giddy. At weekends we toured Tyneside's dance halls, youth clubs, working men's clubs and night clubs, often enough having bookings both Saturday and Sunday. I even got my own back on the organisers of the Whitley Bay Carnival Go-As-You-Please who never gave us a prize. The culmination of the carnival was a massive dance at what was in those days the highly impressive Empress Ballroom. They pulled in some big name bands and that year it was the John Barry Seven, a band perhaps best known as being a frequent backing group for Adam Faith. We were the filler band occupying the stage between the performances of the John Barry Seven. Having heard my passable renditions of some Adam Faith songs, they invited me to do a couple of numbers with them. Giddy heights indeed, and sucks to all the winners of the Go-As-You-Please singing 'I Belong to Glasgow', and to the compère in the top hat and tails that effectively selected the winners. So, with all that and capitalising on the girl-pulling power of being a local 'pop star', I had a pretty busy life.

To put not too fine a point on it, I bombed my A-levels, which surprised nobody including me. On our final day of seven years at St. Cuthbert's, the Headmaster assembled his upper sixth. He spoke always through clenched teeth; indeed the only time that his teeth were unclenched was when he had a cigarette inserted between them. That day they were clenched harder than ever as he delivered his farewell speech:

'Whenever I think of this year,' he said, 'I will have a bad taste in my mouth.' It seemed very unfair, for we had some highly able and hard working pupils some of whom went on to achieve great things, but there was no doubt that this parting shot was aimed primarily at me and a gang of close friends linked directly or indirectly to the band. My parents pleaded with the school to take me back to re-sit my A-levels. I will never understand why they agreed to it – some twisted sense of catholic moral responsibility? A sadistic sense of watching me suffer for another year? Who knows, but they agreed, subject to one condition – I gave up singing with the band.

It was a tough choice. Calculated at today's monetary values it was probably the best-paid job I have ever had – certainly in terms of a daily rate. I was doing what I had always wanted to do since my days as an altar boy – being on stage – and I revelled in the local celebrity status that it brought me, not to mention the girls. The truth, however, was that we were probably going nowhere much further, two failed TV auditions and a demo record that nobody seemed interested in. There were a number of groups like us touring much the same circuit around Newcastle and its environs. Eventually only one really made it to the big time; they were called the Alan Price Rhythm and Blues Combo, better known by the name they subsequently adopted (Price having been told that their name was 'passé') – The Animals. I had always seen myself as a student at what in those days was the King's College of Durham University, with my blue, red and white scarf round my neck, doing deeply irresponsible things during rag week and probably taking a star role in Rag Revue. I grasped the nettle, did an emotional farewell performance that even my mother attended and went back to school. I would like to say that, freed from my commitments as a pop singer, I flourished academically but the truth is that after another year battling with physics, chemistry and biology I scraped three low-grade passes and squeezed into the Agricultural Faculty of Kings College, soon to become Newcastle University.

Surrounded then by an impenetrable gang of Aragarças girls refusing to release you till you had regaled them with the English pop songs of the day, many young men may have frozen and been thus incarcerated for who knows how long. But the altar, the Panama Dip, the Silver Swing, the Black and White Club and numerous other clubs, pubs and dance halls had equipped me for just such an occasion. I sang for half an hour, earned my release and headed back to base camp. No experience is ever wasted.

# CHAPTER 12

# ... AND CREATURES LARGE

Returning to camp in late January, at the height of the wet season, the weather made it impossible to plan my work. It was largely a case of getting out into the field when the rains didn't render it impossible to work, since working involved having to write extensively, an impossibility on soggy paper, and make constant reference to manuals, charts and aerial photos which tended to disintegrate in the rain. I tried various devices for protecting notebooks and manuals, but none proved very successful.

Covering the top of the soil pit with a sheet of plastic was an approach that held some promise for doing my soil descriptions, but was abandoned when I was joined at the bottom of a six foot deep soil pit by a large and highly poisonous snake, a 'fer-de-lance', which had inadvertently slithered onto the plastic sheet and, losing its grip on the smooth plastic, been precipitated into the pit. If you never thought it was physically possible to jump six foot vertically from a standing start consider the following: the 'fer-de-lance' is the most dangerous snake of Central and South America and causes more human deaths than any other Latin American reptile. On average, a 'fer-de-lance' injects 105mg of venom in one bite; the fatal dose for a human is 50mg. As a companion in a soil pit it is definitely not to be recommended and the sheer explosion of adrenalin certainly put springs in my legs that afternoon. After that I abandoned the little plastic roof over the soil pits.

Encounters with snakes were not uncommon and were largely unwelcome, although in fact the majority of the snakes that we encountered were relatively harmless. However, the one that fell from the rafters of the eating 'casa' narrowly missing Angie's head was a distinctly poisonous 'jararaca', and there were regular encounters with coral snakes, brilliantly marked in bright red, yellow and black, although many of these might well have been the harmless false coral. Apparently you could tell the difference because the false coral had a broader head and larger eyes, but how far did you trust your assessment of eye size? You didn't, you got out of the way fast.

While snakes were seen everywhere and by more or less everybody, those of us working on the soils encountered more birds and mammals, and often at closer quarters, than most other people on the expedition. Our work involved both covering considerable distances on foot and also sitting, often for hours and in virtual silence, in soil pits. So as I walked I would stumble across the wildlife and, as I sat, the wildlife would stumble across me. The business of describing soils is of itself not exactly uplifting, but in doing it I was brought into a proximity with nature that I would probably have had no other way. So, I had my soil/ornithological days, my soil/reptile days, my soil/mammal days and simply sometimes my soil/scenery days.

Not even the Guinness adverts had prepared me for what truly impressive birds the toucans were. On one occasion as I sat in a soil pit I could hear their calling, so clambering quietly out of the pit I made my way in the direction of the noise. I got to within a couple of feet of three of them. They really were magnificent with their huge beaks, brilliant yellow chests with a broad red stripe, and maroon heads. They seemed almost unaware of me, apparently feeling safe in this remote location. I returned to my soil pit to find that a group of parrots had settled in the trees surrounding the pit, beautiful green and blue plumage exploding into the sky as I approached, screeching loudly. I could definitely classify this as a top soil/ornithological day.

Yet two of my favourite birds were rarely seen. Walk through the forest and you would frequently find that there was another person or animal crashing through the undergrowth a little ahead of you. The issue of whether this was animal or human would get quite quickly resolved, when the crashing through the bush became accompanied by a pig-like snorting. But try to see this crashing, grunting beast and you will probably be frustrated for you need very sharp eyes and to know what you are looking for, if you are to spot the small nondescript bird that is the source of this amazing set of noises. Quite how it formed this variety of sound and how a bird so small was capable of producing so many decibels I never did understand, but the 'pig bird', as I dubbed it, epitomised the fascination of this wild area and I felt privileged to have seen it. No doubt as this part of Mato Grosso followed in the footsteps of the south of the state this bird would disappear as the forest disappeared.

Then there was the 'wolf-whistle' bird. Again we rarely saw it and, like the 'pig bird', it produced a sound out of all proportion to its size and otherwise uninteresting appearance. What would precipitate a wolf-whistle so loud, so true and so piercing that any bare-chested brickie would have given an eyetooth to be able to match it, was a sudden loud noise. And there was no noise more sudden or louder than that emanating from our petrol drums. These stood on a large plinth protected by a thatched roof but as the day heated up so the drums expanded and as the day cooled they contracted. This expansion and contraction would cause the drums to produce the most almighty bangs and you could guarantee that each bang would be followed immediately by the cry of the 'wolf-whistle' bird. The number of cries reflected the loudness of the bang and a really good implosion could produce six or seven whistles. For me an abiding memory of base camp will be this sequence of sounds – the crash of the petrol drum followed by a piercing wolf-whistle.

The Mato Grosso was no African plain with vast roaming herds of herbivores or prides of lions. Mammals were few and far between but what were there were almost certainly strange, and their sheer rarity made encounters with them some of the highlights of my time in Mato Grosso. Three close encounters stick particularly in my mind. Returning one day along a forested trail, I noticed that on the ground were some eaten out shells of fruits that I was sure had not been there on the way in. I asked one of our Brasileiros what had done that. As a response he started to make the strangest sound; before long the sound appeared to be echoed and indeed an echo was what at first I thought it was. But the echo got closer and I realised that what we were hearing was a troop of howler monkeys. The howl was not what I had assumed, as in the howl of a dog, but rather a moaning like a distant wind. Eventually they were almost directly above us, gazing down to try to find the source of their own cry. On a number of subsequent occasions, and only in that same type of forest, I would hear their haunting sound. Try as I might to mimic it, I lacked the skill and never saw them again.

More frightening, and unique for the expedition, was my encounter with the jaguar. Walking through a wide strip of gallery forest, I became aware that I was being watched and suddenly a jaguar burst from cover and stood not three yards in front of me. I was rooted to the spot and, armed only with a soil auger, realised that I was effectively defenceless. We gazed at each other for what seemed an age then the jaguar turned and started along the path. A few yards on it stopped, turned back and once again stood staring at me before finally and to my massive relief turning once again and disappearing into the forest.

Perhaps my most extraordinary encounter was not out in some remote area of forest or cerrado but in base camp. It was late one evening, and three of us were making our way over to the sleeping quarters, when I became aware that an animal, seemingly of some considerable size, was moving about amongst the sleeping 'casas'. In the dim light I could make out a bulky form and we tried to surround it. Becoming suddenly aware of our presence, it panicked and moved at some speed into an empty sleeping quarter. I followed it in and realised that what I was confronting was a giant armadillo that must have been about four feet long. They are harmless creatures, living on a diet of termites and ants, and I tried to get hold of it. Its strength was amazing and it almost brushed me aside, broke through the palm leaf wall of the sleeping 'casa' and, with a remarkable turn of speed, disappeared into the bush. In truth I might now admit that perhaps I didn't try too hard to hold onto it. The zoologists had a job to do which was to make a scientific study of the mammals which, it was hoped, would in the long term help to conserve populations that were being threatened from all sides. That this entailed killing a proportion of specimens was a fact of life but one that I was never happy with, particularly as I was a major source of some of those specimens. Perhaps the thought that this fantastic creature might end up as a pickled specimen made me weaker than a very fit 24-year-old should have been.

The closest mammalian encounter that anyone on the expedition had was with the capybara. On Iain's Christmas trip in search of funds, he had returned with a young capybara, diagnosed to be female, as a Christmas present for Angie. The capybara is the largest rodent in the world, capable of reaching a weight of 140 lbs; it is semi-aquatic with slightly webbed feet, its Latin name meaning 'water hog' and its local name meaning 'master of the grasses'. She was a sort of reddish-brown, which together with her short but heavy head gave her something of a look of a miniature donkey. She couldn't have been more than a few weeks old and was really quite sweet, showing little sign of fear in her new surroundings. As she grew to her full potential, it left no doubt that the capybara was indeed the largest rodent in the world.

Being in its natural environment a highly social animal, it craved company and would follow anyone around who happened to be in camp during the day. Angie was her favourite, but in Angie's absence she would simply latch on to whoever was around and scamper around your ankles wherever you went. At night it would follow Angie to bed, but in the absence of Angie it was my duty as the acting camp manager to make sure that at night she had moved across the stream to the sleeping area, where she would usually then take up station outside my 'casa'. The capybara enjoyed nothing more than joining us in our swimming pool and had such sharp ears that as soon as she heard the splash of someone entering the pool she would be off and into the pool like a shot.

Unfortunately as she grew she became increasingly aggressive. For those of us that had been around since she was small she never presented a problem, and very rarely did she attack females. However, any new male arrival at the camp was potentially in serious danger of being attacked and an oversized water rat four feet long and weighing in at nearly ten stone was not something you wanted to be attacked by. She was in fact quite selective in which males she attacked and I regarded some of her choices as highly discerning. It was at this point that an embarrassed Iain – a professional zoologist you will recall – admitted that it was not after all female, but a male that now resented other males. Our 'sex-changed' capybara became something of a liability and there was increasing pressure to get him removed from the camp. Not long after I had left camp he was shipped back to Xavantina. Sadly his life in Xavantina did not last long. He was placed in an enclosure, but after just a few days a small child broke into this and was attacked by the capybara. Poor old 'Capy' was promptly shot.

However, my involvement with the fauna in Mato Grosso was about to take on a new dimension that would have much greater significance than befriending a capybara.

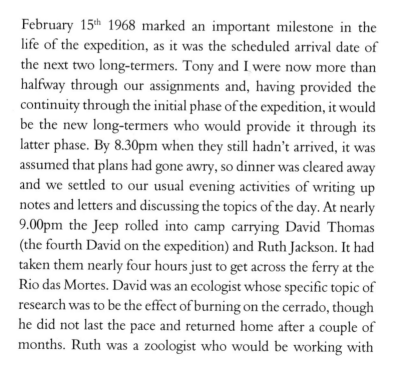

February 15th 1968 marked an important milestone in the life of the expedition, as it was the scheduled arrival date of the next two long-termers. Tony and I were now more than halfway through our assignments and, having provided the continuity through the initial phase of the expedition, it would be the new long-termers who would provide it through its latter phase. By 8.30pm when they still hadn't arrived, it was assumed that plans had gone awry, so dinner was cleared away and we settled to our usual evening activities of writing up notes and letters and discussing the topics of the day. At nearly 9.00pm the Jeep rolled into camp carrying David Thomas (the fourth David on the expedition) and Ruth Jackson. It had taken them nearly four hours just to get across the ferry at the Rio das Mortes. David was an ecologist whose specific topic of research was to be the effect of burning on the cerrado, though he did not last the pace and returned home after a couple of months. Ruth was a zoologist who would be working with

Iain. David and Ruth had travelled out by sea, bringing with them large quantities of equipment for the expedition. This was the Royal Society's latest ploy in trying to get round the Brazilian customs, believing that as accompanied freight it could all be spirited through the system without the endless delays that our cargo had suffered. Needless to say customs immediately impounded it. On this occasion their grounds for not allowing the equipment to go through under the terms of the agreement between the British and Brazilian governments was that along with the scientific equipment was a not inconsiderable amount of ladies' underwear. It took six weeks of intense negotiation for the customs to be persuaded that a lady zoologist could not be expected to undertake field work in Mato Grosso without a plentiful supply of suitable underwear and that on this basis the underwear could be justifiably classified as scientific equipment. Eventually thus designated and stamped the shipment was released.

Ruth had a first class honours degree in zoology, had just completed an MSc in Ecology, and was obviously the intellectual type. Unlike me who had prepared for the expedition by reading 'How to Tango', Ruth had studied the taxonomy of Brazilian mammals, preparing lists of what animals she might expect to see with relevant taxonomic data all neatly cross-referenced. To my astonishment she had apparently not even heard of George Mikes' 'How to Tango'. Importantly, however, she was very pretty, with short black hair, brown eyes and magnificent long legs. Having spent the last few weeks on a boat, she had acquired a healthy suntan; in fact she looked more like a Brazilian than many Brazilians do. Her name presented our Brasileiros with a particular challenge. While a throaty rolled 'r' would be heard in Rio or São Paulo, in Mato Grosso it simply became an 'h', and there was just no concept of the 'th' sound. So 'Ruth' became 'Hoot' and I have addressed her as nothing other than that for the last 47 years, for on that fateful February day in Mato Grosso I had met my future wife.

The potential value of a suitably motivated soil scientist to a zoologist in the Mato Grosso simply cannot be overestimated. The study of soils requires the digging of deep pits – usually down to two metres, but sometimes to nearly twice that depth so that to describe and sample them involved hanging for half a day on a rope ladder. Into these soil pits would stumble all manner of small animals. Some would burrow their way out, some expire from fright or the fall and some survived. Although Iain had nominally been the zoologist, the task of running the expedition left him no time to pursue any zoological studies, so when I did find animals in my soil pits I simply helped them out if they were still alive or deposited them somewhere as food for a passing carnivore if they had not survived the experience. But now with a young attractive zoologist to impress, I went out to my pits with an assortment of live traps and would frequently return with some manner of rodent or, on a really good day, with an armadillo. As with the plants, Taituba was the expert in identifying these small mammals. The nickname that Taituba had bestowed upon me was 'saraway'; I had never enquired as to the meaning of the word but confidently assumed that it meant some sort of great leader. One day the 'catch' from my soil pit included a small, yellow deeply unattractive rat with a long snout. Taituba was summoned to identify it and broke into his cackling laugh.

'Saraway', he pronounced.

And I had two other trump cards in my hand. I made the best 'gin-tonico' in camp, probably the best in Mato Grosso, maybe the best in Brazil, although the barman in the Gloria in Rio might have challenged that. This may seem strange, since before coming to Brazil, while I had undoubtedly heard of gin and tonic and very probably seen one, I had certainly never drunk, let alone mixed, one. It is difficult to define what makes the perfect 'gin-tonico', for its preparation is more an art than a science. The proportions have to be right, of course, and the lime sliced sufficiently thinly to maximise flavour but without bits of fruit breaking away and floating in the glass; the tonic should be poured carefully to allow for some mixing with the gin but still leaving a higher concentration of gin in that last mouthful. But at the end of the day when it comes to making the perfect 'gin-tonico', you've either got it or you haven't; I had it and Ruth was partial to a 'gin-tonico'. Indeed my making of her evening 'gin-tonico' remains a ritual to this day.

Finally, I was blond, and she had a fatal weakness for blonds. The multi-talented Arjimeiro was the camp barber and anybody who spent more than a couple of months at camp would have to avail him or herself of his services. Arjimeiro had only one style of cut and that was essentially based on the hairstyle favoured by the Xavante Indians. So my crowning glory was a great mop of blond hair much in the same style as that with which I had arrived, given certain strong similarities between Xavante and Beatles haircuts. When Ruth and I were reunited in the UK at the end of her year on the expedition, she was appalled to find that her blond had mouse brown hair. It was simply that working all day and every day in the sun had bleached my hair far more effectively than peroxide would ever have done, but after six months back in the cold climate of Newcastle it had grown back to its normal mouse brown. She still maintains that she was hoodwinked.

# CHAPTER 13

# WELL, NOT QUITE LIKE IT IS ON THE TELE

It was the great divide within the expedition over which emotions ran high and the nearest we came to a reality TV show (not that they had been invented in those days), with factions lined up against each other and no small degree of personalisation of the issue. Were we there to 'explore' or to carry out 'scientific investigation'? Where you stood in the argument was fashioned by your subject matter of study and your age. At one extreme were the entomologists. Barely moving from camp, they could gather enough material to provide a lifetime of research material and scientific papers. Tony Matthews, whose studies focussed on termites, ruefully pointed out that if you plunged a trowel anywhere into the soil you would come up with termites; he need barely leave the campsite. Open up one of the giant termite mounds that formed such a prominent feature of the landscape and you would probably find a dozen different species, at least some of which were previously unknown to science. Roger Beaver, a world authority on bark beetles, needed only a few trees to produce more specimens than he could have dreamed of.

At the other extreme were the medics. While they were there to provide a degree of on-site medical facility for the members of the expedition, this hardly represented a full time job. Even at its height there were never more than 25 scientists on site, and the Royal Navy doctor had carefully checked out all members of the expedition and had their ears syringed, so the expedition doctor wasn't going to fill his time treating dodgy hearts or de-waxing ears. Even allowing for dealing with the medical problems of the highly hypochondriac Brasileiros, they were expected to pursue their own research. The medics' interests largely lay in making contact with Indian tribes, learning about their resistance or lack of resistance to the diseases that came with increased contact with the outside world, and the roles played by traditional medicines. You couldn't just hope that some Indians might happen to venture into camp – the medics needed to travel. Those of us whose remit was to develop an understanding of the relationship between the vegetation and the land sat somewhere in between. A worthy piece of research could have been conducted within a radius of two miles of camp, such was its strategic location at the great divide between the cerrado and the forest.

Age, however, also played its part and the younger element like me always backed proposals for exciting jaunts into the unknown. We could usually come up with some pseudo-scientific argument in favour of the jaunt. One such was what we called the 'pincer movement'; it was planned while Iain was on one of his trips away from camp and I was again in temporary charge. It involved two parties, one travelling by boat and one on foot into an area which on the aerial photographs looked most strange. It would have taken at least a month and needless to say it was immediately scotched on Iain's return.

The one side of the argument is well illustrated in quotes from Roy Montgomery, the soil scientist on the advance party. On his return from the expedition and having 'explored' no further than Xavantina, Roy is quoted as saying:

*In my comfort zone: singer with The Invaders.*

*Out of my comfort zone: Barra do Garças, our nearest 'town' – 300 miles from Base Camp.*

*Our staging post in Xavantina on the safe side of the Rio das Mortes.*

*View of the Rio das Mortes from our staging post.*

*Preparing to cross the Rio das Mortes on a pontoon.*
*Something always went wrong!*

*A clearing in the forest - my home for a year.*

*A jaunt on the Rio das Mortes with Ruth Jackson,
one of the expedition zoologists.*

*The Gambia - a
river so sluggish
that tides reached
hundreds of miles
upstream.*

*The Lady Wright
- even then a vital
means of transport
and a floating post
office.*

*Our house at 'stink corner' – shunned by the old colonials but luxury to us.*

*A magnetic attraction for naked Swedish girl – the baby in the pram, not the pusher.*

*Yundum airport arrivals/ departure lounge and social meeting place for the weekly BA flight. Our daughter in pram.*

*My camp cook, surrounded as always by adoring young ladies.*

*At least Mungo Park got a monument at his point of disappearance.*

*The walrus look…*

*Dhows on the Nile.*

*Drilling – not for oil but to determine where to put drains.*

*Sprinkler irrigation turning the desert to puddles as my 'trial' had predicted.*

*Massive foreign input went into producing a plot of sugar beet.*
*The Director demanded an economic analysis.*

*The loneliness of the Neutron*
*Probe operator. The rest of us*
*kept well away.*

*The big machines move in.*

*We did not always enjoy the food in Ethiopia....*

*Carving agriculture out of rugged terrain.*

*Lake Tana, the source of the Nile – the water leaves on its journey to our irrigation plots*

*'I don't consider myself to be out there doing a David Livingstone. We are carrying out scientific research. I am a family man with two children. I wouldn't have gone if there had been any danger.'*

This contrasted starkly with some of the hype that surrounded the early days of the expedition. Just one month in, The Times carried an article winding up the adventurous side:

*'The expedition is to go to what promises to be one of the most exciting and adventurous fields of exploration of the century apart from the purely scientific aspects... Reaches too difficult to explore in the past will be investigated... They will explore from tracks cut into towering forest and jungle.'*

And no opportunity was missed to summon the spectre of Colonel Fawcett and others who had disappeared in the 'green hell' of Mato Grosso. On the eve of the departure of Iain and his wife, *The Times* described the location of the expedition in adventurous terms:

*'Two earlier expeditions – one led by Colonel Fawcett – disappeared not far from where the British scientists are setting up a base camp at Suià.'*

Stealing a march on The Times, the Sunday Mirror despatched its own reporter to see what was going on and described the situation in rather more unrestrained terms than The Times:

*'A dangerous land of nightmare forests, deadly snakes and savage Stone Age Indians. Two British expeditions have met disaster in this almost unexplored jungle... Colonel Fawcett disappeared in 1925, and as recently as 1961 the 26 year-old explorer Richard Mason was ambushed and killed by a native tribe.'*

Writing his article at the time of the establishment of the base camp, Anthony Smith reports:

*'Somewhere within that area, probably within a hundred miles of the base camp, Colonel Fawcett died not too far away from his own Dead Horse camp.'*

Anthony Smith, of course, led the campaign for the expedition to be more adventurous. After all, he had copy to write, and feelings between him and Iain frequently ran high. Breaking with the tradition of Fawcett, who had refused to permit his wife to accompany him despite her pleas to be allowed to do so, the expedition leader had taken his wife of six months with him. Anthony saw Iain, and to a very significant extent Iain's wife, as the stumbling blocks to the expedition fulfilling much more of its exploratory role. He would accuse Iain of being more concerned with building up the base camp than setting out to explore the uncharted territories that lay on our doorstep and would refer to base camp as 'the boomtown'. To some extent he was right, for there was no doubt that what Iain saw as the right balance between exploration and scientific investigation was significantly influenced by not wishing to leave his young wife on her own. A city girl stranded in the middle of Mato Grosso had it hard enough, without also being asked to stick around camp while her husband paddled off up the Suià Missu into the unknown.

It was profoundly unfortunate that Angie should have come to be seen as a major stumbling block to the expedition taking a more adventurous approach; the odds were stacked against her anyway. It was obvious that totally surrounded by scientists – even I in those days would have to have classified myself as such – Angie had little contribution to make. In the early stages somebody, quite possibly The Times, came up with the notion that she was going to supervise the food. In an early article it stated that:

> 'His wife, Angela, will supervise the cooking for the expedition and the helpers.'

The notion that a young girl who had barely travelled abroad and had probably never cooked more than for herself should supervise the sustenance of a large number of people in primitive conditions was a nonsense and, despite the fact that there was little if any real suggestion that Angie had any responsibility over the cooking, she still provided a focal point of grievance for the generally uninteresting diet. She did provide some input to the medical care of the members of the expedition on the back of her relatively brief stay in the nursing profession, but even this won her few supporters.

Underlying some of this antipathy, there was undoubtedly an element of male frustration. Whether or not there was bromide in the porridge, the expedition largely comprised men in a sexually active stage of their life temporarily cut off from their normal relationships. Angie, who had basically nothing to do, would spend much of her time lying around the camp sunbathing in her swimsuit. Male hormones came into play and frustration would frequently manifest itself in attacks on Angie, of which the major criticism was that she was preventing Iain from leading the expedition in a more exploratory – or to be more blunt – more adventurous way. And when they shied away from direct attacks on her, they would attack her through the medium of her capybara that became an increasing bone of contention in the camp. As the newly-discovered-to-be-male capybara nipped at another pair of ankles, the campaign to remove it mounted but in reality the damage that it did was little. This was for some just another way of getting at Angie.

Anthony Smith, certainly the most frustrated by the expedition's lack of adventurous spirit and even perhaps by Angie's attraction, could be vicious in his attacks on her. From the outset he did little to hide his antipathy towards Angie. In his 'First Dispatch' for The Times in December 1967 he writes:

*'...the woman is the expedition leader's wife. Angela Bishop's former home was in Bermondsey, and her experience of foreign travel has been sketchy – a school trip to Holland and Belgium, an au pair assignment in Denmark and then a swift transplantation to what Colonel Fawcett called the green hell.'*

And in listing the personnel at base camp during one of his visits his article in The Times concludes with:

*'and the woman from Bermondsey who types out their notes.'*

Did those first two years of their marriage leave deep scars? It is impossible to say. Iain and Angie returned to the UK, had two boys and the Mato Grosso was behind them. But for whatever reason – including or not the stress of living for two and a half years in the totally alien conditions of base camp, hundreds of miles from anything resembling normal civilisation plus the associated impossibility of starting a family – the marriage fell apart. Divorce followed and Iain was given custody of the children. Angie was supposed to have access but in reality there was no subsequent contact between the children and their mother. Angie rebuilt her life in a tiny house with a job, a new husband and his children. For a while she seemed to have found a degree of contentment until, without warning, her husband removed himself and the family to whom Angie had given so much.

Thereafter she led a sad and lonely life, with Ruth and myself her only old friends, and that was largely a relationship conducted over the phone. Our invitations for her to join us for Christmas or a summer barbeque or just a weekend away from her solitude were always enthusiastically accepted, but never in the end accomplished. It was on her birthday in 2007 that I called her as I ate my picnic on the bank of a reservoir round which I frequently cycled. She was feeling very down so I told her that I would get myself immediately back home, get in my car and make the two hour trip to where she lived; I should be there in about three hours. We talked on and Angie assured me that she felt much better for the chat and better that Ruth and I came another day with a little more advance notice – again putting off.

The next day I took a call from the Cambridgeshire police; Angie had been found dead at the foot of the stairs. For sure she had taken a dangerous combination of alcohol and sleeping pills which might well have caused her fall, it might have been a feigned cry for help or had she reached a point where life was too much for her? The coroner returned an open verdict. Ruth and I went through the painful process of sorting her home, reflecting on how nobody on the expedition had disappeared like Fawcett or was clubbed to death like Mason, but if the expedition did have its tragic side then surely it was the woman from Bermondsey.

The boundaries of the expedition's exploration were eventually extended to an area of 400 square kilometres. While it provided relatively little of a sop to Anthony Smith and The Times, it did at least move people's focus away from the immediate environs of base camp. The area was perfectly located at the junction of the cerrado and the forest and, in a landscape largely untouched by man, the reason for this sharp and dramatic change from open shrub and bush to tall closed-canopy forest was one of the great scientific mysteries. Aside from this major change, there were patterns of vegetation within each broad community. Most notably in the cerrado, along every stream or small river there was tall gallery forest with its dense lower storey of thorny bushes and razor-sharp grasses. To either side of the gallery forest were strips of completely open grassland that then gave sharply away to the cerrado. In places the cerrado merged into the taller somewhat denser 'cerradão' and to the south of the camp the aerial photos indicated patches of a quite different forest to either the forest to the north or the gallery forests. All of these features could be encompassed within a square of 20 km long sides with base camp near to its centre. Of course it was unlikely that within our 20 km square we would encounter previously unknown tribes of Indians or discover the lost city that Fawcett was so convinced existed in this area. However, in his article in The Times of 7th December 1968 Anthony Smith does concede that:

> *'A square whose sides are twenty kilometres long is a minute fragment of this huge Mato Grosso (a state which dwarfs even Texas), but it is big in walking terms.'*

Our first exploratory foray in the 20 km square was to take us to the east of base camp. At first light an intrepid band of three Davids – myself, Gifford and Thomas and two Tonys – Matthews and Young, together with three Brasileiros, inevitably including Taituba, stood ready to depart. It was a democratic system that we ran and certainly the concept of 'porters' was one that had by-passed the Brazilians. The distribution of loads actually strongly favoured the Brasileiros and, having politely waited to the end to be allocated my part of the communal load, I ended up with the heaviest pack of the lot. I was unaccustomed to carrying heavy weights on my back and for the first two kilometres I seriously doubted whether I was going to make it. After about an hour the heavens opened and for the next three hours it poured torrentially. This made you tend to forget your other discomforts, accelerated the walking pace and made any sort of stop sufficiently unpleasant that we just kept going. Coming to two large streams, each about ten metres across there was no hesitation, we just waded in, fording through water waist deep – we couldn't get any wetter. Despite the discomfort there was a strange sense of exhilaration; I was walking where no man other perhaps than a wandering Indian tribe had ever walked before. I looked at one point at our little column crossing a steep strip of grassland. Through the pouring rain I could see the towering gallery forest at the bottom of the grassland, the scrubby cerrado at the top and there filing across the brilliant green grass was a little line of people hunched up against the rain under their grey rucksacks.

We reached our proposed campsite about eight hours after leaving base camp having covered 15 km on a highly circuitous route avoiding the bigger streams and densest forest. Here we established our sub-camp consisting of a flysheet, mosquito net and a hammock for each person. Taituba went foraging and came back with branches of a tree that he assured us would always light quickly because of its resin. It did, and in no time he had a blazing fire going at which we could dry ourselves out a bit and heat up a sort of soup. We spent two days reconnoitring over an area in a five kilometre radius of our sub-camp. Taituba was the ultimate bushman, with a quite uncanny sense of direction and unerring ability in spotting birds, animals and insects which we would all probably have missed. In one place, he pointed out to us that there had obviously been a temporary Indian settlement as evidenced by signs of some remnants of a shifting cultivation crop; we looked a little more nervously over our shoulders after that. Returning to the camp the second day, Taituba chanced upon some wild pineapples which were quite delicious, and another day he suddenly seized a very non-descript looking small tree, hacked it down and from inside poured out copious quantities of the most superb honey. The nights were bitterly cold and we all regretted economising on the weight that we had to carry by not bringing blankets. Sleeping in my rain cape improved things a little, but I vowed that in future I would bear with the extra weight and bring a blanket.

On the third day we struck camp, retraced our steps some way, then headed south. The rains had abated and now it was hot and very humid, and the discomfort of the heavy pack seemed so much worse in the heat. We came to a delightful river and we all had but one thought: to drop our packs, strip off and plunge into the cool clear water. In an instant we had the complete compensation for being at wilting point with sore feet and an aching back; now everything seemed worthwhile after all. I even found some exposed rocks in the riverbank and was able to hack out a geological specimen, which unfortunately more than made up for the reduction in the weight of my pack as food had been consumed.

If our selection of the first sub-camp had been a good one, the second was a disaster. As we arrived at the proposed location the rains returned with a vengeance. In an attempt to retain some dry clothes to sleep in and wear the next day, we all stripped down to our underpants and dumped clothes under a flysheet while we set up camp. Within minutes we were invaded by bees that crawled over and into everything. Again we were grateful to Taituba, who selected some shrubs to put on the fire which gave off a fairly pungent smoke; it got our eyes watering a bit, but did drive off a large proportion of the bees, though we continued to get rid of them from our clothes for half the evening. When I retired to my hammock, I discovered that I had not slung it quite right and as it swung it scraped my backside on the undergrowth which, in the haste to get the camp set up, I had not cleared adequately. It was pitch dark, cold and I was dog-tired and I just couldn't face the idea of getting up again, so I just had to go along with an uncomfortable night.

During the night the leaf-cutting ants arrived. These creatures are awesome; they seem to appear from nowhere in vast numbers and will demolish great swathes of vegetation. Tens of thousands of ants quickly form a track, with ants each carrying a segment of leaf usually considerably larger than itself travelling in one direction, the ants going to load up travelling in the other direction. Although they don't travel in separate lanes they all somehow contrive to miss each other, a bit like the traffic in Rio. David had hung his underpants on a bush in the hope that they might dry out a little overnight and, showing a most remarkable lack of discernment, the ants had completely demolished all but the elasticated waistband that was presumably a little too rubbery for them. Thereafter we always referred to the leaf-cutters as the pant-cutting ants.

We spent two days carrying out our reconnaissance of the area, taking turns to lead the column on these forays, and it always seemed to me that it fell to my turn just when we hit a strip of gallery forest. The spiny palms were vicious and at times it felt as if they had minds of their own – 'you lash at me with your machete, I lash back at you with my spines' – and so in a very short time I would become a mass of cuts and scratches. As always Taituba knew the right leaves to rub my cuts with to stop them bleeding. It was with some relief that we set back on the long hike back to base camp, arriving in the early evening to a hero's welcome and two ice cold bottles of beer.

In March 1968, nearly a year on from the start of the expedition and six months since moving to base camp, Anthony Smith reports on the difficulties caused by the rain – a total of twelve inches in February, an inch a day for days on end in March – bridges down, roads flooded, a tree falling on the campsite (though causing little damage and yielding a rare specimen of a mistletoe). He concludes, however:

> 'The rainy season will end when the English summer starts. The expedition will then think of moving farther afield than has been possible in recent months... Many at camp want to concentrate on a twenty km square area feeling that such a bite will give them more than enough to chew on. Others, when the dry weather comes, will inevitably wish to see – which means cutting their way through to – at least those areas which look exciting from the aerial photographs, the only real maps of the region.'

The expedition never really did, though the medics did slip the leash to some extent.

Dr John Guillebaud, who had replaced Phil Rees, was the first to provide the Times with some small measure of adventure. He also provided us with some of the best light entertainment in camp.

John's research included a study into the relative stress levels suffered by us Brits living in the Mato Grosso, native Indians living in the Mato Grosso and us Brits going about our normal working lives back home. Stress was assessed by the level of some hormone or other which could be measured in the urine, but to get a meaningful measurement required that you collected a full 24-hour output, making it imperative that on your test day you were never out of easy striking distance of your plastic bag. The site of eminent scientists wandering round the campsite carrying their 24-hour sample plastic bags never ceased to amuse. Importantly, however, the same process had to be undertaken by native Indian tribes and so John disappeared into the Xingu National Park with his supply of plastic bags. Given that one of the tribes that he hoped to contact was the Kalapalo, the tribe widely considered to have been responsible for the demise of Colonel Fawcett, one could not help but wonder if the Chief, on being presented with some fishhooks and bullets and hearing John's requested favour in return might not fix him with a steely stare and ask: 'Are you taking the piss?' Anthony Smith quotes in The Times extracts from John's diaries:

*'Parrots ate two bags; mice? ants? caused leaks from five bags; indelible marker numbering volunteers on their wrists proved delible; husbands and wives started exchanging bags at Kalapolo.'*

And so it went on, with a telling entry in John's diary one day saying:

*'Another depressing day – really of all the nasty and difficult fields of research.'*

For what it was worth, the experiment appeared to show that the Indians and ourselves suffered a similar level of stress in dealing with the hardships of the Mato Grosso, but we were much more stressed back home. I was never convinced; it seemed to me that stress varied on a daily basis according to such factors as how bad the insects were, whether we had run out of beer and whether there had been enough bromide in the porridge. Having participated so willingly in John's experimental work, it seemed fitting that when the doctors came out who were to study leishmaniasis I should be found to have the disease. It wasn't a nice thing to have; vectored by a species of sand fly, it attacks soft tissue and cartilage and at best could create most unsightly scars and at worse could destroy your nose or your palate. Fortunately it was diagnosed early and, having persuaded the doctors that I was not prepared in the interests of science to allow it to run its course, a treatment with antimony cleared it up.

In September of 1968, Iain finally succumbed to the pressure for the expedition to 'explore' and a medico-anthropological thrust up the Suià-Missu – the river that would have been one side of the scotched pincer movement plan – was sanctioned. The exploration was to be undertaken by Dr Philip Hugh-Jones, from Kings College Hospital, a young American anthropologist, Kenneth Brecher, who was a Rhodes Scholar at Oxford, a Times staff photographer, Geoffrey Bridget, who took many of the magnificent photographs that appear in the book 'Mato Grosso', and of course Anthony Smith. One of our Brasileiros, Andrelinho (selected perhaps because – as his name implies – he was about the smallest of our team), accompanied the party. Under a headline of: *'Preparing a venture into the Mato Grosso'* (did he mean adventure?) Anthony Smith describes the preparations and start of the journey. He says:

> *'No one is certain whether we will meet Indians en route, but if so the danger is their enthusiasm at walking off with the stores and equipment.'*

Sadly his venture came to a premature end, as it became obvious that they were simply not carrying enough fuel to transport the whole party. Clearly the doctor and the anthropologist had to continue and it was decided that a photographic record was essential; so after three days of slow progress Anthony Smith and Andrelinho took the smaller of the two boats and returned whence they had come, though unable to communicate this change of plan they were obliged to walk the thirty miles back to base camp from the original starting point of the river journey. The site of an exhausted, dishevelled Anthony Smith staggering into base camp, mission not accomplished, perhaps gave a certain sense of vindication of Iain's policy that our scientific purpose was not to be served by 'adventures'. I am certain that beneath a façade of concern over Anthony Smith's condition, Iain was having a little smirk. Anthony Smith's article of 14th September covering his premature return concludes:

*'As for the other three, I do not yet know what has happened to them.'*

– the sense of adventure was being maintained.

A week later, following Geoffrey Bridget's return to camp, Anthony Smith was able to file a report on the continuation of the journey. The river had proved an immense challenge with its unpredictable rapids and meandering course, which made navigation a highly fraught activity. However, none of the party was kidnapped or clubbed to death, though in predicting that one of the dangers of the venture being the Indians' *'enthusiasm at walking off with the stores and equipment,'* Anthony Smith had it spot on. He reports that after a stop at Diauarum, the small outpost of the Indian protection service at the confluence of the Suià Missu and the Xingu, the party continued its journey to the administrative headquarters of the Xingu National Park:

*'What they did not have was a large quantity of their stores. Carelessly they had left their boat unattended for a while, and the Indians were quick to seize the opportunity and the stores. Principally these were the gifts brought for the Indians (but with different ideas for distribution in mind), much food, various clothes and other sundry items. The experience was costly, but this particular ill wind did at least mean that the boat was materially lighter on its journey.'*

Anthony Smith concludes his report:

*'For the time being, the arrival by boat in this distant spot has been satisfactorily achieved.'*

The immediate adventure over, it is not until December that The Times affords its readers another glimpse of what is happening on the expedition. Spicing up his laudable attempts to attribute to the expedition a little greater sense of adventure than for the most part it offers, Anthony Smith harks back to Philip Hugh-Jones' foray to the Xingu National Park:

*'(he) had hoped to go on a large scale pacification mission to bring an uncontacted tribe within the park's compass. Sweets and coloured wools had been dropped by air and the 45 man mission, then hacking a path towards the village, had cooking pots and knives to hand over as soon as contact has been made … Unfortunately these particular Indians – the Kran Akorore – proved initially unfriendly, time ran out and Dr Hugh-Jones had to return to King's College Hospital.'*

One feels that at this point The Times rather lost interest and, apart from the publication of some of Geoffrey Bridget's stunning photographs, Anthony Smith's dispatches dry up until in June of 1969 he reports on the striking of camp in the Mato Grosso.

To this day it is impossible to say whether the expedition took the right course. Certainly for The Times and its reporter it was a crashing disappointment, though the publication of the spectacularly illustrated book – Mato Grosso – might have been some compensation. There is no doubt that a great deal of scientific information was gathered. I, and others, gained their doctorates from it, and large numbers of scientific papers were published. Dr Bill Hamilton, unquestionably the expedition's most brilliant scientist, went on to become widely recognised as one of the greatest evolutionary theorists of the twentieth century, moving evolutionary science on from the work of Charles Darwin. His theoretical work, expounding a rigorous genetic basis for the existence of kin selection and altruism, drew in part from his studies in the Mato Grosso of the social order amongst wasps.

But there on our doorstep lay vast tracts of totally unexplored land which, beyond our four hundred square kilometres, remained unexplored. Might a more adventurous approach, one not constrained by the unadventurous ambitions of a team leader and his young wife, have yielded more spectacular new discovery – perhaps a new mammal unknown to man, perhaps a totally insulated Indian tribe? Perhaps we would finally have unearthed the truth about the disappearance of Fawcett and his companions, or the discovery of his lost world.

# CHAPTER 14

# ALL THINGS MUST PASS

I was spending less time at base camp, which did somewhat curtail my wooing of Ruth. First, the arrival of my successor Peter Searl meant spending time back in Xavantina, as it had been agreed that together we would finish off the work that had been started in that area while waiting to move to base camp. Then I had to manage the development of a network of paths and sub-camps that would give me and others adequate access to the 20 km square. I enjoyed the trailblazing; it called for a great amount of physical exertion and virtually no thinking. In all we established seven sub-camps and a substantial set of trails, so that all sub-camps could be reached within a day's walk from base camp or with no more than a one night stopover at another sub-camp with an interlinking path.

My favourite was our camp in the southeast, which was the second one that we established and in the most remote and unexplored part of the 20 km square. We had learned a bit from our first long trek and this time I made sure that my pack, while no lighter, was better packed and settled more comfortably on my back than the previous time, with some help from Ruth who, I came later to learn, was something of an expert when it came to sorting out backpacks. The departure of the five Inglesas – basically the soils team and the botanists – and the supporting seven Brasileiros was accompanied by much hilarity, if not to say a slight hysteria. Perhaps this was the chance for The Times to get some more interesting copy from the expedition. We planned to be away for a week or so to establish a camp with a little more permanence, as it was an area with many interesting features. We settled on an idyllic spot for the camp at the upper edge of a grassy slope. At the bottom of the slope was a delightful stream, with a waterfall that formed a natural bathing pool at its base. We quickly set up some rudimentary shelters to provide dining and working areas, with flysheets slung to provide individual sleeping areas. That first night we watched a most magnificent sunset, the sky turning a quite brilliant red across a 200–degree arc. Less idyllic was the attack that we suffered that night from both 'maruims' and mosquitoes. Despite supposedly the protection of sand fly netting, the 'maruims' came through it in droves, while thousands of frustrated mosquitoes gathered on the outside of the nets and created a wall of sound with the 'zinging' of their wing-beats. In fact so dense was the coverage of mosquitoes on my net that when I first woke, after finally managing to get to sleep as the 'maruims' departed, I thought it was still dark when in fact the sun was already up. After that night we kept a fairly smoky fire going and suffered relatively little from the insects.

On the fourth day we returned from our reconnaissance of the surrounding area to find that our camp had been invaded, not – unfortunately for The Times – by marauding Indians but by Iain, Ro and Ruth, the latter having taken over my sleeping quarters, dispatching me to share the dining hut with David Gifford. Perhaps this takeover was a portent of what was to come. Suspicions as to my intentions were aroused the following day when Ruth opted to join the soils party. As was the norm I led the way, but on the return to camp I managed to get our little party badly lost. I blamed it on what I called the right-hand swing factor. Because as a right-handed person

I carried my 'machete' in my right hand and cleared the path to my right side so there was a tendency to veer to the right. We must have turned through nearly 45 degrees and only after having slashed our way through a dense bamboo thicket did we get back on track.

Ruth was a good walker and was frequently lauded by Taituba as a 'mulher dura' (a hard woman), comparing her favourably with some of the weaker of the males who were 'homen molé' (soft men). What he didn't know was that her frequently expressed desire was to lie on a cold stone floor. We would be walking through brilliant sunshine in open rolling countryside or towering forest where no man had probably ever walked before when she would announce to me:

'What I would really like to do is lie down on a cold stone floor.' This always struck me as deeply illogical. If what you like is lying on cold stone floors then why come to Mato Grosso, a place singularly not noted for its cold stone floors, whereas a job in, say, the north of Scotland would have provided almost endless opportunity for lying on cold stone floors. The answer of course was the animals. So, given a balance between northern Scottish animals + cold stone floors and Brazilian mammals + sun baked cerrado, it was the latter that won out. But she would still have liked to lie on cold stone floors.

Our detour, however, had been very demanding (and utterly without breaks to lie on cold stone floors) and by the time we got back to camp, Ruth felt that she could not tackle the walk back to base camp as had originally been planned, so of course she had let the rest of her party go without her while she stayed another night. The tongues were wagging. Had getting lost and having to hack through dense bamboo thicket all being cunningly contrived by me, to keep Ruth at the camp for another night? I would like to pretend that my navigational skills were such that I could have stage-managed such a demanding detour, but alas the truth is that I am a useless navigator and I quite simply got lost, as I still regularly do when Ruth and I are walking.

I was spending increasing amounts of time at my sub-camps, sometimes just myself and my Brasileiro helpers, sometimes with other members of the expedition. It was generally accepted that the soils team saw more animals than anybody else because we walked great distances, we sat still for long periods of time and because the damned things fell in our soil pits. It was not unreasonable therefore that Ruth should appear on a fairly regular basis at my sub-camps armed with her traps and binoculars. While she was a welcome sight, she was somewhat upstaged by the botanists, who would come out on plant collecting forays. This required using a small team of carriers to take the day's specimens back to base camp; since they were travelling out light, with a little persuasion they would bring out a few bottles of beer when it was available at base camp. Wrapping the bottles in the newspaper that the botanists used for pressing their specimens, soaking this and hanging them somewhere for the water to evaporate out of the paper would bring down the temperature of the beer to an entirely drinkable level.

Not that life at sub-camps was all beer and skittles. We continued our never-ending battle with the Class 'Insecta'. One day I descended into one of my deeper soil pits which had been dug some time previously. As I started to hack away at the face I realised that there was a wasp nest there, and from it started to emerge a stream of angry wasps. My exit was rapid, though not rapid enough to prevent a substantial number of stings. When I eventually stopped hopping around to assuage the pain, I peered down into the pit and realised that I had left my camera there. I had no intention of descending into the pit again, so from the lid of my lunchtime sardine tin I fashioned a hook that I attached to a length of string, and spent the next half hour trying to fish the camera out of the pit. Food could also be a problem, though this was to an extent my own fault as I couldn't really be bothered to get involved, and left it to the Brasileiros that accompanied me to organise it. We hit rock bottom one day when my evening meal was a warm-up of what my two labourers had had at lunchtime. I decided that the three of us should make an analysis of the shortcomings of the meal and we concluded as follows:

*Rice – dry and hard*
*Beans – mainly water and not many beans*
*Meat – mostly bone*

It was all done in good humour; indeed the Brazilian sense of humour places a great deal of emphasis on someone's misfortunes, and the suffering caused to me by the awful meal was of itself a reason for much hilarity. So I dug into the secret store I kept of little luxuries and pulled out a can of peaches which we shared, on the understanding that I would never again be dished up with quite so grim a meal as that one.

I needed to spend some time at base camp as I still had work to do on my very detailed transect adjacent to camp. Also, whenever Iain was away, and that seemed to be quite often, I was *de facto* team leader, responsible for running the camp, now generally aided and abetted by Ruth. On 1st August 1968 I was celebrating exactly one year in Brazil. On that important anniversary I was working on my base camp transect, with Iain again away, and since I was within easy walking distance of camp, my advice could quickly be sought on all the major issues affecting its management. So it was that on that notable day, not long after getting set into my soil pit description, Ruth arrived wearing some very short shorts and knee length boots – pretty kinky for the Mato Grosso – and requiring a high level consultation. It transpired that a man had appeared at camp with eggs to sell. Well, not exactly to sell, but what he wanted was to barter them for coffee and sugar, and guidance was being sought on the relative values of eggs, sugar and coffee. To think, a year ago to the day I was just an ordinary Geordie lad who knew a lot about football and was not that interested in much else, and now twelve months later I was the fountain of knowledge on the relative values of basic commodities in central Mato Grosso. I made the computations and Ruth returned to camp to complete the deal.

I hadn't made much progress when one of our Brasileiros appeared to say that an injured man had pitched up at the camp and was in urgent need of medical attention. This clearly required my return to camp. The number of squatters had been steadily increasing in the area and it was known that we often had a doctor on site and had medicines there. It was a difficult balancing act between wanting to help poor people with all manner of often appalling ailments, while accepting that we were not there to run a local health service and our medical supplies were very limited. The man was sitting in our medical 'casa'. He had put an axe through his foot, splitting it longitudinally. This was clearly well beyond any medical skills that Ruth and I between us could provide and our current doctor was away on a study of the incidence of leishmaniasis in Indian tribes. The man had walked 40 km to get to our camp, and I felt that we had to do something. On the expedition at the time we had the two scientists from Belém who were leading the leishmaniasis study – Ralph Lainson and Jeffrey Shaw – and although neither were doctors I concluded that, since they spent their lives dealing with diseased people, they might have more clue than I did as to what to do with a semi-severed foot. They were in the forest trapping the insects that vectored leishmaniasis, and so a runner was sent to fetch them. I felt that I should spend a little time with this unfortunate man so tried to make some conversation. Pressed for things to talk about I came out with one of my greater inanities:

'Does it hurt?' I asked him.

'Only when I walk,' he replied. That exchange will live with me forever.

The duo returned, and demonstrating quite remarkable skills they cleaned and disinfected the wound, sewed it up and shot the guy full of antibiotics, giving him a further supply to take away. He was instructed to come back if it didn't heal; he never did, so hopefully my idea of getting a couple of parasitologists to act as doctors had worked.

While football remained a vital part of my life whenever I was at base camp, a new sport had come to the fore. I had invented a sort of cross between water polo, rugby and volley ball which we could play in the camp pool, refurbished in a massive Anglo-Brazilian cooperative venture when everybody in the camp gave up their Sunday to basically rebuild our swimming pool. We were eaten alive by insects, but the end product was a truly splendid pool, cleared of many of the snags that tended to trip you up in the original. The big difference between playing football and playing water-volley-rugby-polo was that the girls were active participants in the latter, which gave the game an extra dimension.

The numbers at base camp could fluctuate quite considerably as we moved back into the dry season, with short-term visitations from Brazilian scientists and occasional bigwigs, including the British Ambassador and a party from the Royal Society flown in on two light aircraft, which were able to land at the old airstrip 20 km up the road. We had as many as 20 people in camp at one time. The expedition inevitably lost much of its camaraderie when numbers hit those sort of levels and I was only too keen to get out to one of my sub-camps. At the other extreme there was one evening when the females outnumbered the males – there was just me, Angie and Ruth.

As well as being, in Iain's absence, the *de facto* team leader, I was also the camp's unofficial 'orelha compassivo' (sympathetic ear). This role was typified one morning when to my surprise and delight I was woken by Ruth bearing a cup of tea. You get nothing for nothing in this world, and I quickly discovered that this was a case of tea for you and sympathy for me. She poured out her troubles, mainly revolving around Iain being in a particularly bad mood at the time and taking out his problems on her, and the deaths of some of the small animals that we had been trying to keep in captivity in the camp. For half an hour my shoulder served as handkerchief and my ear as sympathetic vessel into which she could pour her woes, and she departed much cheered. She was barely out of my 'casa' when Iain appeared and proceeded to pour out his troubles – with the Royal Society, with members of the expedition, with his domestic situation. He got my ear but not my shoulder, and departed much happier, though on balance I was a lot more sympathetic towards Ruth; after all, she had brought me a cup of tea and Iain hadn't.

Slightly less than a year after arriving in base camp, I was walking back to it for the last time along one of my favourite paths, auger over my shoulder and rucksack on my back. I felt a great sadness. In a year I had bonded in a way that I would never have believed possible with base camp, with my sub-camps, with the paths, with the vegetation, the animals, grudgingly maybe even the insects, and I knew I would never see them again. In my subsequent career I would say goodbye to many places and people, but never with finality; there was always the possibility – no matter how remote – that one day I would be back again. But this was absolute finality. The expedition had only a year to run and once it ended, base camp would cease to exist. The pace of development along the road was already accelerating, and we had had a visitation from a party of surveyors acting on behalf of the people who now apparently owned the land we sat on, and would no doubt soon destroy this wonderful natural environment. So it was with a rather heavy heart that the next day we set off along the little track from base camp, stopped for a last gritty 'cafesinho' at Geraldão's, a last swim in the Rio das Mortes, and a farewell nightcap at the little bar.

I still had the second of my 'study tours' to do. It was a trip that would take me on a four day journey, on a bus with a toilet marked 'in case of emergency only', to the mouth of the Amazon, then in a series of flights down the coast visiting Fortaleza, San Salvador, the famous cocoa research station in Bahia and finally back to Rio de Janeiro. Ruth was due the first of her study tours, and having by that time established the absolute coincidence of interests between soil studies and zoology, it was natural that we should do our study tours in tandem. When we arrived back in Rio we ate in the restaurant of the Gloria, and as we entered it we were spotted by the pianist who immediately went into a rendition of the Bridal March.

The Times may not have got its big story. Nobody on the expedition was killed or kidnapped by wild Indian tribes or attacked by a jaguar or bitten by a snake. Anthony Smith had done his best to create an adventure but it had a somewhat contrived feel to it, and even that resulted in nothing more dramatic than having their goods stolen when they foolishly left them unattended, and we never saw any sign of the missing Colonel Fawcett. But the expedition did have its human side. The pianist in the Gloria was a little ahead of himself, but two years later Ruth and I married. Angie, then six months pregnant with her first child, was Ruth's bridesmaid and all seemed well. How different were our legacies from the expedition to be. For Ruth and me, crossing the Rio das Mortes led to 46 years of marriage and counting; for Angie the adventure ended in a lonely and despairing death.

# PART 2

## THE GAMBIA

*The Gambia rises on the Fouta Djallon plateau in northern Guinea and flows for 700 miles west to the Atlantic Ocean. Leaving Guinea it passes through Senegal before entering the country with which the river shares its name at the town of Fatoto. While strictly the country is The Republic of The Gambia, it is virtually always referred to simply as The Gambia, producing the unique situation whereby the country and the river are known by exactly the same name. For 350 miles the river follows a sluggish meandering course through The Gambia, forming large oxbow lakes, and about 60 miles before reaching Banjul, the country's capital, it starts to widen reaching a width of around seven miles at its mouth. So flat is the profile of the river and so low its discharge that tidal movements can be measured throughout its course within the country, and salt from the ocean intrudes as far upstream as the town of Kuntaur about 160 miles from its mouth. A little like the Rio das Mortes The Gambia river enjoyed a certain macabre notoriety, being the access used by Mungo Park on his ill-fated exploration of the Niger.*

# CHAPTER 15

# TO THE ARSEHOLE OF AFRICA

Ruth and I had married in the autumn of 1970. By then I should have finished my PhD, but I was running behind schedule. The scholarship provided by the then Ministry of Overseas Development (known as ODM to distinguish it from the Ministry of Defence) had run out, but the university was able to take me onto its payroll until I completed the work. It was the only contract of employment that I have ever signed that stipulated the minimum amount of holiday that I should take but no maximum. So we found a very pleasant flat in Newcastle and Ruth got work in the University Zoology Department. Under the terms of the scholarship from ODM, if they were able to offer me employment then I was morally, if not entirely legally, obliged to take it. If they had no suitable post to offer me, I was free to seek employment wherever I could find it.

My *opus magnum* was drawing to a close, culminating in the production of a two-volume tome running to nearly six hundred pages. My research may have lacked a certain incisive brilliance or scientific innovation, but my thesis was undoubtedly one of the longest the university had ever seen. I had hand-written the whole thing and it was typed by a moonlighting department secretary, with some help from Ruth, onto wax stencil paper which formed the basis of producing multiple copies. Every correction required painting over the errant word or letter with a strange pink waxy liquid, realigning the stencil sheet in the typewriter and making the required change. How different things are today. By September I had still heard nothing from ODM and was getting a little nervous as to where my next employment was coming from, when eventually I got the call from the man from the Ministry.

'Ah, Moffatt,' he said. 'We are proposing to assign you to a project in The Gambia. You will need to go through an interview but that is just a formality. We are hoping that you will be able to start in about six weeks.' The Gambia – an idyllic Pacific island. Or so I assumed, since I had never actually heard of it, but I knew that ODM was active in the Pacific at the time and could think only that a place known as 'the' something or other must be an island. I quickly phoned through to Ruth's department. She was demonstrating in a practical so I left a brief message:

'Just tell her that it looks as if we are off to the Pacific, more details later.' I hurried off to the library. The Gambia – a ludicrous looking country on the apex of the bulge of West Africa – the white man's grave. I could not have been more disappointed. I telephoned an acquaintance who had worked in the colonial service in West Africa – what could he tell me about The Gambia?

'The Gambia,' he roared with laughter. 'Arsehole of Africa, and it looks like you are going right up it.' And certainly if you look at a map of Africa and see the bulge as its buttock, then I could understand what he meant.

But in fact The Gambia is a fascinating colonial invention, the smallest country of mainland Africa covering a land area of just 4,000 square miles – about half the size of Wales. From one end to the other it is not much over 200 miles as the crow flies, with its borders more or less following the meandering of the lower half of the River Gambia over a width of twenty to thirty miles. According to legend, the British set its borders purely on the basis of how easily they could be defended; in this instance by working out how far from the river its warships could fire. It was the first and last British colony in West Africa. Britain and France had struggled continually for political and commercial supremacy in the regions of the Senegal and Gambia rivers, and in 1889 the British formally claimed the country at the Paris conference, hoping to trade it at a later date with the French for better land elsewhere. However, Britain had underestimated the wily French and they never did manage to trade it for something more useful. The Gambia would be a 'Crown Colony and Protectorate' (the Colony being the capital, Bathurst,[5] and its environs, and the Protectorate the rest of the country) for over 75 years. It was the last country to gain its independence from Britain, which did not come about until 1965.

Despite its small size and a population at that time of around half a million, there are no less than eight distinct tribes, each with its own language and culture, making it one of the most culturally diverse 4,000 square miles of land anywhere. Even this does not take into account the delightfully named 'strange farmers.' These temporary migrants are brought in by the village chief to provide to him with two or three days of labour per week in his groundnut fields. In return for this they are provided with food, accommodation, tobacco and farming implements, and allocated a small area of land on which to grow their own groundnuts. Usually there will only be one or two per village, some of whom return on such a regular basis

---

5    The capital of The Gambia reverted from its colonial name of Bathurst to its pre–colonial name of Banjul on the 24th April 1973. So, for most of the time that we were there we knew it as Bathurst and that is the name I have used in the rest of this account.

that they end up being granted the status of honorary family members. These 'strange farmers' add further to the cultural complexity of this tiny country.

George Mikes' travels may have taken him to the United States, Australia, Israel, Japan, Germany, Italy and even on a whistle-stop tour of the United Nations, but he appeared never to have been lured to The Gambia. In the absence of any preparatory guidance from this source, I had to start life there from a position of relative ignorance, gleaning only that I was once again to follow in the footsteps of an explorer who disappeared almost without trace, and that you couldn't really buy anything in The Gambia. Hence we started frantic preparations for our departure. It was to be a two year posting and we needed to bring everything required to set up home for those two years. This was a task made even more difficult by having to cater for a possible addition to the family. So, eschewing the superstitions that you never bought baby goods for a baby that had not yet been conceived, let alone born, we embarked on a massive shopping spree, trying to visualise what baby needs might be met or improvised in The Gambia and what we would have to take with us. So loaded into our crates was every imaginable baby need, from a carrycot on wheels and folding high chair to nappies and bottles to jars of baby food. For novices in the business of babies it was a marathon task and met with much disapproval from those who believed one should adhere to the superstition.

While baby things constituted the most complex packing, the largest single item on our shopping list was a car. At the time we were the owners of a Triumph Spitfire – my pride and joy, but not a car to be taking onto the dirt roads of The Gambia. So we made the largest purchase of our young lives and bought a brand new Ford Capri. Informed advice was that the sturdier and rather higher-slung Ford Cortina was really the car to get, but the transition from an open top sports car to a tub like the Cortina was more than I could bear. At least the Capri did have reasonably sporty lines, even if its reduced ground clearance might be a problem. I wanted a white one, the same colour as the Spitfire, and Ruth fancied a bronze colour. We compromised and bought a metallic apple green that neither of us liked.

As a car being bought for export, we were required to pick it up at the main Ford dealership in central London, and stringent regulations decreed how long and how far we could drive it before delivering it to the docks in Liverpool. It was a Friday evening and we had not quite allowed for Friday traffic, nor for the time needed to make a call at the Natural History Museum to collect boxes of equipment for Ruth to continue her mammal work. By the time we had jammed all the equipment in the Spitfire, we reached the dealership as it was about to close. A relieved salesman met us and ushered us into the office.

'And may I have your banker's draft please?' I handed over the biggest cheque I had ever written. The salesman gazed at it in horror.

'This is a cheque' he said, 'not a banker's draft'. I had assumed that the term 'banker's draft' was some fancy name that big car companies used for what you and I would just call big cheques. So, faced with the instruction to bring a banker's draft I simply wrote out a cheque.

Impasse. They would not release the car on the basis of a potentially rubber cheque and I had the car booked onto a boat at Liverpool docks the following Monday, prior to our own departure later that week. It was a long shot at 5.30 on a Friday evening, but we decided to try to call my bank. Amazingly the phone was answered – some junior clerk who, I presumed, had not been able to get her figures to add up, was still there and provided us with the home number of the manager; it wouldn't happen now, even if there was such a thing as a branch bank manager. A conversation between the bank manager and the salesman ensued. The manager had been at that branch for quite some years and knew me well, as during my undergraduate years I had been a frequent visitor to his office begging for overdrafts. It appeared that, amidst the hilarity that the phone call had engendered, the bank manager was able to give the salesman the assurances that he needed, and by seven o'clock we were on the road. We had a slow drive to Newcastle ahead of us, because in those days you had to 'run in' cars, the permitted speed in each gear being rigidly set. Driving a brand new car out of central London on a Friday evening gave a whole new meaning to terror and made some of the sporting bridges of the Mato Grosso seem a doddle.

The flight to The Gambia must have been one of the last in the world to involve an overnight stop during which the plane stopped with you. Barely three weeks before Christmas, we took the flight from Gatwick airport and landed early in the evening in Las Palmas. There we all deplaned and were taken by bus to a hotel in the city. It wasn't the greatest hotel in the world, but Ruth and I had seen plenty worse and we had a good meal. Accompanying us was a senior member of the division of ODM for which I was working. He would become my guide and mentor for the next five years and my friend for many years thereafter. Alan Stobbs was ex-navy and one of the last of the old colonials. He continually puffed on his pipe and carried a monocle on the pretext that a spitting cobra had damaged one of his eyes, but he used it only when he felt the need to intimidate some African official. In those politically incorrect days he referred to it as his 'wog[6] basher'. Being a

---

6    The term 'wog' became an unacceptable derogatory word for black
     people. Its origin, however, was essentially benign. Labourers in Africa
     employed by the government wore shirts on the back of which was
     printed W.O.G.S – 'Worker On Goverment Services.'

singleton on the flight, he complained vociferously that he had spent the night in a cupboard, while Ruth and I had been allocated a pleasantly spacious room.

After breakfast we were bussed back to the plane and continued our journey to The Gambia, arriving at a civilised hour at the wonderful airport of Yundum, which was probably the most relaxed international airport in the world. The terminal building was little more than a hut with a check-in desk, a baggage arrival area and a couple of desks for customs and immigration officials. Outside the hut was a truly delightful garden with tables and chairs under bougainvillea trees and a magnificent 'flame of the forest' tree as the centrepiece. A small café sold tea, coffee and cold drinks and arriving passengers mingled freely in the garden with the friends and family that had come to meet them before going through passport control or customs.

We were driven from the airport to Bathurst along almost the only stretch of tarmac road in the country, passing en route the national prison. This was an extensive compound with imposing iron front gates. As you approached it, you could see that to each side of the gates a heavily armed guard stood to rigid attention under the hot African sun. It was only as you got relatively close that you realised that the ramrod guards stood to such rigid attention because they were made of wood. Escapes from Bathurst prison were apparently a rare occurrence. Indeed the story is told of how a gang of prisoners had been taken to the extreme east of the country to provide labour on a road-building project. They departed from the work site one day without one of the prisoners, who had temporarily disappeared into the bushes to do the necessary. On his return he was aghast to find that the lorry had departed without him. He set off and ran after the lorry, which fortunately had been held up awaiting a ferry, and was able to rejoin his fellow prisoners.

While we awaited the allocation of housing, we stayed in The Gambia's original old colonial hotel, the Atlantic. The informality of the capital airport, the wooden guards protecting the prison, the old colonial hotel; one already started to get the feel of a place that was laid back in a way that not even the smallest towns in Brazil were. The Brazilians were lively, fun-loving people, but there was always a frenetic edge to life. Here one suspected there was an altogether different pace to life. And it was under the mosquito net that draped the large ornate brass bedstead in the Atlantic Hotel that our first child was conceived. We had wasted no time and, with self-satisfied smirks, congratulated ourselves for ignoring the doubters and those governed by superstition and that we had prepared for the inevitable event. We knew that nothing could go wrong.

# CHAPTER 16

# LIFE AT THE RIVER'S PACE

Perhaps it was the pace of the river that set the pace of life in the Gambia for the flow is so sluggish that for much of the year that the tide pushes the river backwards and salt water can be detected throughout much of the length of the river within the country.

Being barely six years since it was a colony, The Gambia had a quite disproportionate number of expatriates filling every post of any seniority or at least sitting alongside the national incumbent as an 'advisor'. It was actually believed that there were now more expatriates in the civil service than there had been in colonial times. Certainly the British Government had had to build additional housing to accommodate them all, and this it had done in a housing complex known to Gambians and British alike as Stink Corner, though rather more formally as Mile Seven. 'Stink Corner' had earned its name because it was adjacent to an area of mangrove swamp on a little inlet creek. As the tide fell the swamp would dry out, releasing sulphurous gases that then pervaded the housing complex. At low tide, and with a prevailing easterly wind, the smell around the houses could be quite powerful and I always thought that the Government official who had released that particular piece of land to his former colonial masters must have had many a quiet snigger about it.

Smarter people than us and the old hands of the former

colonial service knew how to work the system and wangle themselves one of the splendid houses at Cape St Mary, overlooking the ocean and well away from the stench of mangrove swamp. However, the swamp was a great habitat for birds. Pied kingfishers and bee-eaters would sit on the telegraph wires, while osprey hunted for fish over the water. To us the house was relatively luxurious, with a spacious living area surrounded by louvred windows which gave a through breeze in the room – albeit tinged with sulphur – and two decent-sized and air-conditioned bedrooms. Compared to base camp it was luxury indeed. However, it was missing certain fundamentals like furniture and curtains for the vast expanse of windows, so that in early days it was much like camping in a goldfish bowl.

And so we set about establishing home, designating one of the two bedrooms to be the nursery. The system was that the Public Works Department held a supply of furniture left by the departing expatriates and, before sanctioning any new purchases, we were required to take a selection of these leftovers. As a result, the house forever looked like a second-hand furniture showroom, reflecting the widely different houses that the furniture had been originally destined for and the eclectic tastes of the first owners. However, newly built for us was the largest cot that anyone had ever seen, and maybe it was just as well if the early indications were anything to go by.

There are women who seem barely to show their pregnancy throughout the nine months. Ruth was not one of those and to this day I swear that she looked pregnant the next morning. Certainly by a couple of months she was like a ship in full sail and, if this was an indication of the size of the forthcoming baby, then it would need every square inch of the cot that had been supplied to us. Against all advice from every side we had decided that Ruth would stay in The Gambia for the birth of our first child. With one voice the old colonials – most of whom seemed to have spent 25 years in Nigeria before graduating to The Gambia – counselled against the idea, with no shortage of horror stories to back up their advice. But we were the new colonials, young and enjoying the confidence of the young that nothing bad would ever happen, and so Ruth would stay. There was a private doctor in the country, largely serving the expatriate population and the richer Gambian politicians. He had a clinic which was clean and reasonably well, if simply, equipped. He was called Dr Sami and it was to his care that we entrusted the monitoring of Ruth's pregnancy and subsequent delivery.

Surrounding our house was a good-sized garden but suffering from severe neglect, and we realised that finding a gardener was a high priority. We were barely moved into the house when a young man turned up to offer his services. We knew nothing of how the hiring of staff was done and were just relieved to have someone who might quickly restore some order to the garden so we immediately employed him. Our new gardener appeared to have only one approach to gardening, and that was to attack the lawn with a machete. After a couple of days, what had been a half decent looking lawn had been turned into something that looked as if it had been used for Sherman tank training. It was then that Vamara came into our lives.

The rubbish collection cart pulled up outside our front gate and sat atop of it was a grinning Vamara. He took one look at the scene of devastation and announced to Ruth:

'Madam, you need gardener.' He had hit the nail on the head. 'I am good gardener, many references, I come every day after finish rubbish.'

We were desperate to halt the devastation, but we were not confident that he could combine his job as a rubbish collector (what these days would probably be called a Waste Transfer Officer) with looking after our garden so we offered him a trial period of a month. He remained with us till the day we left. Vamara was a great gangling beanpole of a man with a very heavy limp; I wondered whether he had had polio as a child though if he had, in those days in The Gambia he must have been very lucky to survive it. Perhaps he'd indeed had just such a stroke of luck and that accounted for his perpetually sunny disposition. Vamara went about his work with a near constant smile on his face. He may not have been the greatest gardener in the world, but he imposed a degree of law and order. Not that this was always appreciated, as on the occasion when to Ruth's absolute horror he cut back a tree in which delightful weaver birds were nesting, totally destroying the magnificent nests. Still, in my frequent absences Varmara could always be relied upon to provide the brute strength that Ruth could not quite manage in her regular DIY activities, or tackle the dangers like the huge black snake that took to living in the drain on the front drive.

His focus of attention was a productive vegetable plot, though I was always fairly sure that more of the produce went to feeding Vamara's extensive family than ended up in our kitchen. Quite how extensive I could never make out, but judging by the number of birthdays, weddings and other expensive feasts that he was required to attend, it was very extensive indeed. Vamara was almost completely illiterate but was still our most regular correspondent, courtesy of the local scribe. There was barely a week went by that we didn't receive a letter joyously announcing the news of some imminent family event, but ending on a note of concern as to the substantial cost of it. Though in more sombre tone were letters detailing medication that was required by an ailing member of the family, sometimes hospitalisation, or even the occasional death. He must have been the professional scribe's best customer. Not all his letters were basically a request for money. Some addressed some finer point of gardening that he needed to ask or inform us about, but which was too complex for his limited English, while others were simply to tell us how much he liked us and enjoyed working for us. I always suspected that such letters not long preceded one of his more substantial financial requests.

When the hungry mouths of the Varmara family left little for us, there was always the allotment over the road that produced vegetables in shapes and sizes that defied botanical norms, and did lead us to wonder sometimes just how it was manured. And when the allotment failed us, then there was always Bathurst market. This was a fetid place, a crowded jumble of tin roofs and beach umbrellas, sheltering from the glare of the sun or the torrential rains hundreds of stalls selling fruit, vegetables, meat, fish, cheap household goods and clothing.

Despite the heat, the smell and the stifling overcrowding, the stallholders, who were almost exclusively female and virtually always on the extra-large side, were always beautifully attired in colourful local costume, and kept up a constant barrage of cheerful conversation often from one side of the market to the other.

Prominent amongst the clothing stalls were those selling woolly hats. The imperative need apparently felt by every Gambian male to wear at all times a woolly hat was something that I could never fathom. However, second hand woolly hats were big business in The Gambia; Bathurst market was always full of them and they must have come into the country by the shipload, but from where I never could find out.

Like a ship in full sail, Ruth would descend on the market, vying for sheer presence with the beautifully attired stallholders, who would marvel at her enormous bump. However, as time went by, manoeuvring through the stalls became increasingly difficult and, as we were to learn, the market could be a dangerous place. Witness the events described the morning the country awoke to the banner headline in the local English language newspaper:

### 'GAMBIAN BEAUTY QUEEN SPERMED IN BATHURST MARKET'

The report was of a court case and went something like this. A former Miss Gambia had been shopping in Bathurst market when she felt something hard being pushed against her. Turning she saw a man starting to run away and at the same time realised that on the back of her skirt was a nasty wet sticky patch. The market was in uproar with the nearby stallholders shouting:

'The thing is out, the thing is out.' The police were on the scene in no time; the beauty queen was escorted to the police station and a man was apprehended.

At the trial, Exhibit A was produced – a skirt with a distinct tell-tale stain which the judge solemnly declared, following forensic examination, to be male sexual product. The former Miss Gambia was called to the stand and identified the skirt as the one that she had been wearing in Bathurst market that day. The defendant who had, perhaps, aspirations to being a lawyer, had decided to act as his own defence. He approached the stand, and in what he believed was going to be the defining moment of the trial he delivered his masterful question to the plaintiff:

*'Is it not true that there were many men in Bathurst market that day, so what makes you think it was me that soiled your skirt?'*

'It is indeed true,' she replied, 'that there were many men in Bathurst market that day, but you were the only one with his penis out.' This more or less seemed to wrap things up, and the defendant was found guilty and dispatched to Bathurst prison and the watchful eyes of the wooden guards.

So as the bump grew, fresh produce was more often sourced at the much smaller Bakau market. Here Ruth learned the tricks of the buyer's trade, particularly when it came to buying meat. While goats abounded in the country, sheep were significantly more rare and therefore fetched a premium price. Naturally the butchers would always sell you 'sheep meat', whether or not it was actually goat. The butcher's art was not well developed and 'jointing' was little more than a random attack with the meat cleaver, although ODM had recently brought in a master butcher from Sainsbury's to advise on proper butchering. Oddly enough his name was Silverside. It was impossible to tell the difference between goat and sheep meat once it was on the slab in its semi-pulverised state. The only answer was to buy meat from a whole carcass as the secret to knowing whether it was a sheep or a goat lay in the tail. In goats the tail pointed upwards and in sheep the tail hung downwards, though no doubt the cunning butchers had devised ways of making a goat's tail hang downwards.

While we sourced fresh produce from Bakau and Bathurst markets, everything else was bought at the one and only major store – Morel and Prom. Bathurst's trading community was dominated by Gambian Lebanese – from the small shops crowded into the colonnaded shopping streets to what at the time was the country's one and only 'super store'. While the business acumen of these descendants of the Lebanese traders was not in question, The Gambia was the ultimate in feast and famine. There appeared to be no organised stock control and the goods in the shops depended on what happened to be brought into the constantly bustling but apparently shambolic docks.

And so we would go through various crises in basic commodities. Now there was no butter, so when it did come into the shops everybody would create little butter mountains in their fridges. But then for the next few months there would be plenty of butter in the shops, while the butter in your fridge would pass its use-by date, and meanwhile the country had run out of cooking oil.

At the other extreme were the one-off appearances of luxury items, often at knockdown prices because the boat passing through Bathurst port just happened to have a load of something and wanted to get rid of it, or it had been offloaded accidentally. One day Morel and Prom would have shelf-fulls of cheap Russian caviar and for the next month or so you knew that wherever you went to dinner caviar would be the starter. Then the caviar would be gone and you never saw it again.

I came home one day to find Ruth very pleased with herself.

'Guess what surprise I have for you.' I gazed at her awesome bump – maybe it was twins. With a triumphant cry, from behind her back she produced a bottle of Guinness.

Prior to our departure for The Gambia I had spent some weeks at the ODM's Land Resources Division, the organisation that I was working for, based in a grim high-rise tower in Tolworth. I found the southern beers almost undrinkable and took to drinking Guinness, to which I became very partial. Since coming to The Gambia I had had little choice but to drink Heineken, despite never having been a lager drinker, since that was basically all there was. Ruth led me through to the storeroom, where I was greeted with the rapturous sight of three crates of Guinness, which she had located in Morel and Prom. Sundown could not come soon enough and that evening, in eager anticipation, I opened my first bottle of Guinness. It was quite revolting.

I later learned that Guinness was enormously popular in Nigeria, having been first imported there in the 1800s. However, fearing the evaporation of some of the alcohol on the long voyage to Nigeria, the Irish brewed the Guinness twice as strong. In fact, the alcohol did not evaporate, but to this day Nigerians brew their Guinness twice as strong and export this powerful brew to other parts of the world. How a few crates had ended up in Morel and Prom was simply a manifestation of the workings of the Bathurst docks. This super-strong drink lacked the sharp distinctive bitterness of Irish Guinness and reminded me more of an English sweet stout or possibly a cheap cough medicine. Still, the squashes seemed to grow apace after the judicious application of Nigerian Guinness.

Having so recently shed the yoke of colonialism but still being full of old colonials, the social life was a bit like something out of Somerset Maugham. The Bathurst Club was a critical social hub; somewhat dilapidated it did, however, boast a nine-hole golf course, tennis courts, billiard table and darts boards. It also boasted a small library, and if I say that during my time in The Gambia I read everything that Howard Spring had written, then I probably need to say no more about its contents. The club was of course open to anybody that paid the subscription, but in practice it was used almost exclusively by the expatriate population, the most notable exception being the then Prime Minister, Sir David Jawara. He had strong ties to Britain and perhaps more importantly enjoyed a game of golf, if not to say a drink. However in a largely Muslim country, he eventually did what any politician does to secure his position and took the expedient step of converting to Islam, reverting to his original name, Dawda Jawara, and in the process was seen rather less often at the Bathurst Club.

His ties to Britain were to serve him badly ten years later. While attending the wedding of Prince Charles and Lady Diana, a coup attempted to oust him. The coup was put down by a coalition of members of the British SAS and Senegalese troops, at a cost of a thousand lives.

So when I was on a 'home' week, at sundown, maybe after a game of tennis, we would join the odd collection of old colonials, a few new colonials like ourselves, most of the staff of the British High Commission and the odd expatriate working in the private sector. We would talk about the state of the country, the weather, the problems of our respective jobs, the latest tales of what the tourists were up to. But mostly we would talk about our servants – what they cooked well, what they cooked badly, whether they were paying too high a price for meat at the market and how much sugar they stole.

From the outset, Ruth had decided that she really didn't want servants, least of all a male cook, and to the horror of the old colonials we simply employed a girl who did a bit of housework and Ruth did the cooking and shopping. It couldn't last. In The Gambia there was basically no entertainment other than what you made for yourselves – no television, no cinema, no restaurants, nothing. And so we spent our time dining at each other's houses. I would get back from trek on a Friday evening, go straight into the shower and be calling out to Ruth:

'Whose house are we at tonight?' And it was rarely that we weren't being entertained at somebody's house.

Of course entertaining has to be reciprocated, and it was here that our new colonial approach of no cook started to tell. With Ruth getting larger by the day, and after a couple of dinner parties where a vast and sweat-covered Ruth would be serving up the meal that she had cooked herself, we decided that the time had come to do the proper thing and employ a cook/

houseboy. Not only would it mean that we could entertain like everybody else entertained, with the hostess in social intercourse with her guests rather than rushing to and from the kitchen in a muck sweat, but we also ceased to be social pariahs in the Bathurst Club and could compete with the best when it came to how much sugar the cook was stealing.

The employment of cooks was an endeavour in which we singularly failed. I don't remember how many we got through, but we certainly seemed to change them at regular intervals. Potential cooks would always appear with their references, almost invariably hand written in fading ink on paper that was curling and ragged at the edges, and this applied even if the reference was relatively recent. I concluded that cooks felt that a well-worn looking reference somehow carried more gravitas than a pristine one. So recent references were presumably left out in the sun to fade a little and wetted and dried a few times to give that curling well-worn look. They would often list the dishes at which a particular cook excelled and would stress his qualities of honesty and loyalty. However, they were often a bit thin on the identification of the person to whom the reference applied. So, a reference for Momodu was not ultimately that significant, since it might have applied to half the population, with certainly no guarantee that it had anything whatsoever to do with the particular Momodu who was applying to be your cook.

Whatever the references said, we found that cooks fell into two categories. There were those who were useless and we got rid of on such basic grounds as: couldn't cook, couldn't do housework, was overwhelmed by sick and dying relatives at whose bedsides/funerals he spent most of his time, and of course stealing all the sugar. Then there were those who were good, but were using us as a temporary staging post until something came up in one of the big houses at Cape St Mary or with one of the new hotels. The fact was that no cook worth his salt wanted to be employed in a house at Stink Corner; it was a bit like a cook having worked at McDonalds on his CV – we were strictly downmarket.

Usually the ones that left us simply failed to show up and after a couple of days you assumed they had gone for good. There was one, however, who had the courtesy to leave his 'letter of resignation'. We thought that we had really found a good one, and that evening we had thrown one of our more successful dinner parties. He cleared up and appeared smiling broadly at the door of the dining room to take his plaudits from our guests and thanks from us. After our guests had left Ruth went to the kitchen, which had been left immaculately clean, and found a note lying on the kitchen bench. It read simply:

'Madame. I am very happy working here and now I am leaving.' We never heard of him again.

Critical on any cook's CV were his curries. On first encountering a reference which stated that the cook could prepare 16 curry dishes I was deeply impressed – this just about outdid my local Indian Restaurant – and he promptly got the job. He did, however, look somewhat perplexed when I asked him to prepare a dinner for Ruth and myself, based perhaps on a couple of his dishes, and what did he recommend? Well, he could do a chicken curry and a bowl of peanuts. That seemed all very well but could he not do another curry dish as well. He brightened a little and yes, he could also do a bowl of chopped tomatoes. What transpired was that they cooked only one curry dish, and the remaining 15 were side dishes – peanuts, tomatoes, chopped onions, you name it and it could appear as a side dish. I never worked out quite what determined a cook's limit in 'curry dishes'; why did one do a 14-dish curry and another a 16-dish curry. Perhaps it was all down to the cook's imagination and willingness to experiment. Strawberry jam, for example, I never found enhanced a curry but it may well have put the cook up into the '18-dish curry' class.

What I quickly learned, however, was that what lay behind the emphasis on the curry dishes on the CV of every cook was the West African Sunday Curry Lunch. I am not ultimately a deeply sociable person and, of all the social gatherings, the one that I hated most was the West African Sunday Curry Lunch and every Sunday someone would be doing a Curry Lunch.

To put my antipathy to this feast in some sort of perspective, I would point to the fact that half of the weekends I was away, and on the weekends that I was at home Saturday was a working day, so basically I was looking at one day off in a fortnight. The centrepiece of the West African Sunday Curry Lunch was of course the 16 or 18-dish curry, depending on how upmarket or imaginative the cook was. The gathering would start about 11.00 in the morning, but the first three hours or more were devoted to preparing for the curry by consuming large quantities of booze. Finally around two or three in the afternoon we would be unleashed on the curry, accompanied of course by more booze, and finally round off the afternoon with a drink before teetering home and collapsing on the bed. And that was my once a fortnight day off gone.

If the West African Sunday Curry Lunch was to be dreaded, the social occasion that we awaited in eager anticipation was the invitation to dine at the residence of the British High Commissioner. There were few visiting dignitaries to The Gambia. We once had a visit from Lady Plowden famous for the groundbreaking Plowden Report on primary education, at the time vice chairman of the BBC governors and soon to become chairman of the Independent Broadcasting Authority. However her visit had less to do with revolutionising The Gambia's primary education system or advising the still fledgling Radio Gambia, than it had with visiting her son, who was working in the country for ODM. The odd Under-Secretary of State for something or other would drop by en route to or from somewhere more important than The Gambia, but basically nobody gave a bugger about the place. We imported their groundnut oil, but even that was falling victim to the iniquitous European Common Agricultural Policy; we might have exported a few woolly hats, but I suspect that many of these were in fact illegally sourced from the Eastern Block; and the tourists were all Swedes.

Finding that you had been appointed as High Commissioner to The Gambia was probably a career-defining moment, that is, it defined that you had no career in the Diplomatic Service. However, if you had been polishing up your French with a view to Paris as a possible next stop, then at least it wouldn't be wasted since you could use it on shopping trips to Dakar.

Despite this, there is no doubt that the High Commissioner would have had a hefty entertaining allowance, so he stoically worked his way round all of us who were employed by ODM and invited us to dinner.

The glass was crystal, the cutlery silver and the waiters wore white immaculately laundered and pressed uniforms. Groups of twelve – being the number of people that the table held – had clearly been carefully selected for compatibility, which meant that you were likely to end up with all the people that you regularly socialised with. The highlight of the evening came as we finished the sweet. The High Commissioner's wife rose majestically from the table and pronounced: 'Ladies, I think we may withdraw.'

I had heard that at the High Commission dinners the ladies withdrew and I was looking forward to finding out what happened next, never having previously been at a function where the ladies withdrew. Port was brought by one of the waiters and placed in the middle of the table alongside a box of obviously expensive cigars. Then the waiter also withdrew, closing the doors behind him. We charged our port glasses and lit our cigars. I was agog; now what? Would the High Commissioner give us the low-down on the current state of the political landscape? Would he enlighten us on the government's latest thinking on nude sun bathing by the Swedish tourists? Would he invite us all to give man-to-man appraisals of how our jobs might be benefiting the economy? Or would we sit round telling dirty jokes? I didn't feel that I could contribute much to any discussion of the political landscape; my views on nude sunbathing were probably best kept to myself and I wasn't sure that my job was contributing diddly squit to the economy. But I had written down a few really quite good dirty jokes on a postcard which I had in my inside jacket pocket and was more than ready to kick off the session. What actually happened next was that we went on talking about exactly the same things that we had been talking about before the ladies withdrew, the only fascinating insight being that the High Commissioner's cook also stole the sugar.

While for the first year of our time in The Gambia, 'eating out' meant a dinner party at someone's house or sausage, egg and chips at the Bathurst Club, the growing tourist industry persuaded a Lebanese investor to open a club-cum-restaurant in Cape St Mary. Being located at the site of house number 69 it was imaginatively called 'The 69 Club'. With the tourist industry still in its infancy, there was no ready pool of trained waiters, and the 69 Club recruited pretty much off the street. It was a sharp learning curve. The restaurant was aiming very much up-market and one of its feature specialities was fondue, a dish so up-market I had never previously encountered it. As well as the more traditional cheese fondue, they offered a beef fondue in which you cooked strips of meat in very hot oil with a little burner under the oil bowl keeping it at the required temperature. I ordered the beef fondue. The hot oil bowl was brought to the table and the waiter set to lighting the little candle that would keep it hot. In the course of lighting the candle he also set light to the hot oil. I knew no better and, being aware that some dishes came 'flambé', assumed that this was how a beef fondue ought to be. I dunked my first strip of beef into the flaming oil which inevitably heightened the flames and realised that not only had all the occupants of my table disappeared but the entire restaurant was being evacuated.

For many of the expatriates, one of the great things about being in The Gambia was getting out of it, and that meant going to the Senegalese capital Dakar. This is a city not to be confused with Dhaka the capital of Bangladesh, a confusion that created deep distress to one of the expatriate families that we got to know in our early days in The Gambia. It was common for children attending boarding school in the UK to be routed back to The Gambia for school holidays via Dakar. This gave the parents an excuse for an expenses-paid trip to Dakar, where they could load up on French cheeses, French wine and a host of other luxury items that you would never hope to find in Bathurst except where they had been mistakenly unloaded in the disorganised port. Such a trip had particular value when the children were coming to The Gambia for their Christmas holiday in which case the Christmas shopping could all be done in Dakar.

This particular Christmas, our friends set off as usual to meet their children in Dakar, but to their consternation the children were not on the plane that they were expecting them to be on. Communications from Senegal were not great but were at least a little better than they were in The Gambia, and they were able to contact the school which assured them that the children had been put safely onto the flight, giving the parents the flight details. The parents then contacted British Airways who also confirmed that the children had boarded the stated flight and were now indeed in Dhaka! Unfortunately, BA explained, they could not immediately do much about getting the children out of Dhaka as there was a full scale war going on in Bangladesh, with India having just deployed troops in support of the Bengali 'Mukti Bahini' or 'Freedom Fighters' attempting to gain separation and independence from Pakistan. It was estimated that some ten million, mainly Hindu Bengalis, were trying to get out to India and BA was sure that the parents would understand that it was all a little difficult at the moment. In the end the children did get out and they did get to Dakar in time for Christmas, but the bloom had certainly gone off the brie.

Neither Ruth nor I were that fussed about French cheeses, French wines, pate de foie gras, or cuts of meat that had been properly butchered rather than being simply hacked to bits with a cleaver. But we decided that before Ruth became at risk of giving birth on a bone-rattling ten or eleven hour trip in a badly sprung Land Rover, we should make the journey to Dakar, if only to marvel at the contrasts. It was a journey to another world. Dakar was a bustling, thriving and ultimately French town. Shops had glittering arrays of goods, be it the latest fashions from Paris, modern electrical devices or of course food. You were spoiled for choice for places to eat and the service was impeccable – little chance here of being presented with a flaming fondue. The French colonisation model had been very different to the British and it came as a total shock to find Europeans working as waiters or serving in the shops. The British in The Gambia would never have so demeaned themselves – they were the rulers and never integrated with local society. The French colonisers came to live in what was simply regarded as an outpost of France where they would work in the sort of roles that they might have worked in had they stayed in France. It was all a far cry from scruffy, backward Bathurst.

But there was another side to it. As we sat to dinner on the night of our first arrival, eating moules marinière in a delightful patio restaurant, we were appalled to see hands being pushed through the greenery surrounding the patio as hordes of beggars attempted to attract your attention. The Gambia had its 'pimps, touts and chisellers' that preyed on the tourists, but it was rare to see a beggar on the streets. As I have never been a big city man I found that two to three days in Dakar were plenty and I was more than happy to get back to Stink Corner.

## CHAPTER 17

# GROUNDNUT TALES

In effecting the transition from Brazil to The Gambia, I was following the journey made by the groundnut in the sixteenth century. A native of South America, it was Portuguese traders that introduced a Brazilian species of groundnut to The Gambia. It was intended as a small-scale food crop, with the particular merit of being relatively drought-resistant, and it remained as that for 300 years. However, the toiletry habits of Europeans in the nineteenth century were to bring the groundnut to much greater prominence. Soap was not new; it was known to have been used in ancient Babylon as far back as 2800 BC. However, it was the drive for improved hygiene in Victorian times as the result of a greater popular understanding of the link between health and hygiene that assigned to the groundnut an altogether different role. Groundnut oil became one of the key oils used in the large-scale manufacture of soap. So, from a hundred baskets harvested for selling in 1830, production rose to over 8,000 tons by 1848, and by the 1850s groundnuts accounted for two thirds of the country's exports. It was therefore a little remiss of me not to have mugged up a bit about groundnuts before going to The Gambia, and of course George Mikes' travels never took him there.

The Department of Agriculture assigned to me six Agricultural Assistants. They were all older than me with years of experience, mainly in the agricultural extension service.

However, I was the 'toubab' (white man) with a string of letters after my name so, despite the fact that I was relatively young and inexperienced, I was very much the man in charge and full of an awareness of my own importance. After a brief period of settling in, I embarked on an initial familiarisation tour of the country accompanied by my Agricultural Assistants. We piled into the Land Rover pick-up that had been assigned to me and set off on our whistle-stop tour, myself and Mr. Cisse, the most senior of the assistants, in the front cab and the remaining assistants huddled in the back trying to protect themselves from the red dust kicked up by every vehicle that we passed.

We had driven for many miles through a landscape dominated by fields of groundnuts, when unexpectedly the land use pattern changed and there was not a groundnut to be seen. I called the Land Rover to a halt and we all piled out so that I might better survey the scene. I turned to Mr Cisse:

'Why, suddenly, are we not seeing any groundnuts growing'? I enquired.

'Well, Doctor', he said with due deference, 'it is because the soils here are too hard and it is difficult to pull the plants up from the ground.'

I realised that I was dealing with unsophisticated people. I adopted my most professorial demeanour and looked over the assembled assistants. Since my arrival in the Gambia I had seen thousands of acres of groundnuts, which looked for all the world just like a pea crop. Now, I was something of an expert on peas, having worked for a summer vacation on the pea harvest in Lincolnshire, and knew all there was to know about the harvesting of the *Leguminosae* family. There they simply went through the crop with cutters and then scooped the cut crop up elevators into lorries that carted them to the vining station, where the haulm was stripped off and the peas shelled for dispatch to the freezing plant. I realised that the highly mechanised harvesting of peas in Lincolnshire could not be adopted in The Gambia, but the simplest of knives could surely be driven through the crop to cut the main stem. Amazing that they hadn't thought of it. I paused until I was sure that I had their full attention before delivering my pearls:

'I would suggest, Mr Cisse, that the farmers in this area be equipped with appropriately fashioned cutting tools, and that harvesting be accomplished by simply cutting through the main stems.'

There had been a lot of competition amongst the Agricultural Assistants for secondment to the project. It offered a base in the capital, rather than living in some remote agricultural extension field office. The project was clearly going to be well funded and surely some of the riches would rub off on the selected assistants. And being part of a high-powered foreign team undoubtedly enhanced their status. Nobody wanted to jeopardise their position.

A profound silence followed my pearls of wisdom. Mr Cisse was clearly deeply embarrassed and hopped uncomfortably from one foot to the other, gazing at his fellow assistants silently beseeching their help. However, they had all seen something interesting in the far distance and their eyes were riveted to it. Nobody wanted to be the bearer of unwelcome information.

'So, Mr Cisse, what do you think?' The hopping intensified.

'Well, Doctor, that wouldn't really work. You see, the groundnuts grow under the ground and so you have to uproot them to harvest the nuts.'

That pesky plant.

Almost uniquely, the groundnut goes through a process known as 'pegging'. Once the plant has flowered a 'peg' (in fact a budding ovary) develops from the site of each flower.

Instead of doing the normal thing and growing up towards the light, the pegs turn downwards and head for the ground. They penetrate the ground to a depth of one or two inches and it is here, below the ground that the nuts develop. What do you say? A weak joke about just testing them, or that this would never happen on Tyneside? In the end I settled for a simple:

'Thank you, Mr Cisse.'

He avoided meeting my eyes for the rest of the day, and clearly for some days he worried that he might be the messenger that I had decided to shoot. The incident was never mentioned again, though in a country the size of The Gambia I have no doubt that the story was very quickly round the Department of Agriculture, and probably a lot of other departments as well, of the British 'expert' who came to a country whose economy depended on the groundnut and didn't know that the nuts grew underground.

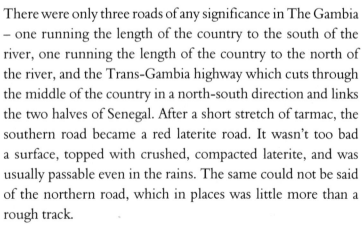

There were only three roads of any significance in The Gambia – one running the length of the country to the south of the river, one running the length of the country to the north of the river, and the Trans-Gambia highway which cuts through the middle of the country in a north-south direction and links the two halves of Senegal. After a short stretch of tarmac, the southern road became a red laterite road. It wasn't too bad a surface, topped with crushed, compacted laterite, and was usually passable even in the rains. The same could not be said of the northern road, which in places was little more than a rough track.

The last town of any size on the southern road was Basse, some 250 miles by road from Bathurst. It was a bustling town, with a lively market and a busy waterfront and some once fine old colonial buildings. It was also the best place to see the rare Egyptian Plover or crocodile bird, so named because the plover will enter the gaping mouth of the crocodile and pick out bits of meat, thus creating a symbiotic relationship, with the bird serving as a toothpick for the crocodile and the crocodile providing food for the bird. At one time Basse marked the effective end of the accessible country, for it was the final port of call for the steamers that plied the river and provided the only access to the far east of the country. Since 1949 that steamer had been the Lady Wright, named after the wife of then Governor of the colony of The Gambia, Sir Andrew Wright. Carrying both people and cargo, the Lady Wright made a weekly round trip of 640 miles on the meandering river, calling at 20 river ports en route. The Lady Wright was one of only a very few floating post offices in the world and envelopes stamped on the Lady Wright were collectors' items.

Continuing beyond Basse to the end of the southern road is the town of Fatoto, marking more or less the boundary with Senegal, and to cross the river to the northern road there was a ferry. The ferry hardly merited the name and was a simple pontoon, capable of carrying one vehicle and an elastic number of foot passengers. It made the one across the Rio das Mortes look sophisticated. Whereas that derived its momentum from a canoe with an outboard engine, the ferry at Fatoto was entirely manual, with the passengers providing the momentum by hauling on the cable stretched across the river. With the Land Rover on board, even with the sluggish current of the Gambia, it could be very hard work.

Having hauled ourselves across the river we set off west, heading back to the mouth of the river on the northern road across a barren landscape comprising mainly massive outcrops of laterite. This is the residual material left after the intense weathering of parent rock in the hot wet tropics which, when exposed, hardens to a rock-like material with a deeply irregular surface and makes for the most uncomfortable of driving conditions. There is an awful lot of it in The Gambia. For hours we bounced across this rocky moonscape, jarring every bone in my body. Dusk was approaching and we had not driven through any villages where we could pitch camp and find accommodation for the assistants and driver. I was becoming concerned, when to my relief I heard the ringing sound of a pickaxe being wielded against rock – signs of life at last. In my relief I turned to Mr Cisse and exclaimed:

'Sounds like they are planting groundnuts.' Without a flicker of a smile he replied:

'Oh no, Doctor, it is not that. Someone is breaking up the laterite for road building material.' I decided that to try to explain that I was having a joke would probably only make matters worse – as if I was trying to disguise another howler. So I left it that they believed their foreign expert not only didn't know that groundnuts grew underground, but thought they could be grown on hardened laterite by smashing holes in it with a pickaxe. It was a lot to recover from.

The men wielding the pickaxes constituted a gang of workers – quite possibly inmates of Bathurst prison; it would have seemed indelicate to ask. They told us that there was a small town nearby called Diabugu. We arrived too close to nightfall for comfort. I clambered down from the back of the pick-up, where I had stood in order to get the best possible view of the terrain. My back ached, my legs were almost locked into a permanent braced position and my head pounded.

'Dear bugger,' I expostulated. Mr Cisse adopted his deferential but corrective tone:

'No, Doctor. It is pronounced Diaboogoo.' It was my final attempt at witticism.

Let me divert briefly from my own journey to that of Mungo Park[7], one of the unsung heroes of early exploration. Moving on from Diabugu the next day, we continued our journey west which, after about 50 bone-shaking miles, brought us to the small town of Karantaba. There was nothing particularly remarkable about Karantaba, but by taking the rough track from the town to the river, we arrived at a must-visit place for someone who had lived so close to the last known location of Colonel Fawcett. For there on the bank of the river stood a twenty-foot high obelisk, marking the departure point of another remarkable explorer who was to disappear for ever – Mungo Park. This Scottish explorer chose the Gambia as his point of ingress to the interior of Africa in his quest to determine the course of the Niger. On his first expedition he departed from or close to Karantaba in July 1795, but before even reaching the Niger he was captured by a Moorish chief and spent four months in captivity. He escaped alone and, undeterred, with only his compass and his horse, he found the River Niger which he followed for 300 miles before heading back to The Gambia and arriving home in December 1797, to the astonishment of all as he was assumed to be long since dead.

You might have thought that enough was enough, and certainly for a while he appeared to have settled down in Peebles to a normal existence, marrying and plying the trade for which he had originally trained, as a doctor. But exploration

---

7   The Last Journey of Mungo Park by Michael Langley, History Today
    Volume 21 Issue 6 June 1971

is in the blood and in January 1805 he was on his way back to The Gambia. Departing from Karantaba this time was a much larger team comprising three officers, forty other Europeans, mostly soldiers from the Royal Africa Corps but also including four boat builders from Southampton. They were tasked with building a forty-foot boat once the party reached the Niger. Making up the rest of the party were the local guides and a number of slaves.

But the trek inland took a massive toll. After five weeks one man was dead, seven mules lost and the expedition's baggage mostly destroyed by fire. By the time they reached the Niger, dysentery and an assortment of fevers had accounted for all but 11 of the Europeans so Park decreed that the remains of the party should rest and recuperate. Two months on and they were down to a party of five, comprising Park, Lieutenant Martyn – who by then had gone mad, probably due to an addiction to the local beer – and three soldiers. Park dispatched a local guide to take his journals back to The Gambia and decided to set off down the Niger in a converted dugout canoe, with the intention of making the journey to the sea without stopping.

Like Fawcett and his party, he was never seen again. However, unlike Fawcett, there appears to be a plausible explanation of his disappearance. Having successfully navigated 1,000 miles, their canoe became stuck on rocks at the Bussa rapids in Nigeria where they came under attack from native tribesmen. All five men were drowned trying to escape and all that was ever found was Park's munitions belt. As with Fawcett, the tragedy was also to embrace the son. 22 years after Park disappeared, in the hope that he had in fact escaped alive and was now in captivity, his second son set off to find him. He was made of less durable stuff than his father and made little headway into the interior before dying of fever.

I stood looking at the slightly neglected monument – not much but more than marked any spot from which Fawcett had disappeared. I was clad for fieldwork, in cool and comfortable gear with well fitting hiking boots. I had always been taken by the thought of Fawcett in his plus fours and hacking jacket. But standing on the spot from which Park set off into the interior, I marvelled at the mental picture of him in his European clothes including his umbrella and tall hat, where reputedly he kept his journal. I climbed back into the Land Rover, the bone-shaking roads put sharply in perspective.

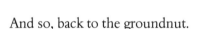

And so, back to the groundnut.

Although by now groundnuts were grown primarily as a cash crop, they still formed the basis of the main local dish – groundnut stew, otherwise variously known as 'domoda', 'durango' or 'mafe'. Recipes vary enormously, but all have in common a liberal quantity of pulverised peanuts. While most recipes do not refer to the inclusion of hot peppers as a key ingredient, pretty much every stew I had was very obviously well peppered, which suited my palate. But hot peppers can be overdone.

Alan was on one of his lightning supervisory missions and I was on trek, so it was agreed that he and John Dunsmore, the team leader, would join me for a couple of days. My team leader was ex-Guards and very much of the stiff upper lip, so stiff in fact that it barely moved as he spoke, nor for that matter did his lower lip. Had he not chosen to devote his post-Guards career to working in overseas agricultural development, he could easily have been a ventriloquist. The locals were totally fascinated by him. When they spoke their mouths moved as if they were chewing on a particularly tough steak, so they would gaze in awe as this stream of sound emanated from John without him apparently moving his mouth.

I was staying during that part of the survey at a rest house on the agricultural research station of Sapu. It was basic but marginally better than camping. Staying there at the same time was the team's socio-economist, also accompanied by his trek cook. My cook had been dispatched in the morning to find fresh meat for dinner that night. Adopting a fairly liberal approach to the word 'fresh' – and thereby no doubt getting it a knockdown price – he returned with meat that was to say the least 'mature'. Realising that his purchase would not meet with my fulsome approval, he decided that he had better use a lot more chilli than usual for the groundnut stew that he was preparing for the evening meal, in the hope that it would disguise the distinctly 'off' flavour. The other trek cook, however, had also noted the smell from the meat and, while not wishing overtly to interfere, he had slipped into the kitchen when nobody was around and chucked a load of chilli into the stew in order to disguise the state of the meat. It is a well known fact that pipe smokers develop rather sensitive tips to their tongues and, as Alan took his first mouthful of the now highly fiery groundnut stew, he just about reached lift-off speed as he headed for the kitchen and a large supply of water. Sadly I didn't have a camera at the ready but we were all agreed that John's upper lip quivered.

# CHAPTER 18

# HE GO TREK, SAAH

I telephoned the Senior Accountant.

'Sorry, Saah, he go trek, Saah,' I was advised by his efficient male secretary. I could see him in my mind's eye, a rather portly figure; I imagined him with a pith helmet and elephant-ear shorts, quite possibly carrying a large cash box as he battled through the bush surrounded by his minions, for people in his elevated position did not travel alone. Then I heard the familiar voice of the Senior Accountant in the office next to mine. In The Gambia, going on trek applied to any journey that involved leaving the city boundaries and, since we were based in Cape St Mary, visitors from the capital were regarded as being 'on trek' when they visited us.

But my treks were of an altogether different calibre. As part of a team commissioned to conduct a study of the agricultural development of The Gambia, my role was to carry out a survey and mapping of the soils of the country. This entailed covering just about every square mile of The Gambia in vehicles, on foot or in a canoe. It may have been the smallest country in Africa but 4,000 was still a lot of square miles, certainly compared to the 400 square kilometres that had formed the basis of my studies in Brazil.

I was presented with a pile of base maps and, since what there was of The Gambia was fairly featureless, one map looked much like another map, showing a few dirt roads and scattered villages, not that any of this necessarily related to what was on the ground. The story was recounted to me of the retiring surveyor who was handing over to his successor. The successor was puzzled as to why on the top right-hand corner of every map there was printed MMBA, as these were not the initials of the retiring surveyor nor seemed to relate to anything else. Eventually he enquired of the outgoing surveyor as to the meaning of the initials. MMBA, he was told, stood for Miles and Miles of Bloody Africa. Looking at my huge pile of maps I felt a certain sympathy.

Since the only part of the country that had already had a soil survey was the bit close to the capital, all my work entailed staying away for lengthy periods. For this I had been equipped from the stores of ODM's Directorate of Overseas Surveys back in the UK. The place was a veritable treasure trove, providing every conceivable item from quaintly colonial pith helmets, umbrellas to shelter your theodolite, and trenching spades for when you got caught short, to the latest mod cons for the discerning camper, such as fluorescent lamps that would run off the Land Rover battery and kerosene powered bush fridges. This treasure trove was presided over by ex-Sergeant Major Kidd, and ex-Sergeant Major Kidd stood no nonsense from anybody. Every item that you requested was carefully considered, in terms of whether you needed it or needed that many of it, or whether what you had ordered was no use unless you had ordered subsidiary parts of it.

'Not much use, Dr Moffatt,' he would say, with a heavy emphasis on my new title, 'ordering a tent without ordering the tent pegs that go with it.' And so it would go on. I would order a water purifier; it required candles.

'So how many candles do you require for your purifier, Dr Moffatt?'

'Oh, just a few,' I would say breezily.

'A few, Dr Moffatt – you mean a few like three or a few like thirty-three?'

I equipped myself with a camp desk, with locking compartments so that it could be transported from place to place and unfolded in front of your tent. It looked just like the real thing that you saw on films about people going on safari in the 1920s. I had a camp bed with metal legs that rolled into a small bundle, a camp cooker that included a bread making oven and, the source of greatest amusement, a camp bath consisting of a canvas bag about three feet by three feet and twelve inches deep, which was held in position by a foldable wooden frame.

My routine was to spend about twelve of every twenty-one days on trek. On this basis I would be finished the first phase of the field work at about the arrival date of the baby, and so be home-based during its first few months. A lorry was loaded up with my camp and survey equipment and the camp cook would accompany this to the village that we had selected as the centre for that survey area. I would travel by Land Rover, accompanied by my driver and the six Agricultural Assistants allocated to me. The driver was called Momodu, as were roughly half my assistants, indeed possibly half the population of The Gambia. He was a fairly serious man with limited education, but still spoke all the local languages with some fluency. I had been told that it was not polite simply to greet someone with a brisk 'good morning', but that you were supposed to enquire as to the health of the family, the quality of his sleep, the state of his crops and anything else that you could think of. On my first meeting with Momodu I set about the traditional style of greeting:

'How is your wife?' I intoned.

'She dead,' he replied. I made sympathetic clucking noises, but undeterred I bashed on.

'How are your children?' I asked.

'They dead,' he replied. More sympathetic clucking noises and I decided not to pursue my greetings any further. Having no wish to hear of any more dead relatives, the next day I thought it better to focus on his crops.

'How are your groundnuts?' I asked him; all Gambians would have a little plot of groundnuts somewhere.

'They dead,' he replied gravely.

'How is your rice?' I tried in desperation.

'It dead,' came the inevitable reply. Momodu had a way of gazing over your shoulder into the distant space beyond you when speaking, and it was difficult to see how distressed he was at the death, apparently, of every living thing that he touched. It did go through my mind that perhaps having a driver with this unfortunate record was not such a good idea. Still, it did explain his rather solemn attitude.

I had had enough of death, and so the next morning I moved to safer ground. 'How was your bed last night?' I enquired.

'It dead,' came the response. I goggled at him.

'Your bed was dead?, I expostulated in exasperation. He looked puzzled at my outburst.

'My bed was dey,' he repeated more slowly.

Use of the word 'dey' (sounding to the uneducated ear much like 'dead') in the local pidgin English apparently meant that all was as it should be. I have to say that as the driver assigned to drive me for many thousands of miles on some very dodgy roads, it came as some relief to find that death did not in fact dog his every step.

Kebba came into my life shortly before I embarked on my first trek. I had put it out on the grapevine that I was looking for a trek cook and had had a fairly steady stream of hopefuls turn up at my office. Kebba arrived with a somewhat equivocal reference from a former surveyor from the Directorate of Overseas Surveys, but he had a twinkle in his eye and I decided to take him on. I fired him at the end of my first trek, indeed at the end of most treks and sometimes midway through a trek. He was a rogue, not that well organised and not a particularly good cook. But he was always cheerful and formed instant relationships with the village chiefs whose permission was required for us to set up camp on their village land – so ensuring that we always got a good campsite. I would reach the height of my exasperation:

'Kebba, you are fired.'

Kebba was an absolute professional at penitence. The depths of his sorrow over whatever misdemeanour had led me to fire him again could not be plumbed. The assurance that never again would he 'disappear when he was supposed to be cooking my dinner', 'not have the camp pitched by the time I got back in the evening', 'fail to fill the jerry cans for bathing water' or whatever, could not have been more persuasive. He was with me for the full two years of my stay. However, the experiment of combining his duties as a trek cook with the role of cook/houseboy at home was a step too far. On the face of it, it made perfect sense. When I was on trek Ruth didn't do any entertaining and was happy to cook for herself, so Kebba would work for us in the house only when I was at home – and double his salary. It didn't work out. Having a lovable rogue as your trek cook was one matter, but the gregarious Kebba around the house all day with an endless stream of, mainly female, visitors was another, so he went back to being just my serially fired trek cook.

Kebba would negotiate with the village chiefs for a site where he could set up my camp; it needed to be near to the village, as this was often the only place to find water, but ideally not too close, as the noise could be quite horrendous.

Mango trees provided the ideal location for my tent; they gave excellent shade with their dense canopies, but which didn't start till some feet off the ground so that the tent fitted completely beneath the tree and, with a bit of luck, a few ripe mangoes might come my way. In return the village was offered the opportunity to provide labour for the survey, often accommodation – for which they would be paid – for my Agricultural Assistants and of course Kebba, and the chance to sell a few vegetables and local chickens. We would start work in the area and hopefully by the time we had finished our first day's work, Kebba would have the camp all set up.

It was my absolute conviction that Kebba used to offer conducted tours of my camp for which he no doubt charged a butut or two (a butut being one hundredth of a dalasi, the primary unit of Gambian currency), as I would occasionally return to camp unexpectedly and find small queues of people lined up outside my tent. I suppose it was like an ideal homes exhibition, what with my fridge and desk and bread oven. My camp bathtub seemed to attract particular attention. The system was for Kebba to fill two very large plastic jerry cans with water that stood all day in the sun. By bath time the water had reached a pretty high temperature and I could use one can-full for soaping and the other for rinsing. Modesty of course dictated that I wore swimming trunks for this process, as there was always a crowd of onlookers placed at what they considered to be a respectably discrete distance.

I never liked the bathtub, which, even for someone of my stature, was cramped and looked vaguely ridiculous, and I eventually got a local artisan to make me a shower. This consisted of a bucket, into the bottom of which was inserted a shower rose; a large bung closed the aperture to the rose until I pulled the string to which it was attached. In theory I could close the aperture at any time, but in practice once started it was best to bash on at high speed through the ablutions. It wasn't ideal but it was better than the canvas bath, and I was able to hide behind a large plastic sheet erected round the shower, so that I could at least wash the nether regions properly. However, on more than one occasion the whole device fell on my head as I attempted to activate it and, although I could never prove it, I strongly suspected that Kebba had so balanced the thing that it was almost certain to fall on me when I pulled the plunger.

In the early part of the evening, just before darkness fell, the village was a cacophony of crying children, barking dogs, the clattering of cooking pots and the shrill voices of women conducting conversations from one side of the village to the other. Shortly after dark it would go quiet – until the drums started up – and they could go on till the small hours of the morning. In these days when it is largely recognised that women surpass men in most things, it would have come as no surprise to me to note the difference in the vigour between the two sexes, but in those days I was shocked at the disparity. The women toiled in the fields, fetched water, looked after children and did all the washing and cooking. Only in the production of the cash crop, groundnuts, did the women play only a minor role, presumably so that the male controlled the income from this. Other than at peak periods of the groundnut season the men appeared to spend much of the day on the 'bantaba'.

From the earliest times in Africa a large tree was the foundation and the base around which the villages were constructed and, because of the shade that this tree gave, a meeting place was founded beneath it where the senior people of the village could rest and engage in conversation. This was known as the 'bantaba', the word in the Mandinka language literally meaning 'the tree where we meet'. In most of the villages in The Gambia the tree had been replaced by a thatched roof, under which was a platform on which the men of the village seemed to spend much of the day lying. However, as the drums pounded out their rhythm it was not the men, rested from their day on the 'bantaba', who found the energy to gyrate to their beat but the women, while the men were simply the passive onlookers. Except that is for Kebba who, despite the demands of looking after me, would regularly be seen dancing with the women, exhibiting a quite enormous zest and very obviously thoroughly enjoying himself.

I was puzzled at how frequent these dances were, since it seemed that they were an almost nightly occurrence. I quizzed one of my assistants about them. His explanation was simple.

'Oh no, such dancing particularly into the middle of the night is a rarity,' he replied.

'And yet,' I said, 'it seems to me that virtually every village we camp at has drumming and dancing going on every night.'

'That', he said 'is because Kebba organises it. A bit of palm wine, some kind of sweet snacks that he cooks up during the day and the party can be kept going for hours.' I had always thought that the sugar went down at an alarming rate.

The men could, however, be tempted off the 'bantaba' by offers of hard cash. As with the groundnut harvest, if cash was involved this was definitely men's work. We needed labourers in quite large numbers to hold survey poles and tape measures, to clear paths through vegetation, to work the auger and to dig holes. While there would have been merit in having a regular pool of labour, it was regarded as politic to employ people in the area where we were surveying. Apart from providing a little instant injection of cash into the local economy, the locals would often know shortcuts to places and could tell us who owned the land that we might want to dig holes in.

We could employ anything up to thirty people and the men insisted that they were paid for their labours at the end of each day. This involved filling in a massive ledger, the format of which harked back to colonial times. On each day you had to write out the name and village of origin of every labourer, the time he started work, the time he finished work, what breaks had been taken, his hourly rate of pay and the sum owing. The final two columns were for his signature and yours, although since most of the labourers could not write their signature they would instead put their thumbprint. Just occasionally one of the men would spurn the inkpad and laboriously but proudly craft his signature.

The whole process was long and tedious, coming at the end of a hard day in the field, and after this lengthy rigmarole I found the sums of money being placed in each man's hand was deeply embarrassingly small. What I would have spent on the beer that I would consume that evening from my kerosene fridge would probably exceed the total sum that I dispensed in wages each day. On occasions, after a particularly long hot day in the field I would be tempted to do away with the damned ledger and just pay them quickly from my own pocket and be done, but I knew that would not be acceptable, particularly to my Agricultural Assistants. Happily, after a short time one of my assistants advised me that he had acted as accounts clerk in one of the research stations where he had been posted, and that he would be happy to take over responsibility for paying the wages – an offer that I accepted gratefully.

Apart from curious onlookers, there was also a fairly steady stream of people requesting that I sell or preferably give to them sundry items of my camp and personal possessions. Requests ranged from my fridge to such bizarre items as a magnetic compass, a corkscrew, a used sardine tin opener, or the book that I was reading. One of the more amusing requests we had was on an occasion that Ruth had accompanied me.

At the outset it had been our idea that Ruth would join me

on trek on a fairly regular basis and hope to do some wildlife studies. However, becoming pregnant almost as soon as we landed in The Gambia largely put paid to that. Although she kept remarkably fit, it was a well-known old wives' tale that if you wanted to hurry along the birth process there was nothing to beat a bumpy ride, and a journey on the roads of the Gambia in a basic Land Rover pick-up certainly constituted a bumpy ride. Little did we know then that it would have taken a lot more than a bumpy ride to have any effect on Ruth's giving birth.

Already six months pregnant, however, she was spending a few days at one of my camps not too long and not too bumpy a ride from Bathurst, and hanging on the washing line was her bra. A lady from the village, of ample proportions, bare-breasted as many of them were, approached Ruth and, through a not very subtle bit of sign language, requested that Ruth give her the bra that was hanging on the line. Now Ruth has a good figure but very much on the slim side, and in the boobs department there is certainly not much to write home about. Ruth's bra, had one found some way of securing it around the lady's massive girth, might just have covered her nipples. Briefly we were tempted to accede to her request just for the sake of seeing the full effect, and perhaps bagging one for the family album, but in the end decided that it would be difficult to contain our mirth and thereby risked being seen as impolite, so regretfully we turned her down.

The soil survey took us to or through pretty much every village in The Gambia. The country may have been the first and last under colonial rule in West Africa but its colonial masters, perhaps particularly latterly, had obviously focussed more on the fleshpots of Bathurst than on the interior. So in many villages that we passed through I was the first European that most of the population had ever seen.

Unlike my surveys in Brazil, a great deal of the area was accessible in a specially equipped Land Rover with a determined driver. We had some pretty basic maps and, if they showed a road then, as far as Momodu was concerned, a road it was even if it had never felt the impact of anything more than a bare foot. For me to get the best view of the landscape that I was surveying, I would always travel standing in the back of the pick-up. A bit like the Queen's, my job entailed a great deal of waving, and I got to develop a certain sympathy with her minimalist waving motion, since there were days when I seemed to spend more time waving than doing anything else.

It seems strange today that in a country where the furthest a village might be from the main roads that ran the length of the country on either side of the river was maybe 20 miles, there were so many people who had obviously had little contact with the world beyond the boundaries of their village. But this was in the days before the ubiquitous television or the massive influx of tourists to The Gambia, and I derived great amusement seeing the looks of sheer astonishment on the faces of the young and the not so young as they saw a white man for the first time. After some time another soil surveyor joined me; where I was small, he was tall; where I was clean-shaven he had a massive beard. With the two of us standing in the back of the Land Rover, looks of astonishment could become looks of terror and, when we stopped in the village to check whether its name matched what it said on the map, terrified children would scatter in all directions.

The low-lying plateau which makes up most of the land area of The Gambia is not by any stretch of the imagination scenic, but it had a certain charm and boasted the most spectacular bird life. South from the deserts of North Africa, The Gambia is about the first vegetated area and is a favoured stopping place for many migrating birds. Over 560 species have been recorded in The Gambia and include some truly magnificent forms like the blue-bellied roller, sunbirds, bee eaters, kingfishers and one of my personal favourites the ground hornbills. These huge prehistoric-looking birds could be descended from the dinosaurs and reminded me of the toucans that I used to watch from my soil pits in Brazil. But if you are more into ugly, then the bird life could also offer you the marabou stork. Standing up to five feet tall with its balding, scabby head, pendulous pink air sac and huge meat-cleaver bill, it is one of the ugliest creatures in the world, made no more appealing by its fondness for carrion and its habit of squirting excrement onto its own legs. As if aware of its ugliness, it has a permanently grumpy look.

In the fresh water of the eastern stretches of the river, there were occasional hippos, and crocodiles seemed to live in any patch of fresh water anywhere in the country. Monkeys – particularly the white colobus – were fairly common and from time to time we would see chimpanzees. One of my favourites was to see a family of wart hogs running across the dry grassland at the edge of the swamps, their tails held stiffly erect. Naturally, it had its snakes – some forty species of them, including the puff adder, which is Africa's biggest natural killer after the mosquito, but our encounters with them were happily rare.

While our survey covered the whole of the country, it was to focus on areas with the highest potential for more intensive agricultural development. This inevitably took us to the low-lying wetlands with their more fertile soils, with the potential to be drained and possibly irrigated from the river. I loathed the swamps. Apart from a few small areas that could be accessed up small channels in a canoe, the entire survey had to be done on foot. There was not a square inch of shade and the threat of stumbling across a crocodile was constantly there.

But presenting a more likely threat was a snail that resided in the wetter parts of the swamps. This was the source of a potentially fatal disease called schistosomiasis, also known as bilharzia or snail fever. The snail is the alternative host for the fluke, which in humans attacks the liver and spleen and may spread to other internal organs. These days there is a quick, safe and effective remedy for it, but at that time it had to be killed off by poisoning with antimony. And you could not be too sure whether the antimony would kill off you or the fluke first. The only way to be sure of not contracting schistosomiasis was to ensure that the fluke never got into your system and that meant wearing waders.

Ex-Sergeant Major Kidd had been deeply suspicious of my order for waders.

'Planning a spot of fishing, are we?' had been his response to my request.

He had taken a bit of persuading to order an item that was definitely not regular DOS stock. Because the waders had to be specially ordered, which involved a very long chain of command, they did not come with the other equipment so we had to delay the start of our survey in the swamps until they arrived. Finally they appeared, only for me to discover that someone must have totally misread my size and the waders were sufficiently large that I could have virtually climbed into one of them and would barely have been able to see over the top. So, I got a charm from a local witch doctor and got on with the survey anyway; the charm must have worked because I never did contract schistosomiasis.

Away from the regularly flooded swamps is land that

is flooded in the rainy season and bone dry and hard in the dry season, on which only grass can grow. Borrowing a term from nearby Ghana, I dubbed these the 'bolilands', and 'boli-hopping' became one of my most uncomfortable experiences. We were carrying out our survey at the height of the West Africa Sahel drought of 1968-73. The Gambia lay really at the fringe of the Sahel and the drought was only partial. Because of the ludicrous wait for waders, we were surveying at a time of year when normally you would not have been able to because the area would have been deeply flooded, but with a much delayed onset to the rains we were able to get in. The climatic conditions were appalling. In a normal season, the temperature and humidity would build up in advance of a storm, that storm would come, bringing down both temperature and humidity, and moderately agreeable conditions would follow for a day or two before the build-up started again. However, because of the semi-drought conditions the storms didn't come, and so for day after day we would have a combination of intense heat and 100% humidity.

But the real killers were the 'bolis'. A peculiar characteristic of the ground was that when it was dry it broke up into little roughly hexagonal mounds standing about a foot above the base level of the ground. Each mound was about the size of your foot and the gaps between each mound were of similar size. There was a complete cover of tall grass anything up to six feet high and it was through this that I stumbled day after day. It was impossible to see the ground and, as there was no way of knowing whether your foot would land on top of one of the mounds or between them, progress across the bolilands would be in a series of ankle-twisting falls.

I moaned endlessly to John and, through him, to my mentor Alan. There was no real purpose to my moaning except largely to get it off my chest, though perhaps I harboured a slim hope that ODM would feel that I merited some sort of hardship allowance, because I certainly wasn't paid much for my discomfort.

On the next visit by Alan, it was arranged that he and John would come and join me on my survey for a couple of days; I looked forward eagerly to subjecting them to the horrors of the bolis. Two days before they were due to arrive somebody had set fire to our survey area and the grass was burnt to the ground. The night before they arrived we had a massive storm; the temperature fell, the humidity fell and the smoke that had been hanging unpleasantly in the air since the grass was burnt off was removed. On the day that I took them to visit the bolilands it was cool and clear; because there was no longer any grass you could see if your foot was landing on a mound or in hollow and it was basically just a stroll in the park. I never did get a hardship allowance.

# CHAPTER 19

# A CLOSE CALL

Ruth was just moving into her ninth month. I had been working in the office and had repaired to the Bathurst Club for a couple of beers and was propping up the bar. In the course of general bar conversation, one of the bar-proppers commented that Dr Sami was going on overseas leave the next week.

'Not possible,' I said, 'Ruth is due to give birth next month and he is looking after her; indeed she had an ante-natal session with him just a week ago. We would certainly know if he was planning on going away.' Still, it's always worth checking up on rumours that you hear at the bar and so when I got into work the next day I called Dr Sami.

'Ah yes,' he said, 'I've been meaning to tell you that I am going on leave next week and will be away for a couple of months, but I can pass your wife on to one of the doctors in the local hospital.' I was speechless. Might his forgetfulness in telling us of his plans have something to do with the big fee that we paid each time that Ruth had an appointment with him?

The Royal Victoria Hospital in Bathurst was a truly grim place. The wards were open-sided and without fans or air conditioning. It was constantly overflowing, with crowds of people always hanging around the grounds waiting to gain entry. Patients would usually – though not always – have a bed, but on the floors slept members of their families, who also brought in their cooking pots and prepared meals at the bedside. There was a doctor assigned by ODM to run a programme to upgrade the hospital, but his was an apparently hopeless task. We consulted him, but he simply confirmed what we knew – that this was no place to have your first child. But Ruth was by then over eight months pregnant and airlines are notoriously unenthusiastic about taking passengers at that advanced a stage of pregnancy. It was unlikely that she could disguise her state, as by that time she had a firm but massive bump looking more like triplets than the single baby that Dr Sami assured us it was.

I spent the day shuttling between the BA office, the ODM doctor and Dr Sami. It was clear that if the birth was perfectly normal – and we had no reason to believe otherwise after such a trouble-free pregnancy – then aside from the discomfort of the Royal Victoria and perhaps some risks of infection, there was really no reason why the delivery could not be done there. However, warned ODM's resident doctor, the system would really not cope if anything went wrong. It was a difficult decision, but we were coming to accept what the old colonials had said all along, that this was not the place to be for a first birth. ODM's doctor spoke on our behalf to the BA office where the Manager – inevitably in such a tight-knit community – was well known to us and was sympathetic. He eventually agreed that Ruth could go on the next flight, as long as we had a letter confirming absolutely that it was okay for her to travel – it could probably only have happened in The Gambia, where everybody knew everybody and so such matters could be sorted in an informal way.

I returned to Dr Sami and grasping him firmly by the throat, figuratively speaking, I suggested that he write a most convincing letter for BA. This he did. It gave an unequivocal assurance that Ruth would not give birth on the flight (not

that any such unequivocal assurance could possibly be given).
BA accepted the letter and so, already into her ninth month of
pregnancy, Ruth departed for England.

Communications were very different in those days. We
had, of course, no phone in the house and it was anyway only
possible to phone overseas by pre-booking a call at the office and
transmitter station of Cable and Wireless. Having booked the
call at least one or two days in advance, you then went to their
offices at the appointed time to make the call. Arrangements
were made with Cable and Wireless for a message to be passed
through them when the baby arrived. I did not want to go over
to the UK until then, as I didn't have much leave available
to me; in fact, other than perhaps a weekend, I strictly had
none since my contract carried no annual leave. In those days
the concept of paternity leave might have been alluded to in
the routine of a stand-up comic but would never have been
dreamed of as a serious proposition. It was all made a little
more complicated, as I was committed to being up-country for
some of the critical period, but it was all sorted out that in my
absence John would be given the news and he would dispatch
a runner to where I was camped. The month passed by with
no news, except for a message to say that Ruth had moved on
from her mother to her sister and the baby would therefore
be born in Macclesfield. By the time I returned from my last
planned trek the baby was almost two weeks overdue, but still
no message. I assumed that the communications system had
failed me so I made immediate arrangements to fly back to
the UK. I was able to book a flight the next day from Bathurst
to Dakar, from Dakar to Paris and from Paris to Manchester,
and I sent off a telegram with details of my flight arrival in
Manchester.

I expected to be met by her sister or a taxi driver holding
up my name on a placard. But no, as large as she had been

when I bid her farewell in The Gambia, there was Ruth. I couldn't believe it; she was now two weeks overdue and had apparently given absolutely no sign of intention to produce the baby. I accompanied her to the hospital the next day, and were advised that if nothing was happening come Monday she was to report to the hospital and would have to be induced. That gave us the weekend to try all the old wives' tales methods of inducing labour, but all to no avail, so on Monday it was back to the hospital. They pumped her full of some sort of drug which had not the slightest effect, and for thirty hours she went through pain but not labour, the baby remaining stubbornly where it was. Other women on this induction ward came and went, though for quite some hours she did have the company in the next bed of a woman who chain-smoked through her induction period.

Suddenly there was panic. The nurse monitoring Ruth noted a major fall in foetal heartbeat. The baby needed to be delivered without delay and they would have to do an emergency Caesarean. Nurses and doctors materialised from nowhere as Ruth was prepared for surgery. Having sat all day by her bedside, I was now bundled unceremoniously off the ward and told I could come back in three hours. It was 6.00pm.

Opposite the gates to the hospital there was a pub and to there I repaired, nervously drank Guinness (proper Guinness, not the Nigerian variety), smoked cigarettes and listened to what was being played on the jukebox. Somebody in the pub was clearly obsessed by Don McLean's 'Vincent' (or Starry Starry Night), which came on as every other song. I will never hear the song without it evoking that night. A little under the stipulated three hours I emerged from the pub and made my way a little unsteadily back to the hospital. I found a sleeping wife and there in the paediatric intensive care ward my daughter; she was not difficult to recognise – the poor child appeared to have my nose. Ruth woke briefly to tell me we had a beautiful daughter (she mustn't have noticed the nose) and went back to sleep. I was told that the ward was now closed to visitors and got chucked out. While drinking time was strictly regulated, the pub still enjoyed longer opening hours than the hospital so I returned there, drank more Guinness, smoked more cigarettes, and listened to Don McLean before finally teetering back to my in-laws where I was violently sick. I put it down to stress and no sleep for nearly three days but I certainly didn't drink another Guinness for some years.

These days there is a lot of twaddle talked about bonding. Children born by Caesarean don't bond properly with their mothers. Fathers feel morally obliged to attend pre-natal classes, and of course the birth, so that they bond with their labouring wife, with the newly born child, and probably with the gynaecologist, midwife and other sundry theatre staff. If they were honest, most of them would much rather have a couple of beers in the pub while wife and professionals got on with the job without a terrified husband hanging around and likely to pass out at any moment. No parents could have had a more 'bonded' relationship with their children than we have, to this day, and both were born by Caesarean. And I have a song that will always evoke the night of the arrival of my first-born plus a general antipathy to Guinness, which given its calorific value is no bad thing.

We must have had a guardian angel, and how that night I blessed Dr Sami's holiday. Had that not happened, Ruth would have stayed in The Gambia where the facilities for conducting an emergency Caesarean, even in Dr Sami's clinic, were virtually non-existent, and the chances of them both surviving would have been very low.

Ruth and baby Rachel were released from hospital after a week, not like now when they turf you out more or less directly from theatre, and the bit of unpaid leave I had begged was running out. The baby could not travel until she had had all the necessary injections to survive West Africa and that would take six weeks, so Ruth was to spend the time with various relatives, starting with my parents, partly on the basis that with the experience of five children behind her, my mother could offer the best support. The fact, however, is that my mother was never very good with babies, as was evidenced by her lack of interest in seeing me the night that I was born.

One day Rachel had been crying for some considerable length of time and Ruth was at her wits' end as to what to do.

'Why is she crying all the time?' My mother peered at the baby.

'Well,' she said, 'I suppose she hasn't got anything else to do.'

Rachel had developed an early antipathy to the bath, and for a few days Ruth and my mother battled through it. By about the fourth day as Rachel started up her protest at what she sensed was to come my mother said:

'Let's just leave it today; I'm sure they don't need to be bathed every day.' It may be an exaggeration to say that Rachel wasn't bathed again until Ruth moved on to her next destination, but it would be true to say that it was a bit of a rarity; the district nurse would have been appalled.

# CHAPTER 20

# UNACCOMPANIED BAGGAGE AND NAKED SWEDES

The post office in Bathurst was shambolic; the staff were unhelpful and unfriendly to the point of aggression and the simplest transaction could take an hour. There was, however, an arrangement whereby international mail could be taken to the airport, franked there and loaded immediately onto the weekly British Airways flight. The arrival and departure of this flight was one of the social highlights of the week in The Gambia, making Yundum not just an airport but a vital social hub. The café would be filled by people departing, people seeing off those departing, people awaiting arriving passengers, and people like me who had managed to grab the office mail and thereby justify going out to Yundum. It seemed as if half the expatriate population of the Gambia would make it to the airport on BA day. Sitting under the bougainvillea trees you would have your coffee or your soft drink, or for the hardier old colonials perhaps a gin and tonic, and catch up on all the latest gossip.

The plane would pull onto an apron immediately adjacent to the café. In theory the café was separated from the apron by a wire mesh fence, but in practice the gate was never closed, so that once the plane had come to a halt people would swarm round the steps to greet their arriving friends and family. The system was to escort them to a table, set them up with a drink and then take their passports to the immigration desk. The immigration officer would enquire as to the whereabouts of the passport holders, you would simply point to the table at which they were sitting, which was generally satisfactory. You would collect their baggage on which a customs officer might or might not bother to chalk a cross and away you would go. It was the most pleasant international arrival in the world.

So just under a year from when I had first arrived in The Gambia I was at Yundum, anxiously awaiting the arrival of my wife and daughter. The usual crowd at the airport was boosted by numbers of friends – or simply the curious – keen to see the new baby. All went as it always did. I was something of an expert at handling arrivals and made sure I got prime position at the bottom of the steps as they were wheeled into place. Ruth descended the steps, followed by an airhostess with Rachel in her carrycot. I took them over to our table which was quickly surrounded by people wanting to get a look at the baby, new babies being something of a novelty in an expatriate population which had largely somewhat passed their child-producing days. I took the passport to immigration and, not unreasonably, the Immigration Officer pointed out that he couldn't possibly see Ruth, let alone the baby, through the large crowd surrounding them. So I managed to get the message to her that she should stand up and hold up the baby. Satisfied, the Immigration Officer stamped the entry visas.

The plane was starting to taxi off the apron when I went to the baggage collection area to retrieve Ruth's suitcases. She had pushed three baggage tags into my hand and I quickly found two of the bags; but of the third there was no sign. In something of a panic I rushed to the BA desk and explained the problem, my concern being that there could be things in the missing baggage that were vital to the baby's survival. The staff were most understanding and the plane was immediately asked to return to the apron. A search of the hold revealed nothing, not helped by the fact that Ruth hadn't a clue what the third bag looked like. As we were about to give up on the search, I noticed that hanging on Rachel's carrycot was the matching half of the baggage tag – she had come out to The Gambia as an item of baggage.

Yundum airport was to change dramatically as the Gambian tourist industry took off. The origins of tourism are shrouded in some sort of mystery. Various accounts allude to one Bertil Harding, a Swede, who is described as having been travelling to Capskerring in south Senegal in 1965 when, after some unfortunate personal incidences, he accidentally drifted onto the shores of The Gambia. Quite what personal incidences could lead to being washed up in The Gambia is difficult to imagine and there is no elaboration of these. However, he recovered from whatever trauma had led him to The Gambia sufficiently to imbue in him a determination that his own country people should see this 'paradise' and how friendly the people were.

To achieve this aim he teamed up with the Swedish tour operator Vingresor and later in that year 300 tourists from Sweden followed in the footsteps of Bertil Harding, landing on the shores of The Gambia. An escape from the dark northern European months of October to April to an exotic 'paradise' beach resort proved to be an attractive concept and, by the time that we arrived in 1971, the number of tourists for the season rose to over 8,000, predominantly still from Sweden. Catering for these were two new Swedish-owned tourist hotels, The Palm Beach just outside Bathurst and the Sunwing at Cape St Mary, which was not far from where we lived. Hotels mushroomed and by the time we left in 1973 there were thirteen hotels in the Gambia.

In recognition of his contribution to the development of tourism in the country, Bertil Harding now has the dubious distinction of having a stretch of the coastal highway named after him. But in truth tourism was doing little for the economy; the bulk of what the tourists spent went to the tour operators, airlines and the foreign-owned hotels. The Gambia was quite unable to provide the guaranteed flow of fresh meat, fruit and vegetables that the hotels required, as a result of which they imported most of what they served. The government, in trying to boost the tourism industry, had offered generous tax duty waivers and tax holidays and so little revenue came into the government coffers, which therefore continued to rely for export earnings almost entirely on groundnuts.

Almost the only beneficiaries in the Gambia were what Alan irreverently referred to as the 'pimps, touts and chiselers', and even in those days there were plenty of them. Your arrival on the beach led to a positive explosion of people selling carvings, paintings, cloth and all manner of baubles and beads. They were endowed with a persistence that had to be admired, were it not so irritating when what you wanted was an hour of peace and quiet. Going waist deep into the sea was about the only escape, though after about six months we did become recognised as residents and were largely left alone.

But it wasn't just the carved facemasks, the tie-dye and the trinkets that were up for sale. I was once shown a poster that I was assured was used in the advertising campaign in Sweden for holidays in The Gambia. The message was simple; it read (translated from the original Swedish) 'Come to the Gambia for a Change.' The picture below was of a large, black male organ. Certainly Swedish ladies of uncertain years in the company of young male Gambians became a common sight and today with more than 100,000 visitors per year to The Gambia I gather that the 'pimps, touts and chiselers' are still one of the few parts of the economy that is directly benefiting from the tourists.

Rachel's pram was a simple affair, consisting of the carrycot on a pram base. The carrycot was a vivid red colour and to the head end Ruth had managed to affix a sunshade. Rachel would lie in her pram wearing nothing but a large sunbonnet. Back on one of my 'office' weeks, I was pushing the pram along the beach when I spotted someone frantically waving to me from higher up the shore. Squinting into a setting sun I really couldn't make out who it was, but I turned the pram and headed for the waving figure. As I got closer I realised that it was a very attractive Swedish girl dressed much like Rachel was, except she didn't have the sunbonnet. She ran towards me and gazed at the pram, its sunshade and the baby in her bonnet lying inside.

'Oh,' she exclaimed 'what a beautiful sight; I have never seen anything quite like this before.' I was about to reciprocate the sentiment when she realised that I was gazing at her and probably with my mouth open.

'I am sorry,' she said, 'Of course you are English; you are not used to nude sunbathing but for us Swedes it is very common.' Before I could find the words to assure her that I was one of the modern, broad-minded Englishmen and really didn't mind at all, she ran back to get a towel and wrapped it round herself while she resumed her cooing at the baby.

It was a good two years. We may have lacked the sophistications of life and you had to be able to respond to challenges, but we lived in a largely tranquil environment with, for much of the year, a good climate. Our daughter grew up on the beach and being wheeled round the beautiful shaded gardens of the compound of the Medical Research Council. Changing this for southern suburbs and a tower-block office was something of a wrench.

# PART 3

## THE NILE

*At 4,180 miles long, the Nile is the second longest river in the world, losing out to the Amazon by just 150 miles, though given the uncertainties of identifying the ultimate sources of rivers, there are those who would still argue that the Nile is the longer. The Nile in fact starts and ends its journey as two rivers. Its widely separated sources, the Blue Nile and the White Nile, then flow as a single river from their confluence near the Sudanese capital, Khartoum. The Nile splits again just north of Cairo into the Rosetta branch to the west and the Damietta branch to the east, together forming the Nile Delta. The greater part of its water and most of the nutrients that bestow such fertility on the Nile delta come from the Blue Nile, which starts at Lake Tana and, after a convoluted journey through Ethiopia, heads northwest through Sudan to the confluence. It is, however, to the White Nile that the river owes its prodigious length; its origins are deemed to be in the Nyungwe Forest of Rwanda and it flows through a large swathe of Central and Eastern Africa, feeding into Lake Victoria in Tanzania and out of that lake at the Ripon Falls in Uganda. It is almost singularly to the water and nutrients of the Nile that the great civilisation of ancient Egypt owed its existence.*

# CHAPTER 21

# A SHOCK TO THE SYSTEM

I first encountered the Nile in 1976, as I crossed the splendid Kasr El Nil Bridge in the centre of Cairo. By then I had spent five years in the public sector as an employee of the Ministry of Overseas Development, which, by that time under a new government, had become ODA – the Overseas Development Administration. Maybe I would have stayed longer, but when I heard people not much older than me discussing how they would have to stay in the public sector on account of the excellent pension arrangements, I knew it was time to move on. Anyway, Rachel was coming up to school age and Ruth found being her mother hard enough work without also being her teacher. Our son John would be reaching the same stage in a couple of years, so long term postings overseas would have to come to an end. I had done academia, I had done the public sector, it was time to try the commercial sector. After a false start when I almost joined the consultancy wing of the sugar giants, Bookers, I ended up with a relatively fledgling international development consultancy, Urwick, Lugg and Gould – ULG. The company was born out of a largely dysfunctional partnership between a firm of UK agricultural consultants, Lugg and Gould, and a firm of management consultants, Urwick Orr and Partners which, in its day, was one of Britain's leading innovators in business management practice. The envisaged synergy, like most envisaged synergies, never did materialise and ULG became simply the international wing of Lugg and Gould. For us it meant a move to Warwick, which at least got us a hundred miles or so closer to the Tyne.

Within a month of joining ULG I found myself on my way to Egypt. Against all expectations and in competition with both the major sugar giants – Bookers and Tate and Lyle – ULG had won a contract from ODA to carry out a preliminary feasibility study of a project in Egypt based around a proposed massive sugar production enterprise in the Western Desert. Although the project location was far from Cairo, the responsible Egyptian agency, the General Authority for Reclamation Projects and Agricultural Development (GARPAD) was headquartered in Cairo. As this preliminary study was to be a largely desk exercise, Cairo would be our base for much of the next three months. We stayed at the Khan el-Khalili hotel, which backed onto the famous Khan el-Khalili bazaar in the old city. The bazaar dates back to 1382; it is a vast area densely packed with stalls selling clothing, spices, jewellery, perfumes and souvenirs, some with their own little factories or workshops, and interspersed with delightful traditional coffee houses and street food vendors. Perhaps one of its most famous outlets is Fishawi's café, which has been open 24 hours a day for 200 years and whose menu includes such delights as 'lamp shops' (being, we assumed lamb chops). The bazaar was constantly seething, and noisy with the shouts of vendors competing for customers and the calling of the Mullah from the Al-Hussein Mosque.

The hotel was rather less old but was doing its best to catch up fast; it was dilapidated and scruffy and had been chosen by our Team Leader, Bill Almond, primarily on the basis of price. ULG was not the most extravagant payer in the world and employees looked to save a bit out of their per diems, which in the case of that provided by ODA was quite generous, making the saving a significant supplement to income. The Hotel was on 13 floors and your selection of floor afforded an interesting dilemma. On the lower floors the ill-fitting windows ensured that the occupant might as well be camped in the Khan el-Khalili bazaar, with its near-perpetual cacophony. The upper floors presented a major physical challenge. In theory there was a lift but in practice it was so rarely in working order that a climb up and down thirteen flights of steep and filthy staircases four or five times a day was inevitable. Even on the odd occasion that the lift was working it was a brave soul that would chance getting into it. After one night on the second floor I moved to the thirteenth; I don't say that you couldn't hear anything, but at that height the noise became more of a background hum, at least once you had sealed the gaps round the windows with old newspapers.

If the hotel had one redeeming feature, it was the restaurant-cum-coffee shop. The food was awful but the restaurant had a huge bowed window and, if you got a table at the window, you could look out onto a street along which thronged an endless stream of people and animals. At almost any hour the street would be filled with people carrying heavy loads on their backs, or on poles across their shoulders. Flocks of sheep, herds of goats, even occasionally cattle, would be driven along the road, but it was the carts, drawn by donkeys, mules or horses, that constituted most of the traffic. Occasionally a lorry or a bus would try to force its way through the throng, its air horns continuously blaring despite the fact that there was nowhere for the carts, people or animals to move to.

What made the location of the hotel so unique was that shortly before reaching the bowed window of the restaurant, there was the beginning of what was probably the only incline in central Cairo. Since the city lay at the head of the delta, it was basically dead flat and, although the incline hardly constituted a hill, comparatively speaking it was a significant climb. People would stop, rest their loads and gather strength for the assault on the incline. Flocks of sheep, which had been progressing at a steady speed in an orderly bunch, would lose their footing as the slope of the ground suddenly changed and they would become scattered across the road as they sought to regain the flat, forcing the shepherd – usually a small boy – to chase round gathering them back together. But it was the carts that provided the sport.

In Egypt all carts are loaded to their maximum capacity, this maximum being based on them being driven only on totally flat roads. The incline in front of the Khan el-Khalili Hotel presented an almost insuperable obstacle. Despite this, their drivers would remain doggedly atop the cart until it finally ground to a halt and only then alight. The animal would make a little progress but again grind to a halt, the driver would grab the reins and start pulling the poor animal up the slope. In extreme cases, where the load must have almost exceeded the maximum on the flat, the driver would get behind the cart and push.

One day we were sitting at our favourite table watching the teeming humanity below us when a horse-drawn cart approached the beginning of the slope. It seemed to be struggling even on the flat and the smart money was on the driver having to alight at the beginning. He didn't, but a few yards up the incline the horse collapsed in a heap. For a minute everything on the road in front of us seemed to freeze, including the driver. Then suddenly he was off the cart and rounding up a gang of volunteers. About ten of them surrounded the horse, heaved it into an upright position and suspended it just slightly above the ground. Its skinny legs dangled and its head lolled to one side; its ribs showed clearly through its skin. At the best of times it was difficult to enjoy the food at the Khan el-Khalili Hotel, and watching a horse drop dead in its tracks did little to enhance the enjoyment. The driver grabbed the lolling head and, forcing it into its proper position, he appeared to blow down its nostrils. Suddenly the horse's body quivered and its head gave an almighty lurch. It let out a great snort and the people surrounding it dropped it back on its feet. Minutes later the driver was back in his seat and the horse was battling its way up the slope.

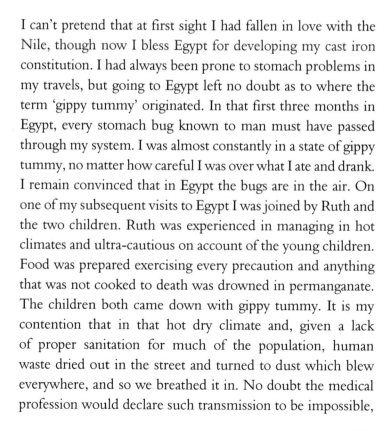

I can't pretend that at first sight I had fallen in love with the Nile, though now I bless Egypt for developing my cast iron constitution. I had always been prone to stomach problems in my travels, but going to Egypt left no doubt as to where the term 'gippy tummy' originated. In that first three months in Egypt, every stomach bug known to man must have passed through my system. I was almost constantly in a state of gippy tummy, no matter how careful I was over what I ate and drank. I remain convinced that in Egypt the bugs are in the air. On one of my subsequent visits to Egypt I was joined by Ruth and the two children. Ruth was experienced in managing in hot climates and ultra-cautious on account of the young children. Food was prepared exercising every precaution and anything that was not cooked to death was drowned in permanganate. The children both came down with gippy tummy. It is my contention that in that hot dry climate and, given a lack of proper sanitation for much of the population, human waste dried out in the street and turned to dust which blew everywhere, and so we breathed it in. No doubt the medical profession would declare such transmission to be impossible, but I just couldn't see where else the bugs were coming from. However, since that first visit to Egypt, and helped perhaps by adhering to the advice that live local yoghurt was the best prophylactic for lively local stomach bugs, I have travelled the world with barely a murmur of protest from my once fragile digestive system.

Alongside the constant 'gippy tummy' there was one other thing about Egypt that, on that first visit, I could not get to grips with, and that was the concept of 'baksheesh' – and Egypt runs on 'baksheesh'. Everywhere I turned there seemed to be an outstretched hand. The slightest service demanded a few piastres (there being a hundred piastres to the Egyptian pound and lots of Egyptian pounds to an English pound); the opening of a door, the direction into a parking space, the offer of toilet paper in the restaurant toilet even if you were only having a pee, or the pressing of the lift call despite it being obvious that you were about to mount the stairs, all led to the expectation of 'baksheesh'.

It was 'baksheesh' that removed obstacles. A table could suddenly be found in a fully booked restaurant for fifty piastres to the man on the door, the guards at tourist sites were not so much guards as unofficial tourist guides, with the added advantage that they had the keys for the places that were supposed to be locked up, and of course for a little 'baksheesh'... I had never worked in a society like it and I found it difficult to live with until, in a guide to living in Cairo produced by some American association of housewives, I came across the advice: 'just look upon 'baksheesh' as a little redistribution of wealth'. Suddenly it all seemed okay and I have been redistributing wealth ever since, producing sometimes rather startled reactions as I press a pound coin into the hand of the man that has come to read the gas meter.

'Baksheesh' of course is simply one manifestation of the

Egyptian obsession with money. During the course of a later project, I came to have dinner with three seriously wealthy couples. The meeting had been arranged by our office manager in Alexandria, a young Egyptian lady from an upper class background. I was amazed that she had so effortlessly gathered together such influential people.

'Do you know everybody in Alexandria?' I joked with her. She took the question literally and responded:

'No, no, but I know all the ones that matter.' It was said without any suggestion of boasting; it was a simple statement of fact that, in many ways, summed up Egyptian society.

About midway through our starters, a conversation started about the price of vegetables in different markets. So absorbing a topic did this prove to be that it was still the main topic of conversation as sweet was served. It transpired that although cabbages in market A were ten piastres cheaper than in Market B – after of course a certain amount of haggling – the potatoes in Market B were the least expensive, so you needed to select your market on the basis of the relative amounts of potato and cabbage that you were going to purchase. The few piastres involved could not have been of the slightest relevance to such wealthy people, it was simply that they loved talking about money, and whether it was piastres or thousands of pounds at stake was almost irrelevant.

# CHAPTER 22

# A GRAND SCHEME

The Government of Egypt wanted to build a massive irrigation scheme in the West Nubariya area of the Western Desert about 30 miles to the south of Alexandria, and to do this they wanted a loan from the World Bank. The scheme would be based on using sprinkler irrigation to cultivate sugar beet on a large commercial scale, with a major processing factory built in the middle of the area. Water would come from the Nile channelled through long canals and lifted by a series of massive pumps at regular intervals; that latter part of the basic infrastructure was already in place, awaiting something to irrigate. ODA had agreed to fund the preliminary feasibility study, which was to run for three months. The head of GARPAD oversaw the project, a relatively elderly gentleman called Dr Rifki Anwar, who had the disconcerting habit of breaking into any discussion at regular intervals to apply eye drops. Dr Rifki was short and heavy with a perpetually mournful expression, a man who was easily disappointed. Indeed almost inevitably he would start most meetings we had with the statement:

'Dr Moffatt, I am very disappointed.'

The Egyptian government of the time had in place a policy that decreed that all agricultural graduates were guaranteed employment. As a result, GARPAD, like other parts of the Ministry of Agriculture, was quite massively over-staffed.

Every office was crammed, with barely enough space to squeeze between the large grey desks. What all these desks had in common was that they had nothing on them except perhaps a newspaper and a coffee cup. It was patently impossible to occupy this huge number of people, and equally impossible to pay them more than a pittance. So, day in and day out, this army of agricultural graduates would sit at their desks, reading the newspaper, chatting and drinking coffee. Of course, they had to supplement their meagre earnings with other income, and 'baksheesh' played an important role in this.

Alfred Shaker enjoyed a dual role on the study; he was our fulltime guide and interpreter and he was the Government's spy. Shaker by name and shaker by nature, his right leg was in a state of near permanent motion whenever he was seated. The speed at which his leg bounced up and down was an accurate indicator of his state of agitation. We would always know when we had asked him to translate a question that he felt was moving into sensitive areas, and in Egypt there were many sensitive areas – this was a country in which it was a serious criminal offence to take a photo of any of the bridges in Cairo. Requests to look at maps or aerial photographs would greatly accelerate leg movement, though not as much as questions about exactly what studies the Russians had already carried out in the area – for we were sure that there had been some. When he felt that our questioning of someone was moving into excessively sensitive areas, he simply changed it in the interpretation. Alfred kept copious notes and we were never in any doubt that everything that we did and said was fed back to the security service.

I was worried about the assignment. The nine years since graduating had been spent working on the soils, vegetation and agriculture of the tropics. I knew absolutely nothing about the arid zone. This was my first job for my new company and, to make matters worse, we were being employed by my former employers, some of whom had seen my defection to the commercial sector as distinctly disloyal. I felt very exposed. Enter Shoukry Morcos. Shoukry was a Coptic Christian and therefore highly unlikely to be promoted from the relatively lowly position that he currently occupied. However, he spoke good English and indeed good Russian, and was designated as my counterpart. He was clearly a devout Copt.

'I pray,' he told me. 'Every day I pray. I pray to my God. I pray, I pray; I pray: God give me money.' Now I am not sure that it works like that. Throughout my life I have dutifully put money on the collection plate in church, but I have to say that I have never seen any indication of money going the other way.

I asked him what he knew about the soils of Western Nubariya. His eyes lit up.

'I have everything,' he said. 'Everything I have. I have ze maps; I have ze analyses – ze physical analyses, ze chemical analyses; ze soil descriptions I have. I have everything.' I felt a great weight roll from my shoulders. The fact that I knew nothing about desert soils would not matter; someone – the Russians, I guessed – had done it all already.

'That's marvellous,' I told him. 'Can I see them?' The light that had shone so brightly in his eyes dulled, and his expression became deeply morose.

'Impossible,' he said. 'Impossible.'

'But that is ridiculous,' I said. 'If you have the information, then surely you can share it with us.' His morose look deepened further.

'Impossible,' he repeated, and shook his head sadly.

'But why?' I demanded.

'Security,' he replied. 'This is classified information.' And nothing would budge him.

Of course it was like the locked rooms in the museum or the fully booked restaurant; what it needed was 'baksheesh', but ODA was not in the habit of doling out 'baksheesh' to get information that the Government was supposed to supply free of charge. And so at that stage of the study we never did get to see it. In a later phase when I was working with a rather more 'flexible' budget, Shoukry did release 'ze information'. It wasn't really worth the 'baksheesh'.

After nearly a month of digging for information in Cairo, we eventually set off along the desert road to Alexandria. The desert road runs for 150 miles through largely empty desert apart from Wadi el Natrun, a valley dotted with oases, and with a small café. This was sufficiently dismal that, in the years to come when I became a regular commuter between Cairo and Alexandria, I very soon stopped bothering to make it a refreshment point and usually just got the journey over as quickly as possible. We stayed in a rather more up-market hotel in Alexandria, from where we made daily forays into the desert and to visit other irrigation schemes that had been developed in the area. Almost without exception the schemes were failing badly. In what seemed like an achievement of the impossible, so grossly had they been over-watered that the Egyptians had managed in the space of just a few years to transform desert into a virtual swamp. This was the driving reason behind the decision that this proposed new scheme in West Nubariya should be irrigated by sprinklers, which made management of the water a lot easier.

On one of our early visits to the site I had detached myself from the main party for a few minutes to answer nature's call, having always suffered a certain weakness of the bladder. To my surprise the 'water', instead of immediately disappearing into the parched desert soil ran off, forming a little rivulet for some distance before being absorbed. I returned to the Russian jeep that had been supplied to us for our fieldwork and fetched a water bottle. If I poured the water gently into the soil from close to the ground it simply disappeared into the earth; if I sprinkled water from a height the soil instantaneously formed a cap and the water ran over the surface. In my report I wrote:

> *'A series of simple experiments has indicated that the highly calcareous soils that characterise much of the proposed development site are liable to cap when water is applied from a height and this may make them unsuited to sprinkler irrigation. Before proceeding with a scheme based on sprinkler irrigation a proper trial should be conducted on this phenomenon.'*

I was popular with nobody. The Egyptians were looking for a quick benediction to their scheme so that they could get their hands as quickly as possible on the World Bank's money, with all the opportunities for 'baksheesh' that that would offer. The World Bank is in the business of lending money and wanted just to get on with it, and ULG was acutely aware of the work that would potentially come its way when the project moved on to a full feasibility study. Now here was I putting a very large brake on the whole thing. Fortunately there were a couple of boffins in ODA who were inclined to agree that there might be a problem and were a bit intrigued at the idea of running some scientific experiments.

After a few days in the relative luxury of Alexandria, it was decided that it would be more efficient if we continued our fieldwork from a base closer to the site, and that meant us moving into the Desert Inn. The Desert Inn was located in a small oasis at the edge of our proposed project area. It could have been a fantastic place; there were still trees and shrubs in the garden and flowering plants growing up the wall, but the place was suffering from years of gross neglect. On our first evening there we were joined for dinner by the Food and Agriculture Organisation's Resident Representative and his wife who were touring the area.

The speciality of the house was pigeon. You knew they were fresh, as you heard the commotion in the pigeon cote on top of the Inn as the cook's assistant went to fetch your order. They were served looking for all the world as if they had been laid on the griddle and flattened with a large mallet – and that is probably how they had been prepared. The Res Rep's wife was suffering from 'gippy tummy' and decided that she would have only a couple of boiled eggs. She asked the waiter if she could have them while we all had our starter. They didn't come.

'Don't worry, Madame, they will come with the main course,' soothed the waiter. We all got served our flattened pigeons. The eggs didn't come.

'Where are my boiled eggs?' she demanded.

'Just a minute, Madame, just a minute please, be patient,' the waiter exhorted. We had just about finished our pigeons when her patience snapped. The Res Rep's wife rose from her chair, marched into the kitchen, and confronted the cook.

'Where are my boiled eggs?' Her raised voice was quite audible from the dining room.

'Madame,' said the cook, 'we have no eggs.'

You see, that is how it was with the Egyptians. They didn't like to admit that something was wrong or that they didn't have something. There was a sort of eternal optimism that the problem would just go away and they would never have to admit to failure or shortcoming. So the waiter was simply hoping that the good lady might just forget that she had ever ordered eggs, or perhaps on seeing the flattened birds on our plates she would change her mind and decide that she didn't want eggs but pigeon, or even maybe that she would conveniently expire on the spot. Anything really could come up which would save having to admit that they had no eggs, and so any such admission was avoided at all costs.

One of our visits took us to an area that had been developed into Egypt's only large-scale winery, which lay to the other side of the desert road from our project area. The Giainaclis winery was founded by Nestor Giainaclis in 1903 and nationalised in 1969. By the time that we visited it, the 10,000 hectares of vineyard were unkempt and overgrown, the buildings in a state of serious disrepair. It produced six different wines with alluring names such as Cru des Ptolemees, Nefertiti, Omar Khayyam and Reine Cléopâtre, but that was more or less where the good things about them stopped. Although some of the first wines in the world came from ancient Egypt, today most people were agreed that the wine from the Giainaclis estate was almost undrinkable. It is commonplace for those who do drink it to suffer from gargantuan hangovers and nausea, and some embassies were warning tourists and foreign residents to avoid Egyptian alcohol which, it was reputed, could cause blindness and even death.

We did a rapid tour of the vineyards and were then ushered into a bar. In those days I never touched wine; I was essentially a beer-totaller and found that wine did not agree with me. But I did know enough about wine tasting to know that it was done in very small quantities and indeed, I had seen gruesome film of wine tasting events where people swilled a bit of wine round in their mouths and then spat it out. On that basis I felt that I could face what was to come. But the staff of the winery had obviously not seen the same film that I had. The first wine was poured out in generous measure, roughly a half-pint glass, and there was no sign of large buckets into which one might have spat out great mouthfuls of it. We were clearly expected to drink it all and our hosts, proud to be demonstrating their wares to this large contingent of important foreigners, beamed encouragingly at us as we downed the wine. Six wines later and the dire warnings of the embassies seemed to be coming true. I had almost moved beyond the nauseous stage and blindness and death seemed to be imminent. The journey back to the Desert Inn was one of the longest in my life and having made it to the bed I remained there for twenty-four hours. The imminent approach of blindness and death seemed to have been halted, but the hangover lasted a week.

Dr Rifki was 'very disappointed' in our report, but I stuck to my position that it would be foolhardy to move to the next stage without further testing of the possibility that the land was unsuited to sprinkler irrigation. Furthermore, I had also fortuitously come across an obscure report that suggested that sugar beet grown on these highly calcareous soils might accumulate impurities that would make it difficult to process. Nobody could have denied my courage even if most questioned my sanity. With great reluctance it was agreed that a short period of trials was required.

# CHAPTER 23

# TRIALS AND TRIBULATIONS

Naturally it fell to me to come up with a design of the proposed trials. I tackled the task with great scientific rigour. We would grow a number of varieties of sugar beet under a small sprinkler irrigation system. Measurements would be made of the pattern of distribution of the water, and we would use a relatively recently developed technique for tracing the movement of water in the soil known as neutron backscatter – basically shooting a weak beam of radiation through the soil with an instrument called a neutron probe, and measuring how much of it bounced back, which in turn gave a measure of how much water was there. This way we would know exactly what was happening to the water that was being applied, and we would also be able to analyse the beet grown and assess the purity of the juice.

We would have to carry out the trials at the periphery of the project area, because that was as far as we would be able to pipe water, but at least it meant that we were closer to Alexandria, which would make commuting easier. ODA agreed to fund the study, and now time was of the essence, because we had to get the sugar beet planted before the start of the really hot weather. We realised that to get all our equipment through Egyptian customs would be a near impossibility, so the grand plan was formulated whereby we purchased a long-wheelbase Land Rover which was to be loaded with all the seed, fertiliser, sprinkler equipment, and scientific apparatus that we would require to carry out the work, including of course the neutron probe. What wouldn't fit inside was loaded on top, and two intrepid members of the team drove this massively overloaded vehicle through Europe to Naples and there boarded a roll-on, roll-off ferry to Alexandria where the vehicle was promptly impounded by customs. It looked as if all our careful planning was in vain.

We had no choice but to employ a 'customs fixer' and for ten days I trailed behind him around the stinking docks into countless squalid offices as he collected dozens of signatures, an appropriate amount of 'baksheesh' being required for every signature. It was as if the system was entirely designed to maximise the number of people who could get a rake-off from releasing goods from customs – and perhaps it was. In theory the letters that we had from the Egyptian government should have ensured that our equipment was released without delay, but then letters can get misplaced and maybe go missing for a week, a month, a year, so wasn't it better just to collect the next signature without fuss and with a little 'baksheesh'? At last our fixer advised me that we had only one signature left to go and that I should come prepared to take the vehicle off the docks.

Our euphoria suffered a serious blow when we discovered that the back door of the Land Rover had been forced open and the contents had obviously been disturbed. When we did our inventory check we found that the only items missing were the bags of sugar beet seed. It was quite bizarre, for the seed can have had no value to anyone. It was sprayed with a poison designed to deter its consumption by the gerbils that we knew abounded in the area of the trials, and I admit that I felt sufficiently vindictive towards the thief that I hoped that he had decided to put the seeds in his soup and poisoned himself. Our conclusion was that he had forced open the crate with the seed first and, assuming it to be edible or saleable, had taken the lot. The only other crate that had been forced open was that containing the neutron probes. These were packaged in special containers covered in radiation warning signs, skulls and crossbones and pictures of people in bandages. It looked as if the thief took fright and decided to leave the rest of the contents alone.

However, without sugar beet we were pretty stymied. I was due to go back to the UK for a couple of weeks and we decided that the only solution was for me to bring a replacement consignment of seed back in my baggage. It was a risky strategy, since it was highly illegal to bring any sort of live plant material into the country without proper certification from the Egyptian authorities. It is something about all of the funding agencies that has always riled me; they are rarely prepared to take a firm stand with the government that is receiving their aid. In theory ODA should have said to the government: 'If you want this project then you must facilitate getting the equipment that it needs into the country or no project.' But do they? Do they hell. They make noises, of course, but when it comes to the crunch they don't have the balls or the clout to take a tough line, leaving suckers like me to take the risks.

So I returned to Egypt, with two suitcases full of sugar beet seed and another two with rather less dodgy contents. In my experience of going in and out of Egypt, the customs officials could rarely be bothered to open all your bags. It was common just to be waved through or for them to demand you opened one of your cases. Weighed down with four cases, I did probably stand out from the run-of-the-mill tourists and, perhaps inevitably, got called to the customs desk. My hopes now were pinned on them not opening one of the cases with seed in it. Luck was not on my side and the customs officer, who spoke some French but not a word of English, pointed to one of the cases containing bags of seed. He was clearly startled by the contents and slit open one of the bags. In French he demanded to know what it was. Now, modern sugar beet seed is pelleted and coated and to the untrained eye looks very much like pelleted fertiliser. Mustering my limited French, I told him:

'Engrais (fertiliser).' He gazed at it, rolling some pellets round in his hand. He seemed convinced and was about to chuck the pellets back in the bag and pick up the twenty-pound note (Egyptian) that I had dropped beside the suitcase, when one of the pellets cracked open revealing the seed inside. Smuggling in a bit of fertiliser was one thing, bagfuls of seed were another, and he burst into a tirade of French in which the word 'graine' (seed) figured prominently. I did what the English do best – look perplexed and say:

'Sorry, I don't speak French,' hoping that he would not have fully taken on board the fact that I had used the French word for fertiliser, fortunately a not dissimilar sound to 'graine'. He called his supervisor who did speak English.

'What is this?' he demanded.

'Sugar beet seed,' I said, 'it's what I have been telling your colleague but he doesn't speak English.'

I produced my letters from the British Sugar Corporation certifying the good health of the seed, and from ODA saying that we were working in Egypt for the Egyptian government and all that sort of stuff. The customs officer read it all carefully and impounded the case of seed. But lady luck had not abandoned me entirely. First, I counted myself seriously fortunate that he did not impound me, for I had been envisaging being cast into the airport prison. Second, so carried away was the customs officer with his capture that he never bothered to open the other suitcases. With only half the amount of seed, we had to do a little trimming of the trials, but we pretty well had enough to do most of what we wanted to do.

The core team of four of us who were to spend a high proportion of the next twelve months working on the trials settled down comfortably enough in an apartment in Alexandria, the greatest feature of which was that immediately around the corner was a bakery producing the most magnificent Egyptian bread. I was chief breakfast maker and there was no greater pleasure at six o'clock in the morning than to be standing in the baker's shop, with the most wonderful smell, awaiting the first bread to come out of the oven, then rushing back the 20 yards to the apartment and starting breakfast with the bread still warm. Other specialists came and went, as we had tacked onto the trials various other investigations, and I spent much of my time commuting between Alexandria and Cairo, and between Egypt and England. Dr Rifki would summon me on his slightest whim and I would have to haul down the desert road to Cairo, sometimes returning on the same day, sometimes spending a night in Cairo in the small Tonsi Hotel that I had found as a significant improvement on the Khan el-Khalili. On one occasion, he had got the idea that instead of growing sugar beet we should be producing vegetables for the European market. I was summoned to Cairo to discuss his brilliant plan.

'After all,' he said, as another bucketful of eye drops went into his eyes, 'the Israelis can do it, so why shouldn't we?' I needed to fashion my response carefully. The fact was that the Egyptians hadn't the slightest clue about quality control, or gearing production to the requirements of the market. The farmers went for maximum production and the consumers bought the produce because there was no choice, and as for what it looked like, nobody seemed to care.

'Well, Dr Rifki,' I said, as he continued to sluice his eyes, 'when the average European housewife decides that she wants to buy cabbages that are so big you need a wheelbarrow to carry one home, or tomatoes that come two to the kilo, then perhaps Egypt should make its foray into the European market. Until then, maybe we stick to other crops that are less dependent on the whims of the consumer.'

The trials were going reasonably smoothly, and the labourers that assisted us had stopped running a mile when the neutron probe appeared, though I have to admit that whenever I was near to it I kept my hands, like a football player in the 'wall', firmly in front of my private parts.

My Managing Director had no compunction in using my leisure time to be the company's general representative in Egypt so I got dragged into all manner of investigations and company promotion activities which further increased the frequency of my journeys on the desert road.

ULG had tendered for another job in Egypt and had been evaluated in the top two, which meant that they were invited to negotiate financial terms. With an ever-watchful eye on company expenditure, the Managing Director decided that rather than go to the expense of flying someone out from England who would actually have known what they were doing, he would simply ask me to do the negotiation in my spare time. I was hardly the ideal person – I even avoided going to the market because I could never be bothered to negotiate – and to the horror of my colleagues would end up paying well over the odds for everything that I bought. However, our Managing Director assured me that it was all quite straightforward and he would courier out all the information that I needed.

The Tonsi Hotel was small – very small – but had been highly recommended to me as quiet, clean and inexpensive. It stood at one end of the Al Gala bridge, at the other end of which was the palatial El Gizera Sheraton Hotel. The Tonsi occupied the first and second floors of a six-storey block, the ground floor being given over to a motor showroom. Rooms ran round the periphery and in the centre on the first floor was a large reception desk. The hotel had a small coffee shop in what was little more than a lean-to, stuck on at ground floor level and reached by a narrow staircase from the hotel proper. It served a simple but moderately good breakfast, but thereafter its opening hours were erratic and, since it anyway didn't serve alcohol, it was not a place that I frequented on more than very odd occasions. The Tonsi lacked any form of communication with the world outside of Cairo so for my communication with the office I used to walk over the bridge to the El Gizera Sheraton where I could use their business centre to send my telexes. I would often then combine my telex forays with having a few drinks in the hotel's fairly lively bar and usually something to eat in the coffee shop.

There are those who may not be familiar with the telex; it was a system of communication that was in use from the 1930s (although ULG, never at the forefront of technological advance, did not have its own telex machine until 1977) until it was effectively phased out in the 1980s, by which time the fax had almost completely taken over. This in turn of course became largely obsolete with the arrival of email, other than for the transmission of some legally binding documents or highly sensitive data. The telex's system of transmission was based on punching the data onto a paper ribbon that was fed through the telex machine. Sending a message therefore entailed me in laboriously handwriting the message in nice clear block capitals, which the operator would then punch onto tape. He would run this off as a paper copy of the text which I would proofread and correct, and then the amended tape would be fed into the telex machine for transmission. It was a deeply tedious process.

The negotiations lasted nearly a week. It turned out that the Egyptians were negotiating with two companies simultaneously. Our competitor's negotiator and I sat in separate anterooms and would get called in turn to the negotiating table. The anteroom was unbearably hot, while the room in which the Egyptian negotiators sat was chilled to north polar temperatures. The constant switching from the furnace of the anteroom to the freezer of the negotiating room made me feel quite ill. There were four of them and one of me, with no sort of refreshment offered, so by the end of each day I was utterly exhausted. The project was quite complex, involving not only the time charges and expenses for the team of consultants, but a massive amount of equipment, mostly to be imported – with all that entailed – and a great deal of travel within and outside of the country.

The ploy seemed to be to negotiate virtually every single line of the bid with each company in turn. Whoever was highest on each item was recalled to the negotiating table and the Egyptians would try and drive their price down to a level below that of their competitor. When they were following this system for a line item costing only a couple of hundred pounds, I started to wonder if this was simply another manifestation of the Egyptians' love of dealing with money, rather than a reasonable attempt to get the price down. At the end of each day I would laboriously write up an account of what had taken place for my Managing Director, take it over to the Sheraton, deposit it at the business centre then repair to the bar for a cigarette and a couple of very stiff gin-tonics while the telex operator punched the message onto tape. I would review and amend the draft and off it would go. With the UK two hours ahead of Egypt I would not get a reply that evening, but was back at the Sheraton at eight o'clock the next morning, when the Business Centre reopened, to collect my telexed instructions.

By the Thursday afternoon we had ground our way through every line of the bid and I sat in my little anteroom in a state of nervous exhaustion, awaiting what I assumed would be the final verdict. My competitor was summoned first. I never smoked 'dry'; for me a cigarette always had to be accompanied by a drink of some sort, but on that occasion I sat in my roasting hot room, having had nothing to drink for many hours, and puffed nervously on a cigarette. I couldn't decide if his being called first was a good thing or a bad thing. Were they simply thanking him for his efforts to then dismiss him and invite in the successful bidder? Or was he at that very moment placing his signature at the bottom of a contract? After an age he emerged from the negotiating room and shot off down the stairs; he did not appear to be very elated and I was filled with hope. But the Egyptians had a final card to play. I was summoned to the negotiating table and, after a long rigmarole about how ludicrously expensive we were, I was told that both companies were now being invited to submit a final offer. Whichever company was the lowest got the job. These final offers had to be submitted in writing at the client's office by 9.00am the following day.

I sat in my hotel room and carefully prepared the telex to my Managing Director, summarising exactly where our bid had got to and what had been said at the final meeting. I had to make sure that there was no room for misunderstanding because a contract of this size could almost break the company if we got it wrong. I read and re-read my childlike printed script to be certain that I had got everything exactly right, then headed off over the bridge to the Sheraton. The telex operator was out of the office, so I just hung around awaiting his return. As I waited the telex machine, which sat on the desk in the middle of the room, suddenly clattered into life and started to spew out a telex. I stared at it in utter disbelief. It was a simple one-line telex from the head office of our competitor to the guy that was presumably their negotiator, and who was either staying at the Sheraton or, like me, was just availing himself of the Business Centre. The telex advised him of the final figure that he was to offer.

I quickly shot out of the Business Centre and went into the bar. With a stiff gin and tonic and a cigarette to settle my nerves, I added a last crucial line to my telex – the final offer price of our competitor to the nearest dollar. It was a figure well below where we had started, or indeed the level we had reached after four days of negotiation but now the matter was out of my hands; it was a decision for my Managing Director whether he was prepared to do the job at a lower price than our competitor and if so, by how much he would want to undercut their final offer without it being obvious that we knew what their offer was. I advised him that I would collect his telex as soon as the Business Centre opened at 08.00am the next morning. A few more gin and tonics, a few more cigarettes and a bowl of peanuts constituted my evening meal and I returned to the hotel Tonsi. There were three girls who worked shifts in pairs at the reception desk, all of whom were extremely attractive with their jet black hair and splendid Egyptian bums – no wonder Anthony was smitten. I had a deal with them that for a rather generous 'baksheesh', supplemented by the occasional bottle of duty-free perfume, they would do bits of typing for me. I prepared our final offer letter and one of the girls typed it up, leaving only the blank space where I was to fill in the figure. I retired to bed.

But the Gods who had smiled so benevolently on me had a last trick up their sleeves.

The rooms in the Tonsi were fairly small, but clean and well kept. In the far corner from the door was a small bathroom. The rooms at the front of the hotel had little balconies which if you were stone deaf might be pleasant to sit on, but the roar of traffic along the constantly busy Tahrir Street made it a largely miserable experience, and I generally forewent the luxury of the balcony and settled for a quieter room along the side of the hotel. The view was uninspiring. The window looked over the flat roof of the bolted-on coffee shop to the walls of the next building up the street – but it was quiet. There was an air conditioner in the room but it rattled and came on and off with a massive shudder which shook the whole room. So for the most part I didn't run the air conditioner, but slept in the buff on top of the bed with a ceiling fan running. Positioning the bed in relation to the ceiling fan was a tricky exercise. I could never decide what would happen if the slightly dilapidated fan should detach itself from its moorings. Would it simply fall like a stone, and therefore I was best not to lie directly underneath it, or would its motion carry it sideways a short distance, so I was best to be positioned directly below?

I slept fitfully that night, over-stimulated by the tension of the negotiations, the excitement of my find in the Sheraton's business centre, and a surfeit of gin and tonic. My stomach groaned its complaint at having been provided with nothing all day but a bowl of peanuts and a large dose of alcohol. Around six o'clock in the morning I decided that it would be expedient to go and sit it out on the loo for a while, as the groaning threatened to escalate to a greater level of protest.

I went to the bathroom and, through force of habit, closed the door behind me. When I came to leave the bathroom I turned the doorknob, only to discover to my horror that it simply spun round and round, without in any way making contact with the bolt. It seemed that in closing the door with perhaps rather greater force than should have been applied I had detached the knob from its bolt.

I was stuck in the bathroom, stark naked – without even a towel. This I had simply dropped in my room after the hasty shower I had taken before going to the Sheraton and – as my wife will testify – I have never been very good at hanging towels back where they belong. I tried banging on the door but it was futile; the walls of the building were thick and the bathroom was against the outer wall of the hotel. I contemplated ripping down the shower rail to see if I could fashion it into some sort of a jemmy to force open the door but decided that I would never get an end thin enough to wedge into the crack of the door. If I had had my Swiss army knife that at one time I kept in my wash bag I might have been able to do something with the hinges, but I'd had two knives stolen from hotel bathrooms and I now kept it hidden in a drawer of clothes. I then turned my attention to the window. It was small but then so was I and, although it was quite high, I reckoned that by standing on the basin I should be able to get onto the window ledge and from there somehow squeeze through the window. Below the window I knew it was only a short drop to the roof of the coffee shop. But what then? I might find some sort of purchase that would let me get down from the roof of the coffee shop to the ground, but I would then be standing stark naked on Tahrir Street, and it was already broad daylight and getting busy.

By now it was nearly seven o'clock. I had to be at the business centre of the Sheraton at eight, collect the telex with my instructions, get back to my own hotel, fill in the critical gap in the final offer letter and have it delivered to the client's office by nine. Desperate measures were called for so I decided that the only course of action open to me was to get out of the bathroom window and go and hammer on the window of one of the adjoining rooms. It carried risk. Having someone called to their window and open the curtains to see a naked man standing on the roof of the coffee shop was going to be a nasty shock. Suppose the person in the adjoining room was female and promptly called the guards to deal with this extreme flasher. Fortunately the hotel largely catered not for tourists but for foreigners and Egyptians doing business in Cairo and that, almost by definition in those days, meant they were male.

I scrambled painfully through the window, trying to ensure that I didn't lose my private parts in the process, and dropped onto the roof of the coffee shop. As I tossed a mental coin to determine whether to go to the room to the left or right it occurred to me that I might just inspect my own windows. With an appalling lack of regard for security, I discovered that the latch which supposedly held the window closed in fact made no contact with it and with a gentle push and near tears of relief I opened the window, scrambled through and collapsed on the bedroom floor. The door to the bathroom could still be opened from that side. I wedged it open with a chair although there was no breeze that might have slammed it shut, showered, dressed my grazes, donned my business suit and shot off to the Sheraton.

We undercut our competitor by a credible number of dollars. I have been involved in many negotiations since then and I have a theory that a good negotiation will usually presage a good project. This project was fraught from the start and, although we stuck it out to the end, I often wondered if it would have been better if I had been less determined and just remained in the bathroom till the chamber maid came in and to hell with the final offer.

## CHAPTER 24

# YOU CAN PLEASE SOME OF THE PEOPLE

We completed the trials and prepared our report on these. I laboured day and night on that report, trying to cast the results in a context that, while not for all time precluding the use of sprinkler irrigation, acknowledged the finding of the trials that serious problems were encountered in achieving an anywhere near even distribution of water with sprinklers. We came up with a whole suite of recommendations that I felt gave the Egyptians a degree of latitude, while ensuring that no funding agency would agree to put money into the scheme as originally conceived. We proposed that the initial phase of the project should be based on smallholder settlement using modified traditional methods of irrigation and with a drainage system installed from the outset, so that even if they did over-water, the desert would not be turned into a quagmire. Meanwhile further trials could be conducted to see if cultivation techniques might be developed in the longer term that could make sprinkler irrigation viable in some areas. I was pleased with my report.

A meeting was set up to review the report with the Egyptian authorities. Dr Rifki expressed himself to be 'very disappointed'. My heart sank. I had gone almost without sleep for the best part of ten days as I wrote and re-wrote the report trying to steer a tricky course between the requirements of the Egyptians and the rigour of the funding agencies and I felt that I had got it pretty well right.

'I am very disappointed,' Dr Rifki repeated, 'there is no economic analysis.' We all gaped at him. I did some rapid calculations on a scrap of paper.

'Well, Dr Rifki,' I said, 'it took about a quarter of a million pounds worth of foreign expertise to produce those plots of beet; we imported extremely expensive cultivation and scientific equipment, and we hired farm machinery at exorbitant prices from an adjoining state farm. Taking it all together, I reckon that it probably cost about a tenner for every beet that we grew. Say each beet produces a spoonful of sugar then we would be costing the sugar at around six million pounds per ton, but I really don't think that is the sort of figure that the World Bank would want to see.' It was one of his characteristics never to concede a point, but if he knew he was wrong-footed he would move seamlessly onto the next topic.

In the end all parties broadly accepted our findings and the project moved on to a full feasibility study, which ran for over a year. The focus of the study had moved away from my area of expertise and I had only a part-time involvement in it. During the last of those inputs my family came out to join me. We got a short term let on a pleasant enough apartment in Alexandria. With total inevitability they all went down with 'gippy tummy', my son managing a most spectacular throw-up in the middle of a busy street and a doctor had to be summoned in the small hours of the morning when he got particularly bad. But they recovered and I took a few days of leave so that we could all go up to Luxor. I had spent a significant part of nearly three years in Egypt and, apart from a brief visit to the pyramids, I had seen none of the tourist sites. We took the train from

Alexandria to Cairo – a welcome change from blasting down the desert road and giving a marvellous view of the Nile delta – and then flew up to Luxor.

Even for a self-professed philistine like myself, one could not help but be awed by some of the remains of this remarkable civilisation and, looking at modern day Egypt, wonder where it all went wrong! We had opted to stay in a large up-market hotel and on our first day there the children were running ahead of us through the hotel lobby and got into the lift. Unfortunately they must have pushed the button for our floor as they got in and the lift set off before we reached it. I started to race up the stairs and midway between the first and second floors the lift came to a halt, presumably because my daughter had found and pushed the emergency stop button. We were fairly panic-stricken, my regard for the Egyptian ability to react to crisis not being of the highest. We could hear our four-year old son bawling, but our ever-unflappable six-year-old daughter said to him:

'Stop crying, John – that just makes things worse.'

An 'engineer' came on the scene and started to try to force the doors open, though had he succeeded it was not clear just what he proposed to do then with the lift clearly stuck between floors. Suddenly the lift burst into life again. A few seconds later it arrived at the second floor and the doors opened. The experience had been sufficiently unnerving that we decided that the lift was best avoided and thereafter we used the stairs – it was like being back at the Khan Khalili all over again.

From the feasibility study, the project moved on to implementation. Alongside the design and construction, we established the expanded trials that we had proposed were needed to refine and develop appropriate cultivation systems. My input to these gradually phased out and by 1982 my involvement ceased entirely as I moved to other areas of the business. Passing through Cairo in the late 1980s I stopped over for 36 hours and made a rapid excursion up to Nubariya. Where there had been an almost endless expanse of desert, now it was green as far as the eye could see. The land had been settled by a mix of the landless poor from the delta and agricultural graduates. Under a scheme whereby, instead of being offered an empty grey desk in some overcrowded Ministry of Agriculture office, they were offered a plot of land of between 5 and 10 acres, many seized the chance. It was difficult to remember how it had looked when I had first seen it twelve years previously and, although the development was clearly not without its problems, I felt a certain sense of satisfaction that I had been part of this massive undertaking.

# CHAPTER 25

# THE UPPER REACHES

My introduction to the upper reaches of the Nile came in Ethiopia some eighteen months after I had first crossed the Kasr El Nil Bridge in Cairo, and it began uncomfortably. The revolution, which had started in 1974, still had Ethiopia in the grip of chaos and violence. In 1977 Mengistu, the new military leader, who had grabbed power with a quite staggering display of ruthless disposal of his rivals, declared Ethiopia to be a Stalinist state and instituted the 'Red Terror', a purge designed to get rid of anybody that the regime didn't like. Ethiopia entered a new phase of turmoil, with bloody civil wars being waged in the provinces of Eritrea and Tigray.

Mengistu gave a free hand to his political cadres to carry out the 'Red Terror'. Thousands of students, teachers and ordinary Ethiopians who were suspected of supporting opposition groups were imprisoned without charge, tortured and executed. A vice-like grip on society was effectively achieved through the 'kebeles', small neighbourhood units in both town and country led by a chief loyal to the Mengistu regime. Nothing in these tight administrative units went on without the knowledge and agreement of the 'kebele' chief. More or less anybody could inform on anybody else, so if your neighbour played his radio too loud or the barking of his dog irritated you, you simply had to inform the chief of your 'kebele' that you suspected him of supporting an opposing political group and in all probability the problem would be removed. Bodies were left for up to three days on the streets, in front of public buildings, schools and universities, in order to scare others into not supporting opposition groups.

In that same year, Somalia invaded Ethiopia and occupied the region of Ogaden. In the merry-go-round of the super powers the USA, taking umbrage at Ethiopia embracing Stalinism, withdrew its support and moved over the border to Somalia to buttress their attack on Ethiopia. A desperate Mengistu then turned to Russia, erstwhile supporters of Somalia, and requested their assistance. Thousands of Russian and Cuban advisors and fighting forces flooded into Ethiopia, initially to support the war against Somalia and later the civil wars in the north of the country. It was to this Ethiopia that I made my way in January of 1978.

My route there was somewhat circuitous. I was required to undertake a short job in Sumatra and I left the UK in early January. I completed my work in Sumatra and started on the long journey to Addis Ababa. Flying into Jakarta I had first to make a detour to Bandung lying around 120 miles to the south, where bizarrely the management and administrative headquarters for the project in Sumatra were located. In those days the only access to this rather fine hill city was on a twisting, tortuous road almost continuously lined with ribbon development along which hurtled cars, trucks and long distance taxis, the drivers of all of which seemed to be intent on mass homicide. I delivered my report and then headed back to Jakarta. A dense fog had descended, which in no way deterred the headlong dash down the road and, given a predominant descent, the trucks could now coax an extra ten miles an hour out of their decrepit engines – terrifying. A night in Jakarta – my thirteenth bed since leaving the UK – and I set off on the next leg of my journey taking me to Singapore. I was pretty knackered and, knowing that I would be fed on the next flight, I resisted the temptation of the Singapore Airlines meal and settled down for a doze. It turned out to be a good decision, as the plane hit massive turbulence for a large part of the journey and most of the meals that had been served ended up on the floor – either before or after ingestion. After a fairly rapid transit I was on an excellent KLM flight to Karachi. The excellence ended abruptly as I deplaned. The airport was a complete shambles and I was led on a merry dance trying to locate my baggage so that it could be transferred to my next flight. It was only by sheer bloody-minded persistence and through a stroke of good luck – when I happened to spot it lying in a corner of the lost luggage room – that I was able to ensure that my baggage and I took the same flight out of Karachi. After five hours in Karachi airport I was greatly looking forward to the next leg of my journey. I shouldn't have been. The flight was Kenya Airways coming from Bombay; it was absolutely packed and, by the time I boarded, the economy class cabin looked like a slum. Remnants of food littered the floor and the toilets had ceased to work. So had the cabin staff, who seemed to have decided to give up the unequal struggle and didn't even attempt to serve a meal. Nearly six hours later I staggered off the plane in Nairobi, to discover to my unqualified delight that Addis Ababa airport was closed for 'security reasons' – presumably a further massive inflow of Russian military hardware and Cuban troops.

I decided that I had earned the best so booked myself into the Norfolk Hotel. I was however faced first with a neat little problem. As I had not intended to stay in Kenya but simply transit to Ethiopia, I had no visa. Visas, however, could be issued at the airport. I was directed to the visa office and after lots of form filling the clerk was ready to hand over my visa on the consideration of $50. I proffered a Sterling traveller's cheque. They only accepted cash – Kenya Shillings or US$ but – no problem – there was a bank at the airport where I could cash a traveller's cheque. I was directed to the bank that inevitably was at the other side of the airport. They wouldn't cash my traveller's cheque because I didn't have my passport. I returned to the visa office; they were sympathetic but pointed out that they could not give me my passport as it now had the visa stamp in it, and what was to stop me simply leaving the airport without paying the fee? There was a period of debate and then the clerk at the visa office came up with a solution. He suggested that I could 'hire a security guard,' who would accompany me and my passport to the bank while I made my transaction. Security guards did not come cheap and a security guard that could be trusted by the visa office would cost a further $20. I agreed to the proposal. The clerk walked from behind his desk, locked up the visa office, and accompanied me to the bank.

In Kenya the Norfolk Hotel is an institution; it is located at the centre of the town and indeed the town and subsequently the modern city of Nairobi almost grew up around the hotel. It has an extensive tropical garden and, sitting that evening on the famous Lord Delamere terrace – probably Nairobi's best known meeting place – surrounded by well-heeled tourists in their brand new safari outfits and drinking an Elephant beer, life seemed to be worthwhile again. A day by the pool and then, sadly, the news that the airport in Addis Ababa had reopened. I checked in for the Kenya Airways flight on the morning of 31st January. I have always had a near obsession about sitting in a window seat, and indeed have been known to swap flights if I cannot get one. The girl at check-in handed me my boarding pass and I saw that it had no seating allocation on it. When I pointed this out to her she shrugged: 'There are only four people on the flight' she said.

I can only assume that one of them took fright, because when our Boeing 707 took off there were only three of us aboard. There was something seriously disconcerting about being one of three passengers aboard a two-hundred-seater aeroplane. I commented to a surly hostess on the light passenger loading. She stared at me as if I came from another world:

'Nobody goes to Addis Ababa these days,' she said, leaving unsaid what she clearly thought – 'not if they are in their right minds, that is.' She exuded resentment toward me, as if I was personally responsible for her having to make what she clearly perceived was an unnecessary hazardous journey. I have to say that when your nerves are a bit taut anyway, the approach to Addis Ababa airport is pretty scary, as the pilot squeezes the plane between the hills to drop precipitously onto the runway.

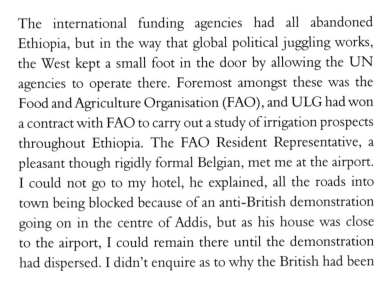

The international funding agencies had all abandoned Ethiopia, but in the way that global political juggling works, the West kept a small foot in the door by allowing the UN agencies to operate there. Foremost amongst these was the Food and Agriculture Organisation (FAO), and ULG had won a contract with FAO to carry out a study of irrigation prospects throughout Ethiopia. The FAO Resident Representative, a pleasant though rigidly formal Belgian, met me at the airport. I could not go to my hotel, he explained, all the roads into town being blocked because of an anti-British demonstration going on in the centre of Addis, but as his house was close to the airport, I could remain there until the demonstration had dispersed. I didn't enquire as to why the British had been singled out for special treatment, but it did little to reduce my overall sense of foreboding.

The demonstration over, I was driven to the Ghion Hotel, where I linked up with two members of the team who had already arrived. Bill Almond had been my Team Leader on that first project in Egypt and I had always found him to be pleasant company. Tony Peacock was a young engineer from the big consulting engineers, Sir William Halcrow and Partners. He had been brought up in Africa and was fairly relaxed about the rather volatile situation in Ethiopia, to such an extent that his new wife was to join him very soon. She also had been brought up in Africa and regarded living in the middle of an ongoing revolution to be quite normal. Despite his constant one-upmanship, he could be a most amusing companion and his wife turned out to be a real charmer.

Addis Ababa lies at 8,000 feet – that is like being more than a quarter of the way up Everest, or twice as high as Ben Nevis. At that altitude the air gets pretty thin and it is wise to move a little more slowly than one might normally do, to mount stairs one at a time, and press the release knob on your shaving foam with great circumspection. Amongst the more alarming effects of the low oxygen levels at that altitude is a serious disturbance of normal sleep pattern, which manifests itself as either having great difficulty sleeping at all or, almost worse, dreaming vividly for what seems like most of the night.

The Ghion Hotel was not the best in town – that accolade going by a long way to the Addis Ababa Hilton. We probably wouldn't have stayed there anyway on price grounds, though given the dearth of visitors even the Hilton was prepared to offer some very good deals. However, my arrival coincided with a decision by the Ethiopian government that foreign reporters were to be allowed in for the first time in many months, and the Hilton was being cleared for the pending arrival of the media. Still, the Ghion was not too bad. Set in some reasonably spacious gardens with a tennis court and a small pool, I had certainly stayed in worse. After nearly a month 'on the road' during which time I had never stayed long enough in one place to make it worth unpacking my bags, it was with a great sense of relief that I emptied my suitcase and grip into the drawers and cupboards, and laid out my toiletries neatly on the shelf in the bathroom. It was going to be a two-month stay, so I might as well make myself at home.

There was an 11 o'clock curfew in force in Addis, and it needed to be taken very seriously, with stories of foreigners caught out spending weeks in gaol before being deported. What made it particularly tricky was that road blocks could appear from nowhere, so that a journey through town that should take twenty minutes could – if you encountered two or three road blocks – take an hour, so by the time you got to the last one you were into the curfew. That evening it had been decided that we would go to the British Embassy club, which was showing the film 'Raid on Entebbe'. In a rare display of generosity, the Embassy was allowing British nationals working in Addis to become temporary members of the Embassy club. Of course there might have been a degree of enlightened self-interest; sitting in the Embassy club you were unlikely to get caught in the gunfire, which would have created a great deal of tiresome paperwork for the Embassy. But perhaps that is slightly churlish, for the club was an excellent place – a good bar serving traditional pub grub, a pool table and darts boards and a comfortable room where films were shown or occasional discos were held. Certainly that first evening, after a month of travelling mainly in the remoter parts of Indonesia, the bangers and mash seemed like Cordon Bleu.

It wasn't going to be too bad after all and I was in a happier frame of mind as we returned to the Ghion. The assistant manager was awaiting us at the door and, with a smile and deferential bow not somehow entirely in keeping with the spirit of 'revolutionary Ethiopia' and the ubiquitous billboards that acclaimed equality of the masses, he handed each of us a white envelope. Almost certainly invitations to some hotel junket, which were usually fun with lots of free booze, and we all opened our envelopes expectantly. The note inside was brief;

'Dear Valued Guest,' it said, 'you must check out of the hotel by 8.30 tomorrow morning so that we can accommodate members of the foreign press corps.' No 'Sorry for any inconvenience caused', or any indication of how long we were to be ejected for. We took the only course of action open to us and repaired to the hotel bar where we imbibed large quantities of the local beer.

High altitude hangovers are somehow worse than those at normal altitude, presumably something to do with the lack of oxygen failing to break down the alcohol as effectively as it should be. So it was a sorry little party that assembled in the lobby at 8.30 the next morning to plot our next move. We were being chivvied to pay up and get out as quickly as possible; it seemed that the government did not want the rank and file guests to end up mingling with the press corps which, it transpired, was to be closely chaperoned. We had no real choice but to take the next step down market and off we set to the Ethiopia Hotel. It might be unfair to describe it as a dump, but then on the other hand it might not be that unfair. It was a gloomy building with no grounds in a fairly noisy part of town, though with the night-time curfew we concluded that this would not seriously disturb our sleep. What we hadn't allowed for was the gunfire, which went on incessantly through the night as the Red Terror continued its murderous course.

I decided against tempting fate and dumped my bags in my room with no attempt to unpack them, though the crashing hangover may also have played its part in that bit of decision-making.

We were working for the recently established Valleys Agricultural Development Authority (VADA) and they were struggling to find accommodation for themselves, let alone find space for a team of foreign consultants. FAO had agreed that we could rent a modest office not far from the centre of town and within walking distance of VADA's offices. For 'modest' perhaps read 'very small'; with just the three of us there it was reasonably comfortable, but when we reached the full complement of six we would be down to sharing desks. But whatever the office may have lacked in space or facilities, it won out all hands down on location, for it was situated on the first floor immediately above a traditional Ethiopian coffee house. There was a constant faint but deeply tantalising smell of roasting coffee and, when the temptation became too much, it took only a few minutes to pop downstairs for a cup of the finest coffee I had ever drunk. Green beans of Arabica coffee fresh from the Ethiopian highlands, roasted and ground in front of you and covered in hot but not boiling water and finally filtered into cups so small that they made the Brazilian 'cafesinho' look like a brickie's mug.

Bill had discovered that there was an Indian restaurant in town that was still functioning, so we ate there that night. We were stopped twice at road-blocks on our way back from what had proved to be an excellent meal. We didn't feel seriously threatened; for the most part we had the impression that the militias manning the roadblocks didn't really want to get involved with us and, once they realised that they had stopped a party of foreigners, they were as keen to see us on our way as we were to be on it. But you never knew when you might come up against someone with a grudge against foreigners and who had possibly had a bit too much tej – the local high octane drink made from fermented honey. It was therefore decreed that a nerve-settling nightcap was required in the hotel bar once we were safely back.

Inevitably the nightcap turned to three or four, and once again I was teetering a little as I went to bed. Was it the curry? Was it the five or six coffees? Was it the altitude? What was for certain was that I was dreaming vividly; there were people in my room, they were opening my suitcase, opening my cupboard. I was trying to tell them to go away but nobody seemed to take any notice and finally the dreaming stopped. In the morning I realised that it wasn't the curry or the coffee or the altitude, but actually there had been one or more people in my room, and they clearly had gone through my belongings. Nothing had been taken – not my little cassette player, not my expensive short wave radio, not even my Swiss army knife so coveted by room cleaners around the world. No, these had not been thieves in the night but some sort of security agents who had pretty methodically had a thorough search of my goods and chattels. It was a deeply uncomfortable feeling that while I had slept there had been someone in my room and I decided to cut back on the nightcaps, though to this day I remain convinced that something had been put into one of my drinks, which is what had really knocked me out. The experience served to remind us all that we were living in a country under the rule of a ruthless regime in which everybody was potentially being spied upon, and we were a lot more careful after that about what we talked about in public places.

Our job was to come up with a ranking of all the known potential irrigation schemes in the country so that VADA could prioritise these in terms of finding the necessary funding to construct them. It was to be a largely desk exercise and every available surface in the office was piled up with reports on over a hundred irrigation schemes that had been identified and studied to some level. The number did come down rapidly when we were told that we should eliminate areas that were currently 'insecure'. Given that international and civil wars were raging in the Ogaden, Eritrea and Tigray, that there was reported military activity in other areas, and that the main road running east from Addis Ababa to Djibouti (Ethiopia's only safe access to a sea port) was effectively closed to everything but the mostly Russian and Cuban military traffic, you started to wonder just how much was left and what we were doing here at all.

Countless hours were spent coming up with a system that attempted fairly to balance considerations of optimum use of natural resources, ease of construction, economic returns, impact on starvation and many other factors so that we could place what was still a large number of disparate schemes into some sort of logical order of priority.

In the original plan we were then to visit a selection of our preferred choices involving extensive overland travel. The Government, in a realistic assessment of their own lack of control over the course of the Red Terror, decreed that it was altogether too dangerous for us to travel by road and proposed to provide us with a light aircraft, from which we could make some sort of aerial reconnaissance and land at selected 'safe' locations. After the inevitable number of false starts we finally arrived at Addis airport. We were the only civilian passengers there. On the apron stood three massive Russian military cargo planes and a little way from them a small twin-engine, ten-seater light aircraft belonging to the Ethiopian air force. Travel by road in that lawless country may have been deemed to be too dangerous, but frankly I had my reservations about flying around, at heights low enough to be able to make any useful reconnaissance of ground conditions, in a light aircraft so clearly marked as belonging to the air force.

By that time we had been joined by Bob Camacho, one of Halcrow's most senior irrigation engineers. Bob hailed from Guyana; he had the looks of an Amerindian and the accent of the West Indies. He had been Guyana's Chief Engineer before being lured away by Halcrow and was by some stretch the most talented engineer that I have ever worked with. Bob had the ability to look at an area of land and sketch on the back of an envelope where water might be impounded, how canals would be aligned and the area that would come in the command of the irrigation system. Of course it would take many months of surveys and of young engineers with their computers to design the scheme, but usually the finished article looked much like Bob's back of envelope sketch.

The four of us were joined by two counterparts from VADA; there should have been more but there had been a sudden outbreak of sickness, domestic crises, urgent work to be completed and whatever other reasons could be found for not spending five days in a military aircraft flying at heights that would probably have been within the range of a blunderbuss, let alone a hand-held rocket launcher. The pilot, however, dressed in the most casual of military clothes, seemed very relaxed. We first flew south more or less following the great Rift valley and the string of massive lakes, the pilot encouraged to keep as low as possible so that we could get the best possible view of the terrain. We had a system whereby we all took our separate notes of what we could see on the ground and, at five minute intervals, Bill would intone a time which we would each note at the margin of the page, so producing a sort of primitive log of what we were seeing. We would later be able to compare observations at more or less the same points. We flew over Lake Koka and Lake Ziway in the north and the spectacular cluster of Lakes Abiyata, Langano and Shala. We finally landed at Arba Minch, a small town surrounded by mountains and lying between the massive Lake Abaya and the smaller Lake Chamo, the isthmus between them forming part of the Nechisar National Park.

Arba Minch was in those days a town of around 20,000 people, deriving its name from the Amharic meaning 'forty springs'. The area's potential for irrigation was regarded by us as being high with this abundance of spring water, a vast area where the shallow ground water table supported an impressive groundwater forest and of course the lakes. We had hopes of scrounging transport from the local office of the department of Agriculture in order to conduct some sort of ground reconnaissance, but we were told that all their transport had been commandeered and they had nothing. It made no difference, they said, because even if they had vehicles they had no fuel to put in them. Here was the reality of the revolution – a once thriving area now struggling for survival and deprived of the basic services that they needed. There had never been any significant European presence and whatever there had been had long since flown the town. Perhaps in days gone by we would have found some little European restaurant, but now we realised that we had to brace ourselves for the local food.

'Injera and wat' constitutes the staple diet of all Ethiopians. Strictly, 'injera' is made from 'teff' – a grass with a very small seed grown in the Ethiopian highlands, though poorer households may bulk up this relatively expensive commodity with cheaper grains. The 'teff' itself has a sour taste and in the process of producing 'injera', the flour and water are left to ferment for several days before being baked into vast flat round pancakes. The end product has the texture of foam rubber and a sharp, acrid flavour. It is matched in its unpleasantness to most western palates only by the 'wat', a ferociously hot stew; of course there are sanitised and up-market versions of it using a variety of tasty spices, but at the level of the ordinary Ethiopian it is essentially a bit of meat and lots of hot pepper. The restaurant where we ate that night was definitely at the level of the ordinary Ethiopian and the food was served in the traditional way. A vast round tray was produced, completely covering this was a single pancake of 'injera' with the 'wat' heaped in little mounds at a number of points on the 'injera'. We arranged ourselves cross-legged around this. There was no cutlery and the idea is that you tear off bits of the 'injera' which you use to scoop up mouthfuls of 'wat'. For those who find acrid foam rubber to be quite irresistible, smaller pancakes of 'injera' are provided at your side to supplement the edible tray cloth. As the mounds of stew disappear there are left little islands of soggy 'injera' regarded by many as the gastronomic climax of the meal. Served with the food was 'tej', very alcoholic and not exactly great for dousing the fires of the 'wat'.

The next day we spent five hours in the air over-flying the very southernmost parts of the country, with the pilot watching the terrain nervously as we got too close for his comfort to the border with Kenya. A wide flat valley floor to the north of Lake Chew Bahir, the southern tip of which touched the Kenyan border, was the focus of much of our interest and the Weito river flowing into this was later to become one of the priority irrigation development areas. We returned to Arba Minch in the late afternoon to find a large reception committee waiting at the airstrip. Our initial arrival had been largely unannounced, given the fractured communications in the country at that time, but word had quickly got round that there was a party of foreigners with the power to dispense large sums of money. Five hours in a light aircraft flying at low altitudes and concentrating hard on recording everything that you can see leaves your head spinning, and the last thing in the world that any of us wanted was some sort of civic reception but that was clearly what we had.

Leading the reception committee was someone that I took to be the head of the region as surrounding him were as many of the 'kebele' chiefs as had been able to make it to the airstrip. A speech of welcome was made by the regional head, somewhat half-heartedly translated by one of our counterparts, though whether he was really translating or just pouring forth a few appropriate utterances of his own we would never know. Bill gave a short impromptu response and we were all loaded into the back of a rickety truck with benches, on which the honoured guests sat while the 'kebele' chiefs stood in a knot in the middle hanging on to each other as we bounced around the rutted roads. They took us first on a tour of the town, pointing out the various civic amenities, all of which appeared to be totally dilapidated. Then to our delight, the truck headed out of town and across the isthmus between the lakes. Here was an opportunity to make some correlation between what we had been observing from the air and what was actually on the ground. Approximately two miles out of town the truck came to a halt and the regional head jumped out of the cab. He made a further little speech, the gist of which was that with apologies this was as far as we could go, because they now had only enough fuel to get us back to town. I felt a twinge of guilt at the thought of the drums of petrol being held in the military compound to fuel our plane.

We were dropped at our hotel and informed that we were invited to dinner that night. The venue was a different restaurant to the one that we had visited the previous night, a little more sophisticated with large tables, but the food was much the same. Huge trays were brought to the tables covered in 'injera' and little mounds of different varieties of 'wat'. There was, however, one difference. Behind each of us stood a girl in traditional dress, some strikingly beautiful, others perhaps showing a little more of the ravages of time. It was explained to us that these girls were to feed us and that etiquette required us to keep our hands entirely off the table.

As babies we had food put into our mouths; it was the only way that we could get it, but most babies are intent on taking over the feeding process for themselves. This may initially be a messy and grossly inefficient business, but clearly regarded by the child as infinitely preferable to having the food shovelled in by somebody else. It is a preference to which most of us adhere for the rest of our lives, possibly only forced to revert to being fed again in sickness or old age. Perhaps a tasty morsel popped into your mouth by a loving partner could seem like fun, but handfuls of burning hot stew scooped up in bitter foam rubber is hard to take. The girls saw it as their duty to get as much food into us as possible, seeming almost to vie with each other as to who was pushing the most food in. It was hard not to gag – which would clearly have been deeply offensive – and the relief as we reached the last soggy bits of 'injera' was indescribable.

In the morning, feeling slightly queasy, we set off on the next leg of our journey. We headed north, but following the lowlands running along the border with Sudan. They looked hot, dusty and forbidding. We refuelled at a military-controlled airstrip in Gambela, a town atypical of Ethiopia, being in the hot and humid lowlands. We had originally proposed to stop and spend some time in the region of Gambela, but the authorities had vetoed that. The region was populated by two ethnic groups that seemed to have little in common with most Ethiopians and it had, in the not so distant past, been a part of Sudan. So, with one eye on a possibly volatile local community and the tensions between the Mengistu government and Sudan, it was decreed that this was not a place to have a group of foreigners wandering around. From Gambela the plains on the Ethiopian side of the border rapidly diminished and it was with a certain sense of relief that we headed once again into the highlands. The prospects for identifying irrigation development sites were negligible and, had the plane come down in that terrain it would probably never have been found, but there was still something oddly comforting about looking down on the hills.

We finally landed at Bahir Dar at the southern tip of Ethiopia's biggest lake – Lake Tana – and here communications had worked, for a crowd of people and, amazingly, reasonable looking vehicles were at the airport to meet us. Bahir Dar was one of the largest towns in Ethiopia which somehow seemed to be divorced from much of what was going on elsewhere in the country. There weren't the same number of scruffily dressed soldiers wandering the streets with machine guns over their shoulders and, compared to Addis or even to what we had seen of Arba Minch or Gambela, there was an air of something approaching prosperity – well, relatively speaking that is. That was the good news. The bad news was that our aircraft had been summoned to return to base. We could either return with it, or spend the two days that we had allocated to the region doing some ground reconnaissance, and then travel back to Addis by road. The previously expressed concerns over our safety on long road journeys seemed to have pragmatically evaporated, in the face of other more important demands for the aircraft.

The local officials who had no intention of having this potential flying carpet being pulled from under their feet, persuaded us that we could see a great deal by road, and they would make all arrangements for our return to Addis. But the clincher was the promise of a trip to the source of the Blue Nile. We spent two days reconnoitring the area around Lake Tana, but the highlight had nothing to do with irrigation. Lake Tana is the source of the Blue Nile, which is known locally in its upper reaches as the Abbai and regarded by some as being the sacred river Ghion, which flowed out of the Garden of Eden. It starts its journey at the southeast corner of the lake and after travelling nearly 25 miles the river tumbles over a 400 yard wide lava dam cascading down 150 feet into the Nile gorge at what is known locally as the 'Tis Issat' falls, which translates as 'water and smoke'. It was a truly spectacular sight, the crashing waters and the haze of spray creating myriad rainbows. Looking at this mighty force of water, I couldn't help but think that a tiny portion of it ended up in our little irrigated plots in West Nubariya. Today the force has been harnessed to generate power and, although there is still some flow over the lava lip, particularly in the wet season, I count myself as blessed that I saw it in all its natural grandeur.

We returned to Bahir Dar to the inevitable news that there was to be a reception in our honour that evening, and the ghastly vision of more 'injera' and 'wat' being force-fed into us took some of the shine off the glorious day that we had enjoyed. It turned out not to be quite like that – just somewhat worse. The table in the restaurant was indeed set with little piles of 'injera', but down the middle of the central long table was a massive quantity of meat and offal – prime beef we were told. Each chunk of meat was impaled on a long knife, which had been stabbed into the wooden table. It was all raw and was attracting a good deal of attention from the flies.

I looked around to locate the barbecue, which I anticipated must be nearby, but as to the means whereby the meat was to be cooked there was no sign. It turned out that I couldn't see the means of cooking the meat because there was none. As particularly important and honoured guests, we were to be treated to the great Ethiopian delicacy of raw meat. Beside each chunk of meat there was a small sharp knife, and now the girls in their traditional costume started to slice off bits of meat onto small plates that they carried to us. Hope for the best and prepare for the worst. It was the latter, and the first piece of raw meat was pushed into my mouth. With the 'injera' and 'wat' it was so spicy hot that there was a massive incentive to swallow as quickly as possible before it burned your tongue off. But the raw meat sort of sat there, while you fought the urge just to shoot it straight out before forcing yourself to swallow. There was an element of illogicality, as I will cheerfully eat a rare steak, which is little more than browned on the outside and heated up on the inside. Maybe it was the fact that the meat was clay cold, maybe it was just the psychology of looking at these great raw slabs of meat, maybe it was having it put into your mouth for you. Whatever, the meal definitely ranked as one of the worst of my life – and that was before the raw liver.

It took us 16 hours to drive back to Addis, including three punctures and numerous road blocks. The latter were always tense affairs. Groups of scruffy soldiers touting rifles or machine guns and without any sense of there being some overall command structure milled around the vehicle, sticking rifles through the windows and shouting at us, occasionally demanding that we all got out. But in the end we were always waved through and without – as far as I could see – money changing hands. It wouldn't have happened that way at the other end of the Nile.

And that was the fun over. Now it was down to the detailed analysis of the sixty potential projects that hadn't been sieved out so we settled to ploughing our way through the mound of what were often appallingly badly written reports. The weather, so glorious when I had arrived, had somewhat unseasonably changed and now it was cold and damp. For the most part we ate in the hotel – a monotonous diet of lentil soup and leathery steak – with occasional forays to the Pizza place in the Hilton now the foreign media had gone, the excellent Indian, a third rate Chinese and of course bangers and mash and a game of darts at the Embassy Club. We were invited twice to dine at the residence of the FAO chief where the food was excellent – all of it imported – but the dining was so rigidly formal that I lived in the fear of letting out a burp or worse, or being caught out buttering my bread with the fish knife, or offending the hostess with my excessive use of the salt cellar. Finally, after nearly three months away from home, I was on my way back to the UK. There was an anxious moment at the end, when I realised that the wording on my exit visa would imply that it had not come into force. I was assured that this was simply a mistranslation of the Amharic original and that it was only the Amharic version that the immigration officials would take any notice of. All the same, I really only relaxed as my flight finally lifted off and snaked between the hills to head for Europe.

# CHAPTER 26

# BACK TO 'INJERA'... AND WHAT?

I blame these upper reaches of the Nile for a period of some years when I became a whisky drinker. I was brought up a beer-totaller; in my youth in the northeast of England the men drank beer. Over the border we knew that whisky was the drink, and down south people drank wine, but on Tyneside real men drank real beer. I had once tried whisky, but even the smell of it made me feel sick. I had an aunt with pretensions to being upper class; we often had Christmas or New Year dinner at her home and she served Spanish Sauternes, which we considered the height of chic, but I found it gave me indigestion. It would be many years before I drank wine again. So apart from an occasional foray into gin and tonics I remained a staunch beer drinker – until Ethiopia that is.

I returned to Ethiopia in 1980. Mengistu's purge had largely subsided and the Somalis had retreated from the Ogaden but, backed by Russian and Cuban troops, the Ethiopian army continued its long battle with the Eritrean independence movement. Our study into the prioritisation of potential irrigation schemes had done the rounds and, after the inevitable interminable bureaucratic delays, FAO had given the report its blessing and agreed to finance the feasibility studies of the Dabus and Weito Irrigation Projects.

A small team assembled in Addis ready to carry out the initial ground reconnaissance. We had negotiated a good per diem, felt to reflect a certain element of discomfort and danger money. In the continuing absence of significant numbers of tourists or businessmen to Ethiopia, the Hilton was offering highly competitive room rates, and we decided that for the days we were to spend in Addis before heading to the field we would treat ourselves to its comfortable rooms and the swimming pool fed by a hot spring. While the room rates were undoubtedly very reasonable, nothing else was. The other members of the team, all of who had been in this game a lot longer than me, had arrived weighed down with their bottles of duty-free whisky. The routine was that before going out to eat in the evening you would all gather in someone's room, bringing your tooth mug, and you would imbibe a few whiskies. Being unable to drink the stuff, I would call room service and order myself a couple of beers. Room service was not only horrendously expensive but desperately slow, so that I found myself waiting around as the others drank their whiskies, then having to gulp down my expensive beer when it eventually arrived.

By our last night in Addis I had become fed up with the system so I took my tooth mug along with me. I found that if I held my nose, the whisky didn't go down too badly. Indeed, returning to the Hilton that evening after dinner, I agreed to join one of my colleagues and continue my education into the delights of whisky. Between us we polished off most of a bottle and certainly by then I was no longer having to hold my nose as I drank it. Whisky became a regular nightcap for me for quite some years after that but, strangely, as suddenly as I had taken to it, I went right off it and it is many a year since I last drank a glass of whisky.

The next morning the party travelling by land started the

long road journey to Dabus. It had, however, been decreed that I should await the helicopter that was due to come in from Kenya a few days later, so that I could first travel with Bob Camacho to an irrigated cotton scheme at Amibara in the middle Awash valley, in the heart of Afar country, that was having drainage problems. It was a delightful four-hour drive through fine scenery, dropping to the floor of the Awash Valley. There were small gazelle, quite a lot of oryx with their ridiculously long horns and a reasonable array of birds that reminded me fondly of my years in The Gambia. These included one of my favourites, the ground hornbill, and one of the ugliest birds around, the marabou stork. The driver told us that there had been a lot more wildlife, but the Cuban soldiers stationed in the Awash valley had hunted much of it out. The team of expatriates from Halcrow and ULG who were supervising the development of the scheme lived in a new compound; attractively laid out, each house with its small garden – but what an isolated existence. The compound included a clubhouse that sold beer and bags of local crisps and had a dartboard and a simple music system blasting out 1960s pop. The appearance of a couple of new faces ensured that the clubhouse was full that night and I was told the next morning that it had got through more beer in one night than it normally got through in a week. I have always seen myself as a victim of other people's drinking habits. I am an amiable person by nature, never liking to refuse a drink for fear of appearing unfriendly, and of course it is a well-known fact that willpower is highly soluble in alcohol. But looking back over a number of fairly heavy drinking sessions in recent years, I did start to come to the realisation that the one common denominator was unquestionably me.

It didn't take a great deal of investigation to come to the conclusion that the reason for the drainage problems was, as it was in most cases, gross over-watering. Unfortunately the rising water tables brought with them high concentrations of salt, so that the deleterious effect of poor drainage was exacerbated by the salinity. There was little option but to accept that a comprehensive drainage system would ultimately have to be installed so I drew up the specifications for the surveys that would need to be undertaken to support the design of the system. After a few days, Bob and I returned to Addis to find that the helicopter had just arrived from Kenya. It was another couple of days before we could leave, as everything had to be put in place to be able to refuel the helicopter halfway to Dabus.

Over the years my job has provided me with many marvellous experiences, but none better than that trip to Dabus. It was a three-seater bubble helicopter, entirely open at the sides. The pilot was more my build than Bob's so, to get the best weight distribution, Bob had to sit in the middle and I got the 'window' seat. There was considerable consternation as the pilot realised just how much equipment we were carrying, and every nook and cranny in the helicopter was filled, with a few more bits and pieces tied on the outside. The reason for the pilot's consternation was quite clear. Addis airport was at an altitude of nearly 8,000 feet – basically the operating ceiling of our little bubble helicopter. At full revs we rose maybe 20 feet above the ground, the pilot pointed it in our direction of travel and off we went. We literally skimmed the treetops, or more accurately we were steered between them. We almost touched the pointed roofs of dwellings as we threaded our way through the villages. I felt guilty at getting a kick out of it, but I just couldn't help enjoying watching men, women, children and animals scatter as we skimmed over their heads.

But it didn't seem so funny as we approached a significant hill head on. The hill rose some hundreds of feet and, given that we were barely ten feet above the ground, I was struggling to see how we were going to get over it, yet the pilot seemed to be heading straight for it. Just as it looked as if we were simply going to run into the hillside, the downward draft of the rotors created a cushion of air between us and the hillside and, rather than run straight into it, we now started to drift up and over it in a phenomenon known as 'ground effect'. And so we progressed, passing over herds of gazelle and oryx and packs of jackals awaiting their chance, all amidst spectacular scenery. We stopped to refuel from a lorry that awaited us on the roadside and resumed our flight. Then suddenly we came off the plateau. One minute we were skimming feet above the ground, the next we were looking at the earth at what seemed like thousands of feet below us. It was like being on the world's greatest roller coaster and we started our descent to the Dabus valley.

It was in 1988 that I made my final visit to Ethiopia, as a member of a team charged with preparing the Awash Valley Masterplan, and there was a point at which I feared that the stay may last a great deal longer than the bar chart showed. I was teamed up once again with Bob Camacho. One of the areas of particular interest was the bottom end of the river system in the area around Dire Dawa. This is the second largest city in Ethiopia but altogether different to the country's capital. Dire Dawa lies at only 3,500 feet; it is backed by a ring of hills but otherwise surrounded by desert. It was known that here the streams braided, breaking up into smaller streams that spread across the desert plain. At times of low flow the water simply disappeared into the ground, and at times of high flow in the June to September rainy season there would be widespread flooding, which often caused considerable damage to Dire Dawa itself. We were looking for ways in which this water might serve a more useful purpose. Major impounding structures were out of the question, and it seemed that the best approach was to harvest the floodwaters, spreading them over as wide an area as possible with a series of small structures to push the waters this way and that, and then grow crops on the moist soil as the floodwaters receded.

Bob and I had spent a long day in a light aircraft criss-crossing the area, looking for places where the natural lie of the land would favour the sort of water harvesting that we had in mind. For the most part we flew over miles of emptiness, but from time to time we would see groups of Afars, the nomadic pastoralists of the region, moving their herds of cattle, sheep and goats in the constant quest for feed and water, and always armed to the teeth. Ethiopia was much more settled by then, though the war with Eritrea continued, and there was discontent amongst some of the Afars as the major irrigation schemes in the Awash valley disrupted their already erratic supplies of water and attendant flushes of growth.

Dire Dawa boasted one hotel, proclaiming itself to be of 'international standard,' and Bob and I went to check in. It was fully booked and, despite a notional booking that we had made from Addis, no amount of cajoling or even dollar bills were going to get us rooms there. Our driver toured the town with us, working ever further down the hotel chain. All were fully occupied, but we finally came to a small hotel with maybe ten rooms with corrugated iron doors built round a small courtyard, which could provide us with two rooms. It wasn't much, but it was somewhere to sleep and the owner seemed very attentive, arranging for someone to go and fetch us some 'injera' and 'wat' and a few bottles of a local beer which was clearly of a most worthy alcohol content. Mellowed by the strong ale, we decided that all in all it hadn't turned out too badly, so we sat downing our beer and me having my cigarette in the warm evening – so very different to the chilly evenings in Addis.

I had probably been in bed for about three hours and was in a fairly deep, alcohol-abetted sleep, lying on top of my bed and as usual in the buff. Suddenly there was a commotion in the little courtyard and, after a certain amount of shouting, somebody came and hammered loudly on my door and then on the door of the adjacent room which was occupied by Bob.

'Out,' someone was shouting, 'Out, out'. I went rigid with fear. My worst nightmare was about to come true, and I could clearly picture myself spending the next few years wandering the desert as the prisoner of some disgruntled and lawless Afar tribe.

I had the strange idea that I should hide in the bathroom. The word bathroom was something of a euphemism for a corner of the room that had been separated from the rest of it with a head-height wall hiding a squat toilet and a bucket of water for washing. I made no attempt to respond to the violent hammering on my door but, still naked, crept into the bathroom and, squatting below the level of the wall, remained motionless and silent, aside from my terrified quaking. It is hard to imagine I could possibly have believed that, having once broken down the flimsy iron door and seeing the bed empty, it would not occur to them that I must be hiding in the bathroom. In the grip of fever we do not always think logically. Bob had taken a different tack and was demanding of them what they wanted, but all he got in reply was:

'Out, out'. A bolder man than me, I heard him pulling the bolt on his door and stepping into the nearly pitch black courtyard. There was a lot of general commotion and I heard Bob saying:

'Where are you taking me?' My sense of foreboding deepened. Now I pinned my slender hopes not so much on them not spotting me hiding in the bathroom but, deciding that one prisoner was enough and, having escorted Bob away, they would not bother returning for me. The noise started to move away, but five minutes later I could hear the party returning with voices raised even more excitedly. There was further hammering on my door; obviously Bob was not sufficient of a prize on his own. But then it was Bob calling out:

'David,' he said, 'you had better get out quick, the place is on fire'. Throwing on a pair of trousers, I shot out of my room. Now I could smell the smoke and, over in the far corner of the courtyard, yellow tongues of flame were licking up behind the bedrooms. The generator that supplied some feeble light to the hotel had taken fire and the owner was concerned that it was going to spread to the rooms. It didn't; a chain of people emptied what seemed like hundreds of buckets of water onto the burning housing that covered the generator and, fairly quickly, there was nothing but the smell of acrid smoke. It was actually difficult to imagine that the rooms could possibly have taken fire, since they were made of concrete with tin roofs and doors, but maybe sparks could have blown into the rooms. I don't usually have a beer and cigarette at three o'clock in the morning, but there was a bottle left over from the evening before and I decided that my nervous system needed a little calming down.

In this strange business in which I worked, you always believed that you would return and so, apart from the Mato Grosso that would for certain disappear as I knew it, I have never said 'adieu' to anywhere that I have worked, never more than an 'au revoir' and an 'à bientôt'. So, as my Lufthansa flight rose from the ground and headed for the gap between the hills, I had no idea that my twelve-year acquaintanceship with the countries of the Nile had come to an end. Indeed, after so many years during which the Nile and the lands that it ran through dominated much of my life, my involvement with that river had ended forever.

# ACKNOWLEDGEMENTS

I will be forever grateful to the Royal Society and Royal Geographical Society for mounting and managing the expedition to Central Brazil, and to the Leverhulme Trust for awarding me the scholarship that allowed me to spend a year as a member of that expedition.

I am deeply indebted to my university tutor, Peter Askew, who believed that – even without a paddle – I would survive the exceptional demands of the 'green hell.' His faith in me changed my life.[8]

To the late Alan Stobbs, that larger than life ex-naval commander turned colonial officer, with his pipe, his elephant ear shorts and monocle, I owe a huge thank you for helping me through the transition from academia to the realities of international development.

I spent 25 happy years with a rural development consultancy, ULG. The demands of the work could be extreme, but nowhere could you have found greater teamwork. Everybody, from the consultants spread across the globe to the support staff in Warwick, worked together to achieve shared aims, and nobody watched the clock! From people too numerous to mention, I learned so much and

---

8   Just as this book went to print we had the sad news that Peter had passed away. I am so sorry that he did not get to read something of the life on which he launched me but hope that his family might enjoy some of what I have written.

found a camaraderie that could never have been bettered.

My greatest debt of gratitude goes to my wife, who provided the bedrock to which I returned from my travels. Largely homebound once the educational demands of our children meant that we could no longer travel overseas together, Ruth forged a wonderful home and brought up two marvellous children, while never losing sight of her passion for wildlife, and continuing to contribute in many ways to its conservation. It was a marvellous place to come home to.

My heartfelt thanks to Rachel and John who took having a part-time father in their stride and always gave me a rapturous welcome home. My involvement in their many sporting activities provided a normality to an abnormal life.

# PHOTO CREDITS